# SpringerBriefs in Environment, Security, Development and Peace

Migration Studies

Volume 14

*Series editor*

Hans Günter Brauch

For further volumes:
http://www.springer.com/series/11825
http://www.afes-press-books.de/html/SpringerBriefs_ESDP_MiS.htm

Liliana Rivera-Sánchez
Fernando Lozano-Ascencio
Editors

# The Practice of Research on Migration and Mobilities

Springer

UNIVERSIDAD NACIONAL AUTONOMA DE MEXICO

CRIM

*Editors*
Liliana Rivera-Sánchez
Fernando Lozano-Ascencio
The Regional Centre of Multidisciplinary
Research (CRIM)
National Autonomous University of Mexico
Cuernavaca
Mexico

ISSN 2193-3162 ISSN 2193-3170 (electronic)
ISBN 978-3-319-02692-3 ISBN 978-3-319-02693-0 (eBook)
DOI 10.1007/978-3-319-02693-0
Springer Cham Heidelberg New York Dordrecht London

Library of Congress Control Number: 2013954844



Printed on acid-free paper

Springer is part of Springer Science+Business Media (www.springer.com)

# Contents

# Chapter 1
# Introduction: Interdisciplinary Dialogues and Methodological Debates

**Liliana Rivera-Sánchez and Fernando Lozano-Ascencio**

Over the last two decades, the volume of academic publications and news articles on migrations around the world has been remarkable. The acceleration of human mobilities is inherent to the current stage of the globalization process. In academic and political spheres, the topic has been the focus of numerous seminars and debates on the impacts, effects and consequences accompanying these international processes of accelerated migrations.

In contemporary social sciences we have also witnessed an intense exchange among academics in many parts of the world regarding how to theoretically address the current migration process and identify the analytical perspectives—in other words, the conceptual structures and epistemological meanings—that can contribute toward fully understanding the multiple facets and dimensions of a process which, by its very nature, demands interdisciplinary and multidisciplinary perspectives (Morawska 2003). The emergence of debates on this topic—especially on how to address it—reached one of its most critical points in the academic community in the early 1990s, with the first works from a transnational perspective and its subsequent reformulations during the second half of the same decade (Glick Schiller et al. 1992; Wimmer and Glick Schiller 2003; Khagram and Levitt 2008). Also contributing to this debate, without a doubt, were academics who did not find *anything new* in these reformulations (Waldinger and Fitzgerald 2004; Waldinger 2008), and this led to the emergence of other perspectives.

The revitalization of post-colonial studies, reformulations of critical anthropology, studies on global coloniality (Grosfoguel 2006) and on *coloniality of power*, in the words of Aníbal Quijano (2000), contemporary studies by neoassimilationists, and also a refinement of the original proposals made by theorists from the transnational perspective, among other proposals linked to the field of

L. Rivera-Sánchez (✉) · F. Lozano-Ascencio
Centro Regional de Investigaciones Multidisciplinarias (Regional Center for Multidisciplinary Research), Universidad Nacional Autónoma de México (National Autonomous University of Mexico), Cuernavaca, Mexico
e-mail: rivesanl@yahoo.com.mx

L. Rivera-Sánchez and F. Lozano-Ascencio (eds.), *The Practice of Research on Migration and Mobilities*, SpringerBriefs in Environment, Security, Development and Peace 14,
DOI:10.1007/978-3-319-02693-0_1, The Author(s) 2014

migration studies, all contributed to expanding the range of modalities for addressing this topic (see Rodríguez and Martínez 2008).

More recently, concern lies with reformulating analytical strategies that will permit interdisciplinary dialogue for constructing new research agendas in the study of contemporary migrations—not necessarily because this involves a *new* phenomenon, but rather with the objective of recognizing the heterogeneity of the process, its contingency, and the multiple interconnections with contemporary social transformation processes, thereby enriching the disciplinary approaches from which this phenomenon is addressed in the social sciences (Foner et al. 2000; Morawska 2003; Glick Schiller and Levitt 2006; Glick Schiller 2007; Pries 2008; Feldman et al. 2011).

Research questions on the migration process vary according to discipline and theoretical approach (Brettell and Hollifield 2000), but they also, of course, attempt to respond to the modalities and accelerated changes experienced in the migration process itself. Clearly, the social sciences and their consequent epistemic change respond to a slower rhythm than the changes and dynamics of social processes and their effects, since they are intrinsically nourished by and linked to these changes (Kuhn 1962; Bourdieu 1976). In other words, the acceleration of migration flows, changes in migration patterns, emergence of new regions of origin and destination, and social transformations associated with them, have clearly contributed to the new research questions and theoretical proposals currently accompanying the evolution of academic debates (Glick Schiller and Faist 2010; Glick Schiller and Caglar 2011).

Interdisciplinary and multidisciplinary dialogues can enrich this effort, with a focus on discussing not only theoretical and methodological perspectives for addressing the contemporary migration process, but also the units of analysis and epistemic consequences of studies conducted in recent years. With this objective, scholars studying these topics in different regions of the world have been brought together. Still, it is a challenge for dialogue between academics from the *north* and *south*—to speak generically of two locations that are not only geographic, but also epistemic and sociological in nature—to become an exchange among equals. On the one hand, language imposes certain limitations in terms of communication and dissemination of knowledge, or at least this is more clearly evident among academics that communicate and publish their findings in Spanish in particular. Generally speaking, at least some of us in the *south* have assumed the task of continuously reading publications from the *north*, particularly those in English. However, it should be said that academics and students in countries in the *north* fail to do the same. Most of them do not read publications in other languages, and particularly those in Spanish, to mention one example. Nevertheless, significant efforts have been made to establish a dialogue between academics from the *north* and *south*, with the aim of understanding the viewpoints, conditions and perspectives from which knowledge is generated in this field (Ariza and Portes 2007; Delgado and Castles 2007; Feldman et al. 2011).

In summary what we would like to emphasize is that the migration process is interpreted in a different way when researchers live in so-called societies of origin, than when it is interpreted from societies of destination—even when research work is multi-situated. The location of researchers in this field involves numerous factors that influence the modalities for conducting research: national and/or regional academic traditions, education in a given discipline, gender, nationality, access to resources, institutional affiliation, the way research teams are formed, and the position/role of researchers in the field of study, to mention only some (see Bourdieu 1976, 1984; and also Gray 2008; Kaltmeier 2012). Research agendas are clearly mediated by these locations, and it is necessary in our work in contemporary social sciences to bring awareness to these mediations, and to break with the dichotomic readings that are implicit in this migration process (origin–destination, north–south, cause-effect, to mention a few).

It is important to clarify that for the purposes of this book, an interdisciplinary dialogue was carried out primarily among academics in the American continent, with study focused particularly on groups of Latin American migrants in the United States, Canada and Spain, together with inter-regional migrations within Mexican territory and Colombians who migrate to Ecuador and Canada, particularly. In other words, a dialogue was established between the *north* and *south*, focusing on a specific region of global capitalism. What remains as an academic challenge for the future is a reflexive, comparative, multidisciplinary exercise focused on migration experiences in other geographic regions and with participation by researchers from other continental and regional academic traditions.

With the objective of establishing an interdisciplinary dialogue among research teams working in the field of migration and human mobilities studies, in both the northern and southern regions of the American continent, a Seminar was initiated in 2006, entitled *Theoretical-methodological challenges in migration studies: between comparative analysis and interdisciplinary*. The Seminar was coordinated by the Migration and Social Transformation research Team at the Regional Center for Multidisciplinary Research (*Centro Regional de Investigaciones Multidisciplinarias*) at the National Autonomous University of Mexico (*Universidad Nacional Autónoma de México*). One of the Seminar's founding principles was to consider the field of migration studies as *a strategic field* for researching the dynamics of the configuration of contemporary societies and their social differentiation and transformation processes. In other words, the point of convergence for participants was a perspective from the same field of study, which is by nature both interdisciplinary and multidisciplinary, beyond the research problems and objectives proposed. The Seminar participants, who have written the chapters in this book, came from different disciplines: sociology, demography, anthropology and history. Our research teams were at different stages in the research process. Some had already completed their field work and were processing the information gathered; others were writing up their research results or had already concluded and even published some of their findings; and one team was just initiating a new project. The different points in time characterizing the various research studies also enriched the dialogue in Seminar sessions and facilitated the writing of documents that demonstrate the methodological dilemmas experienced in the various stages of research. This can be highly useful for students, who find themselves at different points in the preparation of their research proposals, and to whom we especially dedicate this book.

This methodological Seminar was initiated at the first meeting held in June 2006 in Cuernavaca, Morelos, Mexico. The purpose of the meeting was to bring together researchers working in interdisciplinary or multidisciplinary teams, engaged in comparative research on issues related to migration processes in various countries and regions, and related to different national and ethnic groups. Two of the primary objectives that led to this initiative were, first of all, to develop a forum for theoretical and methodological discussion on analytical strategies that contribute to the development of comparative analysis in migration studies, and in general, human mobilities' studies; and secondly, to share the challenges of research work confronted in interdisciplinary teams (Bryman 2007; Mills et al. 2006). Clearly, one of the main concerns of Seminar participants was the fact that, despite a significant volume of literature related to migration studies—and not only in this field, but also in other social science fields—there are few contemporary methodological texts that manage to combine reflection on the way that research is carried out in practice, while manifesting the position held by participating researchers, with reflection on the actual process of the research carried out.[1] In short, authors either present the findings or results of studies carried out, or design methodological texts that fail to include any examples of the dialectic exercise that social research allegedly fulfills.

This concern also arises from the daily experience of Seminar participants with our students, as we demand clarity in their methodological proposals, however we cannot easily provide them with texts containing a *map of the route* that our research work or that of our colleagues has followed. Nonetheless, the objective of bringing together texts with these characteristics does not suppose that social research is conducted on the basis of a certain formula, and we are certainly not suggesting that the chapters contained in this book constitute a handbook with prescriptive formulas for undertaking research. To the contrary, the texts we have compiled here illustrate the diversity of methodological and analytical strategies that were designed, from the same field of study, to conduct research with different objectives, interests and approaches to the research problem.

Over these years we have held three Seminar meetings, the first in June 2006 in Cuernavaca, Morelos, Mexico; the second in May 2007 at the Latin American School of Social Sciences-Ecuador in Quito, Ecuador; and the third in June 2008 in Taxco, Guerrero, Mexico. This book is composed of the final products generated by this working group. The chapters are the result of dialogue and debate among the participating teams and have been in a continuous process of re-writing, with the objective of offering final documents that will be useful for systematic methodological reflection, not only in the field of migration studies, but in general

[1] There are, of course, notable exceptions. See, for example, some recent publications that manage to achieve this exercise: Masseroni (2007); De Sipio et al. (2007); Ariza and Velasco (2012).

for social science scholars concerned about the methodological and conceptual rigor of research work.

The essays compiled in this book were written throughout the various stages experienced by this group of researchers constituted in a Seminar, following a methodological guide that proposed questions and problems—which were resolved among the members of each group, who responded from their varying research contexts. These methodological guidelines were prepared collectively and constitute a methodological instrument in and of itself. As a result, we are now offering a compiled book that is not merely the sum of disconnected chapters, but rather an integrated product constructed around a series of focuses that guided the discussion and development of the final texts.[2]

The methodological reflections contained in this book's chapters followed two primary routes: (1) demonstrating the research process through the design of an analytical, methodological strategy for testing a research hypothesis, and on the basis of testing such an hypothesis, discussing the ways through which results or findings are generated, or in other words, the diverse modalities used in data construction; or (2) demonstrating the research process through the design of an analytical strategy and then, describing the way in which certain initial suppositions were re-conceptualized and/or certain analytical categories were reformulated, as well as bringing attention to the theoretical-methodological implications of this process and its reformulation.

The main focuses around which discussion in the methodological seminar revolved were: (a) interdisciplinary or multidisciplinary in research teams, (b) the design of research strategies with methodologies that combine quantitative and qualitative methods, (c) the relevance and utility of comparative analysis in social sciences, and (d) the division of labor in collective research, reflexivity and the dialectic nature of research (Ragin 2006; Smelser 2002).

Interdisciplinary was one of the topics addressed in the seminar, underscoring, on the one hand, the richness obtained when analytical perspectives from different disciplines enter into dialogue through members of the research team, making it possible to use different approaches, by incorporating analytical categories and instruments from varying fields of study. On the other hand, emphasis was placed on avoiding the risk of losing rigor in disciplinary work and in the rules imposed by the use of certain research methods or techniques (Siltanen et al. 2008).

One of the routes taken by participating research teams was a multidisciplinary approach, that is, with specialists from different disciplines coming together in a

[2] The methodological guidelines developed and circulated prior to each Seminar session made it possible for documents to be read before the session and organized around defined focuses of discussion, and facilitated the systematization of debates among researchers. In addition, because topic and problem-based minutes were taken of each Seminar session, the most relevant debates were systematized and the pending tasks and commitments made by each research team at the end of work sessions were identified. These minutes were taken by a person outside the Seminar group and were sent to participants in the days following the work sessions. These minutes constitute a valuable record of the discussions among participants.

team to resolve a research problem, share common language and even agree upon the use of certain analytical categories—by constructing them. One of the keys in this multidisciplinary work was to acquire and develop habits of ongoing communication among the members of each team, with the aim of respecting the specialization represented by each discipline, but also incorporating elements from the other disciplines in order to enrich the perspective from which a given matter was being analyzed.

According to González Casanova (2004), the term *interdisciplinarity* applies strictly to studies on self-regulated systems in which there is a constant intersection or integration of knowledge from different disciplines. However it also applies generically to new divisions and collaborations among specializations within the same discipline. In other words, this concept can relate to the intersections among different fields of study or different problem-based specializations.

Today, interdisciplinary has multiple connotations, from institutional conceptualizations that refer to work carried out in research centers with academics from different disciplines, to the development of sub-fields or hybrids of knowledge that cross fields of different disciplines, also referred to as transdisciplinary (Smelser 2002). Thus, one of the challenges proposed by the research teams was the articulation and complementary nature of research work, not only because borders between disciplines have been permeable, but also because reflexive work in teams makes it possible to construct analytical structures and concepts for defocalizing the hierarchal organization of the social sciences and also the exclusively discipline-based debates (Siltanen et al. 2008). In addition, the complexity of social reality demands integral or integrated explanations and not only partial perspectives on empirical phenomena. Nonetheless, this explicit acknowledgement of the need to construct and carry out interdisciplinary research constitutes a challenge in research practice. A researcher cannot carry out interdisciplinary work on his or her own. Dialogue with others is of course necessary, and so is coordination, which involves more than one division of field work or merely the use and application of certain methodological techniques or instruments. Rather, this process involves the construction of analytical structures and certain methodological tools that facilitate transversal readings of the phenomena under study (cf. Corona-Berkin and Kaltmeier 2012). In other words, an option for conducting interdisciplinary work consists of designing a research problem to be addressed through different levels of analysis.[3] In this case a transversal reading does not necessarily signify that methods must be combined, and in fact a multi-method (both qualitative and quantitative methods) strategy used in a study does not necessarily imply interdisciplinary work, unless instruments are explicitly designed to achieve such a dialogue (see Bloomraad 2007; Onwuebuzie and Leech 2005). In the same way, the mere combination of methods in a single instrument does not represent an interdisciplinary strategy, but it does open up the possibility that research results or

[3] This practical modality of interdisciplinary work is notably illustrated in the chapter in this book by Coubes, Velasco and Zlolniski.

findings can also be the product of an interdisciplinary dialogue—with diverse levels of analysis—and readings made with different instruments.

Research and data construction in the social sciences are dialectic processes, independently of whether their construction is interdisciplinary, multidisciplinary or disciplinary. In the end data are the product of an exercise in conceptual and analytical reflexivity. The production of scientific knowledge is clearly related to researchers from different fields taking epistemological positions. In other words there is no single way to construct data or present research findings. Innovation in a scientific field—according to Pierre Bourdieu—is not produced without breaking with current assumptions, and scientific capital is the most exposed to challenge (Bourdieu 1976, p. 56).

The validity of knowledge produced in social sciences is associated with the validation of procedures through which certain evidence and factual information is generated, and through which certain assessments have been made with regard to the significance of findings. Consequently, in the chapters of this book, priority is given to presenting the modalities through which research is conducted in multidisciplinary or interdisciplinary teams. In other words, the focus is on the narrative of methodological experience, the way in which certain findings were obtained, the methods and instruments designed for this purpose, the methodological difficulties and the processes followed in order to prove an hypothesis. In most of the chapters the reader will find some retrospective reflection that facilitates systematizing methodological practice and demonstrating the research process to the reader.

In addition to this exercise, which shows how research is being conducted, authors also discuss how investigative strategies are reformulated. In fact throughout the chapters the reader can observe how the dialectic element is present in both the data construction process and in the research process itself. Through methodological narrative, some chapters indicate basically how hypotheses are proven, and how the production of research findings or results is not subject to approval or confirmation of hypotheses—since the refutation of hypotheses is one of the possible results of research. In other cases priority is placed on the process of reformulating concepts and analytical categories.

One of the focuses that can be found transversally across the different chapters of this book is a process of reflecting upon the construction of complex units of analysis, which lead to the development of certain analytical strategies for studying the multiple facets of contemporary processes from a social science perspective. In some cases authors explicitly resume the discussion on methodological nationalism, and fundamentally, the discreet units of analysis that do not permit dynamic comparisons and detailed readings in diverse and sometimes simultaneous times and spaces are problematized. This methodological tension becomes apparent in the study of settlements through mobilities, expressed in the relation between residence and mobility (in the Chap. 2); the comparative exercise and *contextual* analysis of two migration flows of women in global markets located in two large cities (in the Chap. 3); the *relational perspective* for understanding variations in experiences of fear and forced migration in the different migration journeys, and in incorporation into the different receiving societies (in the Chap. 4); the problematization of nationality or a national group as an analytical unit for subsequently explaining organizational identities, practices and modalities, as well as the historic complexity of contexts of departure and of reception (in the Chap. 5); the substitution of urban and rural places of origin with urbanized and ruralized contexts of departure, as well as the development of an analytical category like *oriundez*, to explain the interrelation between internal migration and international migration, as well as the historic links among regions (in Chap. 6); and finally, the development of a methodological strategy that recuperates the historicity of migration processes and the construction of their own contexts, based on understanding transnational social space, also from its origin (in the Chap. 7). All these methodological dilemmas lead to a process of re-thinking all cases, and re-thinking the units of analysis that are useful for reformulating analytical strategies that facilitate the construction of comprehensive explanations of complex processes. We will now closely examine the contents of each of the chapters included in this book.

## 1.1 Focus of the Chapters

The idea is not only to emphasize the main contributions derived from interdisciplinary reflection and the use of comparative methodology, but also to present a brief summary of the contents, scope and objectives of the studies around which each team engages in theoretical-methodological reflection.

Chapter 2 by Marie Laure Coubês, Laura Velasco and Christian Zlolniski on *Residential Settlement and Mobility in the San Quintín Valley: Methodological Reflection on an Interdisciplinary Study* is a clear example of what it means to carry out a research project based on a strategy of interdisciplinary collaboration. The authors use a study of the residential settlement of contingents of agricultural day workers in the San Quintín Valley in the Mexican state of Baja California as a base for analyzing and discussing ways to construct and design a research project with interdisciplinary aspirations. The authors found it necessary to adopt an interdisciplinary investigative strategy due to the complex way the research problem was proposed, specifically the process of residential settlement as the result of global, regional and local economic processes, which at the same time lead to new forms of geographic and migratory mobility, generating new social actors and new processes of identity and rootedness.

The research team, composed of a demographer, sociologist and anthropologist, found it necessary to constantly resolve the tension created by their disciplinary specializations, and at the same time, to constantly promote interdisciplinary dialogue. This dialogue and the continuous crossing of disciplinary borders was a central factor in defining the units and levels of analysis in the research, in designing the questionnaire, in the theoretical discussion (especially at the macro level) and in interpreting research results. Nevertheless, despite the significant level of interdisciplinary integration achieved in certain areas and at certain moments in the research, team members maintained the rigor characteristic of each of their respective disciplines, especially in carrying out their individual work. In this sense, the challenge of interdisciplinary work lies not only in maintaining a spirit of teamwork and ongoing dialogue—which implies defocalization from individual disciplines—but in knowing how and when to use the rigor and strength of each discipline represented on the team, that is, knowing how to combine collective (interdisciplinary) work and individual (disciplinary) work.

Beyond teachings and experiences in the arena of interdisciplinary work, it is worth mentioning the way an analytical strategy of this type makes it possible to propose research problems related to certain social processes, in more complex, contextual manners. A traditional, or we might say classic, study of the process of residential settlement will identify the San Quintín Valley as a place of final destination of geographic and migratory mobility that originates in southern Mexico. Apart from the emergence of new social processes in the region under study, for example the fight for land and for urban services, or for recognition of certain cultural practices (a result of the significant presence of the indigenous population among new residents) we can see in this research a conceptual link between residence and mobility, elements that make up the settlement process. At the origin we find mobility, since only on the basis of mobility can we explain the region's population process. Nevertheless, once new inhabitants manage to establish themselves, new forms of mobility and migration emerge, or in other words, the new residence does not inhibit mobility and in fact it may facilitate or promote geographic and migratory mobility, especially to destinations like the United States. Consequently, as the San Quintin Valley is established as a point of arrival, it is at the same time a point of exodus, revealing the relation or interweaving between internal and international migration, processes which some disciplinary perspectives do not consider to have or have had any relation.

It is precisely the analytical, methodological strategy of an interdisciplinary nature proposed by Coubês, Velasco and Zlolniski that allows them to propose and prove their study's hypothesis, specifically that once migrants achieve their residential settlement, the circular patterns of mobility are transformed toward less frequent migrations of longer duration, at both national and international levels.

Marina Ariza's Chap. 3 on *A Comparative Approach to Global Domestic Service in Two Cities. Methodological Notes* belongs to a group of chapters that reflect upon analytical and methodological strategy, in this case on a comparative strategy based on the comparative method, oriented toward testing specific hypotheses. Based on the study of the relation between female migration and labor insertion, in the context of social transformations associated with globalization, the author discusses and proposes a strategy for comparative analysis in the study of two clearly-identified female migration circuits: women from the Dominican Republic in Madrid, and women from Mexico in New York.

In this chapter the reader will find a systematic, clear discussion on the limitations and advantages of the comparative method and its different meanings, both in social sciences in general and in the field of migration and mobilities' studies in particular. Especially noteworthy is the need to achieve an adequate comparison of similarities and differences between the cases under study, and the importance of identifying the number of cases to be studied, the selection of those cases and the equivalence of the indicators for comparison.

The author suggests three advantages from the use of the comparative method in the study of migration processes. The first is that it minimizes the risk of tautological statements, since by incorporating a second or third group in the study, or by analyzing the same social group but in different contexts, it is possible to relativize statements and avoid inappropriate generalizations. A second advantage is that it reduces the tension between micro and macro levels of analysis, since by expanding the scope of the first and the specificity of the second, it incorporates explanatory factors that are not necessarily associated with one or the other level of analysis. The third advantage is that it combats methodological nationalism, since analysis of human mobility and migration from a transnational perspective breaks with the nation-state referent and challenges the origin–destination dichotomy.

The idea of comparing two migration flows of women originating in two countries (the Dominican Republic and Mexico) and arriving in two urban contexts that attract the Latin American and Caribbean labor force—specifically Madrid, Spain and New York, US—is highly pertinent, due to the increasingly global nature of domestic work, as a feminized labor market. However, the study is even more unique because of the type of comparative perspective selected by the author, by suggesting that each of the two circuits has a set of inter-systemic differences and similarities, associated with what takes place in the countries of origin and destination. As for differences in the country of origin, especially worth noting are the presence of dissimilar family structures, and more independent female migration in the case of women from the Dominican Republic and more associational (following family members) migration in the case of Mexican women. With respect to the context of reception, the author underscores differences and especially similarities between the two feminized migration flows. The key differences are established in the different types of immigration policies, regulations in labor markets for foreigners, and in the welfare state policy applied to migrants. In contrast the author points to a set of similarities associated with the contexts of reception, such as two developed economies, with tertiarized productive structures, aging demographic structures, and a significant demand for female migrant labor in activities such as domestic services and caretaking work in general. The author focuses on developing a comparative analytical strategy that allows for delving more deeply into the analysis of inter-systemic similarities than differences. She indicates that the research design proposed is similar to that of the *maximum similarity systems* suggested by Przeworski and Teune (1970), to the extent that there are a significant number of variables in both migration systems that are postulated as causal variables.

In terms of methods and techniques used in gathering information in the field, the author proposes a qualitative analysis strategy that includes interviewing migrant women as well as another type of informant in the four points (localizations) where the study was conducted. The tendency is clearly toward studying diversity (key criterion in the selection of informants), beyond attempting to discover patterns. This is not a study oriented toward examining 'two cases', and to the contrary, the feminized migration circuits selected are not limited to only the national groups considered. The author proposes developing a comparison of the two migration trajectories in a context characterized by globalization and the creation of specific labor markets that require the female migrant labor force. This perspective is what allows the author to break with methodological nationalism and propose "a type of causal explanation that is more complex and contextual one". It is important to point out here that unlike the other chapters included in this book, in which teams of two or more researchers have participated, this study was led exclusively by Marina Ariza. Her methodological reflections, nevertheless, reveal the enormous potential of the comparative analytical strategy in the study of migration and human mobility.

Chapter 4 by Pilar Riaño and Marta Villa on *Forced migration of Colombians: a relational perspective*, is a reflection on the study of forced migration of Colombians (both internally displaced and refugees) in three national contexts: Colombia, Ecuador and Canada. While the chapter has been written by these two researchers, the team that carried out this complex, broad-based research was composed of ten researchers from different disciplines, and from the three countries mentioned. The purpose of the research was to analyze the social integration process of Colombians who cross internal and international borders, while taking two key analytical focuses into consideration: the *social fears* and *experiences* of individuals in displacement and refugee situations. The research was conducted in nine different sites (three in each country) in order to develop a broad universe for examining modalities, differences and similarities in the insertion of Colombians who are displaced or refugees.

After presenting a detailed characterization of the concepts of internal displacement and refugee status, the authors discuss some relations and variations in the fear and forced migration experienced by refugees and the displaced. The research is basically qualitative, multi-situated and focused on receiving societies, and confronts enormous methodological and disciplinary challenges. In the nine localities selected, a total of 21 workshops were organized to the refugee population, eight discussion groups were held with representatives from governmental and nongovernmental organizations linked to providing services to refugees and the displaced, and 22 interviews were completed with functionaries and those providing services to refugees and the displaced.

Although the research suggests using a comparative analytical strategy, what it actually uses is a *relational perspective*, with the aim of understanding certain variations in the experiences of fear and forced migration in the different journeys taken and in the incorporation of individuals in the particular receiving societies. The analysis and discussion among the three national teams made it possible to establish diverse 'types' of forced migration in each country, constructed on the basis of displacement experiences, systems of relations and types of journeys taken. Nonetheless, the main contribution of this research, in methodological terms, is not focused on the typology of forced migrations for each country, but primarily on the conceptual scheme known as the *field of relations in the forced migration of Colombians*. In this scheme the authors analyze characteristics of the sending context (violence, war, conflict), the receiving context (public policies and institutions associated with services to refugees and the displaced), and the central role played by the migration journey and the elements of which it is composed, such as the social mediating organization in these displacements, social and institutional resources used along the way, social networks, transit spaces and migration routes. A very important strategy adopted by this research team, from both methodological and ethical viewpoints, was the presentation of study results to the population of refugees and the displaced who participated in the workshops. The impact of this effort to socialize the findings made it possible to confirm the similarities and differences in the experiences of the refugees and the displaced in the various receiving sites.

Unlike the study conducted by Marina Ariza, whose comparative strategy is oriented toward examining some structural characteristics of labor insertion by two groups of immigrant women working in domestic services, the research led by Riaño and Villa demonstrates another modality of comparative analysis, specifically of subjective processes, such as social fears and the way in which such fears shape the way refugees and the displaced become integrated in another place of residence. The authors call this process an analysis of *experience*.

Closely associated with the previous chapter is the work of Luin Goldring and Patricia Landolt in Chap. 5 on *Transnational Migration and the Reformulation of Analytical Categories: Unpacking Latin American Refugee Dynamics in Toronto*. This chapter offers a rich discussion on the ways that original research suppositions (hypotheses) are transformed—especially during field work—and the ways in which concepts and analytical categories are modified and reframed in the process. The initial objective of this study was to build a map of the patterns of transnational engagement and the integration process in the society of reception (the city of Toronto, in Canada) for four national-origin groups of Latin American exiles and refugees: Chileans, Salvadorans, Guatemalans and Colombians. It was assumed that the groups selected were composed of refugees with a specific national origin, defined by the centrality of their country of origin. Based on a comparative analysis strategy, the idea was to contrast the characteristics of the social incorporation and transnational engagement of these national groups, with the assumption that organizational forms based on national and sub-national identities would be found. The essay analyzes the way in which the original categories and lines of analysis were reframed, leading the authors to also reformulate the study's initial assumptions and hypotheses.

An initial problem confronted was that in the original proposal, the contexts of departure for the four national groups of refugees were homogenized as a single 'type' of context, assuming the situations characterizing forced migration were the same. In other words, it was assumed that if all migrants had the same condition or characteristic as refugees, then a similar situation (violence, war) would have led to their emigration, and what migrants had in common was their national origin. The error, which was rectified during the process, was to consider only one context of departure, instead of four.

The second field or node is related to the independence of the cases studied and the notion of temporality. Since the place of arrival and/or reception for Latin American refugees in this case is Toronto, the way in which the authors differentiated between the contexts of reception was almost exclusively on the basis of the period of arrival for the waves of refugees. For example, they identified specific cohorts or periods of arrival, dominated by certain national groups. The authors were able to reformulate the 'context of reception' category and the notion of temporality by theorizing and anticipating that the waves of migrants were modifying the characteristics of the contexts of reception. Given the structural difficulty in comparing groups of refugees arriving at different times to the same destination, it was necessary to unravel the context of reception, since the emergence and consolidation of Canadian organizations assisting Latin American refugees and the very arrival of new refugees implied changes in the context of reception.

The third node is related to the tendency to define 'groups' or populations according to a shared nationality. At the beginning of the study, national origin was a key category, a fundamental unit of analysis. Nationality was considered to be a valid 'container' or basis for generating identities, practices and organizations. However, field work assisted the authors in recognizing the importance of organizations without a shared nationality, in the social and political incorporation of the Latin American refugee population in Toronto. The authors found organizations bringing together artists, women and professionals, as well as religious organizations and *umbrella* organizations made up of Latin Americans of diverse nationalities, with significant levels of integration and transnational engagement.

When the authors abandoned the idea of developing catalogues of different individuals or national organizational cultures, they moved on to a much more detailed analysis of the cultural practices and features that migrants bring with them when they are displaced to other countries. This cultural and political 'toolkit'—described in this way by the authors—may be more important than national origin in terms of the generation of identities, practices and organizations.

Chapter 6 by Liliana Rivera-Sánchez and Fernando Lozano-Ascencio on *Between the contexts of departure and modalities of the social organization of migration: a radiography of the research process*, presents a meticulous reflection on a process through which the analytical and methodological strategy of a study on international migration dynamics in the Mexican state of Morelos was enriched and modified. This is a chapter that describes changes in direction and key reformulations in the research methodology, process of construction and transformation of some analytical categories, and methodological designing of instruments employed in the corresponding field work. The framework for this reflection is a study that was focused on studying the differences and similarities in the flow of migrants to the United States originating in Mexican rural and urban localities in a state considered to be part of 'emerging' international migration. The central hypothesis was that the profile of migrants with rural origins was essentially different that the profile of migrants with urban origins. At the same time, the rural or urban nature of the locality of departure played a part in creating differentiated migration patterns. The idea was to prove, from a comparative perspective, whether the rural or urban environment had an impact on migrants' selectivity and on the dynamics of migration to the United States.

There were two important changes in the orientation of the analytical strategy used in this research study. The first was substituting the 'place of origin' category (rural or urban) with the *context of departure*. The idea was to move beyond the simplistic notion that rural or urban features are automatic attributes, defined according to the size of the population or the predominance of certain productive activities. The 'context of departure' category implies a complex perspective of migrants' place of departure that takes into account not only the local geographic space but also social space, that is, the presence of historic processes and economic, social and political relations that extend beyond the locality's physical space. The second change in the orientation of the analytical strategy was replacing the category of 'migration dynamics' with the *social organization of migration* category. This change signified moving away from the idea of identifying and comparing rural and urban migration patterns, toward the need for analyzing a wide range of processes such as migrants' strategies for crossing borders, the selection of places of destination, the presence and use of *coyotes* and *polleros*, the forms of migrants' social and family links with their places of origin, and the modalities of concentration or dispersion of migrants in different points within the United States. This complex aggregate of processes was identified as the social organization of migration. In rigor, the changes in strategy allowed for refining the study's central question, specifically to describe the relation between the *ruralized* or *urbanized* contexts of departure and the modalities of the social organization of migration in Morelos.

In order to explain the relation between these two analytical categories (contexts of departure and social organization of migration), the authors defined a set of complex variables such as the historic formation of territory, the history of emigration to the United States, the link between internal and international migration, the role of social networks, and modalities of settlement in the place of destination. This made it possible to not only operationalize the study of the relation between contexts of departure and the social organization of migration, but it identified the need to construct new analytical categories that incorporate elements of complex variables such as those mentioned. One of these analytical categories is *oriundez*. In this chapter the authors present a detailed discussion of the process of construction and transformation of this analytical category, and it is one of the main strengths of this particular work.

Chapter 7 on book, *Investigating the 'origin': rethinking the transnational social space from contexts of departure* by Alicia Torres and Gioconda Herrera offers a reflection on a research study in process on a social space with a long migration tradition. The theoretical and methodological reflection is developed around a study in the Cañar province in the southern Andean region of Ecuador—a region that has presented different modalities of internal and international migration: journal workers traveling within the country to work in the sugar cane harvest, migrations to the United States, and more recently, migrations to Europe, especially Spain. The authors review the original proposals of their research project, and the way in which collective discussion and reflection signified a reformulation of the methodological strategy, units of analysis and the way to propose the universe under study,

The purpose of this research is to analyze the way in which the migration experience in the Cañar province has influenced the reconfiguration of relations of inequality and social exclusion, as well as the reconfiguration of the transnational social space, in terms of its effects on hierarchies of class, gender, and ethnicity. Initially, the objective was to follow the trajectories of migrant families in order to analyze the way in which the experience in the place of destination influenced both the type and characteristics of the transnational practices and links carried out by migrant families, and in the processes of inequality and social exclusion in the place of origin. This was a proposal that over-represented the influence of the receiving country in the forming of local social spaces, without delving deeper in the study of what took place in societies of origin. Even more so, since emigration from Cañar is directed toward two clearly-identified international destinations (New York, in the US, and Murcia, in Spain), the authors proposed comparing the effect from the experience of migrating to these two specific destinations (based on a multi-situated research) as a way of understanding the social dynamics of the context of departure. In rigor, what this chapter presents is the rectification of the path to be taken by the research, by proposing to abandon the relation with receiving societies and instead further study the social fabric of the societies of origin.

One of the most important changes in the orientation of the methodological strategy was the decision to reconstruct the migration dynamics in the Cañar province from a historic perspective. This would facilitate observing the process of construction of transnational social spaces, not only on the basis of studying transnational practices and links, but fundamentally on the basis of analyzing how the transnational forms of *being* and *belonging* (based on Glick Schiller 2004) are interwoven and constitute forms of reproducing local social spaces. In this sense, the study of local spaces is central, however in relation to what takes place globally, although the focus is on local occurrences. In the words of the authors, theoretical-methodological reformulation signifies "moving toward a more dense perspective of the contexts of departure".

The comparative perspective in this research study is clarified when the authors reflect upon the study's units of analysis. Since the authors' interest is to further develop its analysis of local society, in relation to its global insertion, the units of analysis proposed are precisely the transnational modalities of *being* and *belonging*. This implies that the comparative perspective is focused on homes with migrants, and homes without migrants—in this case migrants inserted in a context of international migration. The reflection contained in this chapter provides a set of theoretical and methodological tools for identifying and studying transnational social spaces, with special emphasis on contexts of departure.

The seminar, which led to this book, was financially supported by the William & Flora Hewlett Foundation, the Regional Center for Multidisciplinary Research (*Centro Regional de Investigaciones Multidisciplinarias*—CRIM) at the National

Autonomous University of Mexico (*Universidad Nacional Autónoma de México*—UNAM), and the Latin American School of Social Sciences (*Facultad Latinoamericana de Ciencias Sociales*—FLACSO) campus in Quito, Ecuador. In particular, the last Seminar meeting and the publication of this book were financed in the framework of the Program for Assistance to Projects for the Innovation and Improvement of Teaching (*Programa de Apoyo a Proyectos para la Innovación y el Mejoramiento de la Enseñanza*—PAPIME) at the UNAM.

Lastly, we would like to express our appreciation to all the collaborators who co-authored this book, who worked with particular dedication during this long period of time, generously sharing their knowledge and experience in research. In addition we would also like to express our gratitude to Luciana Gandini, who carefully prepared the Seminar minutes, and to Rosa Lilia Álvarez, who has accompanied us since the project was created and who was responsible for the Seminar's operational coordination.

## References

Ariza, Marina, Alejandro Portes, 2007: *El País Transnacional* (Mexico: Universidad Nacional Autónoma de México).

Ariza, Marina; Velasco, Laura, 2012: *Métodos cualitativos y su aplicación empírica. Por los caminos de la investigación sobre migración internacional* (Mexico: Universidad Nacional Autónoma de México-El Colegio de la Frontera Norte).

Bloomraad, Irene, 2007: "Of Puzzles and Serendipity: Doing Research with cross-national comparisons and Mixed methods", in: De Sipio, Lois; García y Griego, Manuel; Kossoudji, Sherri (Eds.): *Researching* Migration. Stories from the field (New York: The Social Science Research Council); at: http://www.ssrc.org/pubs/researching_migration.pdf.

Bourdieu, Pierre, 1976 [first Spanish Ed., 2000]: "El campo científico", in: Bourdieu, Pierre, 2000: *Los usos sociales de la ciencia. Por una sociología clínica del campo científico*, (Buenos Aires: Ediciones Nueva Visión).

Bourdieu, Pierre, 1984 [first Spanish Ed., 2008]: *Homo Academicus* (Buenos Aires: Siglo XXI editores).

Brettell, Caroline B.; Hollifield, James F., 2000: "Introduction. Migration Theory. Talking across disciplines," in: Brettell, Caroline B.; Hollifield, James F. (Eds.): *Migration Theory. Talking across disciplines* (New York: Routledge): 1–26.

Bryman, Alan, 2007: "The Research Question in Social Research: What is its role?", in: *International Journal of Social Research Methodology*, 10,1 (February): 5–20.

Castles, Stephen; Delgado Wise, Raúl (Eds.), 2007: *Migración y desarrollo: perspectivas desde el sur* (México: Miguel Angel Porrúa – Zacatecas: Universidad Autónoma de Zacatecas).

Corona Berkin, Sarah; Kaltmeier, Olaf, 2012: *En diálogo. Metodologías horizontales en Ciencias Sociales y Culturales* (Barcelona: Gedisa Editorial, Col. Herramientas Universitarias).

De Sipio, Louis; García y Griego, Manuel; Kossoudji, Sherri (Eds.), 2007: *Researching Migration. Stories from the field* (New York: The Social Science Research Council); at: http://www.ssrc.org/pubs/researching_migration.pdf.

Feldman, Bela; Rivera-Sánchez, Liliana; Stefoni, Carolina; Villa, Marta Inés, 2011: *La construcción social del sujeto migrante en América Latina. Prácticas, representaciones y estrategias* (Quito, Ecuador: Facultad Latinoamericana de Ciencias Sociales, Consejo Latinoamericano de Ciencias Sociales – Universidad A. Hurtado de Chile).

Foner, Nancy; Rumbaut, Rubén; Gold, Steve (Eds.), 2000: *Immigration Research for a New Century*. Multidisciplinary Perspectives (New York: Russell Sage Foundation).

Glick Schiller, Nina; Basch, Linda; Szanton, C. Blanc, 1992: *Towards a Transnational Perspective on Migration: Race, Class, Ethnicity and Nationalism Reconsidered* (New York: New York Academy of Sciences).

Glick Schiller, Nina; Levitt, Peggy, 2006: *Haveńt we heard this somewhere before? A substantive view of Transnational Migration Studies by way of a reply to Waldinger and Fitzgerald*, Working Paper No. 06-01, The Center for Migration and Development, Working paper series (Princeton, NJ: Princeton University).

Glick Schiller, Nina, 2004: "Transnationality", in: Nugent, David; Vincent, Joan (Eds.): *A Companion to the Anthropology of Politics* (London: Blackwell).

Glick Schiller, Nina, 2007: *Beyond the Nation-State and its Units of Analysis: Toward a New Research Agenda for Migration Studies. Essentials of Migration Theory*, Working Paper No. 33, (Berlin: Germany: Center on Migration, Citizenship and Development).

Glick Schiller, Nina; Faist; Thomas; 2010: *Migration, Development and Transnationalization*. A Forum for Social Analysis, Vol. 12 (New York: Berghahn Books),

Glick Schiller, Nina; Caglar, Ayse, 2011: *Locating Migration. Rescaling Cities and Migrants* (Ithaca: Cornell University Press).

González Casanova, Pablo, 2004: *Las nuevas ciencias y las humanidades. De la Academia a la política* (Barcelona: Anthropos/Instituto de Investigaciones Sociales-UNAM).

Gray, Breda, 2008: "Putting Emotion and Reflexivity to work in Researching Migration", in: *Sociology*, 42,5 (October): 935–952.

Grosfoguel, Ramón, 2006: "La descolonización de la Economía Política y los estudios postcoloniales: transmodernidad, pensamiento fronterizo y colonialidad global", in: *Tabula Rasa* (January–June), No. 4, (Bogotá, Colombia Universidad Colegio Mayor de Cundinamarca): 17–46.

Kaltmeier, Olaf, 2012: "Hacia la descolonización de las metodologías: reciprocidad, horizontalidad y poder", in: Corona Berkin, Sarah; Kaltmeier, Olaf (Eds.): *En diálogo. Metodologías horizontales en Ciencias Sociales y Culturales* (Barcelona: Gedisa Editorial, Col. Herramientas Universitarias): 25–54.

Khagram; Sanjeev; Levitt, Peggy, 2008: *The Transnational Studies Reader* (New York: Routledge).

Kuhn, Thomas, 1962, 2006: *La estructura de las revoluciones científicas* (Mexico: Fondo de Cultura Económica).

Masseroni, Susana (Ed.), 2007: *Interpretando la experiencia. Estudios cualitativos en ciencias sociales* (Buenos Aires: Colección Investigación y Tesis Mnemosyne).

Morawska, Ewa, 2003: "Disciplinary Agendas and Analytic Strategies of Research on Immigrant Transnationalism: Challenges of Interdisciplinary Knowledge", in: *The International Migration Review,* 37,3 (Fall): 611–640.

Mills, Belinda; Van de Bunt, Gerhard G.; de Brujin, Jeanne, 2006: "Comparative Research: Persistent Problems and Promising Solutions", in: *International Sociology,* 21,5: 619–631.

Onwuegbuzie, Anthony J.; Leech, Nancy L., 2005: "On Becoming a Pragmatic Researcher: The importance of Combining Quantitative and Qualitative Research Methodologies", in: *International Journal of Social Research Methodology*, 8,5: 375–387.

Pries, Ludger (Ed.), 2008: *Rethinking Transnationalism. The Meso-link of Organization* (London: Routledge).

Przeworski, Adam; Teune, Henry, 1970: *The logic of comparative social inquiry* (New York: Wiley-Interscience).

Quijano, Aníbal, 2000: "Colonialidad del poder y clasificación social", in: *Journal of World-Systems Research*, Vol. 6 (summer/fall): 342–386.

Ragin, Charles, 2006: "How to Lure Analytic Social Science out of the Doldrums: some lessons from Comparative Research", in: *International Sociology,* 21,5: 633–646.

Rodríguez, Ileana; Martínez, Josebe (Eds.), 2008: *Postcolonialidades históricas: (in)visibilidades hispanoamericanas/colonialismos ibéricos* (Barcelona: Anthropos-Colección Pensamiento crítico-pensamiento utópico).

Siltanen, Janet; Willis, Alette; Scobie, Willow, 2008: "Separately Together: Working Reflexively as a Team", in: *International Journal of Social Research Methodology*, 11,1 (February): 45–61.

Smelser, Neil J., 2002:"On comparative analysis, interdisciplinarity and internationalization in Sociology", in: *International Sociology*, 18,4: 643–657.

Waldinger, Roger; Fitzgerald, David, 2004: "Transnationalism in Question", in: *American Journal of Sociology*, 109,5: 1177–1195.

Waldinger, Roger, 2008: "Between "Here" and "There": Immigrant Cross-Border Activities and Loyalties", in: *International Migration Review*, 42,1 (Spring): 3–29.

Wimmer, Andreas; Glick Schiller, Nina, 2003: "Methodological Nationalism, the Social Sciences, and the Study of Migration: an Essay in Historical Epistemology", in: *International Migration Review*, 37,3: 576–610.

# Chapter 2
# Residential Settlement and Mobility in the San Quintin Valley: Methodological Reflections on an Interdisciplinary Study

**Marie Laure Coubès, Laura Velasco and Christian Zlolniski**

**Abstract** This chapter examines the settlement and mobility practices of farmworkers and families in the San Quintin Valley in Baja California, Mexico from a multi- and interdisciplinary perspective. Its goal is to open the 'black box' of interdisciplinary collaboration as research praxis to expose its nuts and bolts. The praxis of interdisciplinary research can be conceptualized as a process consisting of different stages requiring various approaches and research strategies. Each stage poses a distinct set of challenges but also presents opportunities for enhancing dialogue across disciplines. Interdisciplinary research means both specialization and defocalization, with each of these logics dominating in a different way at the stages of theoretical conceptualization and methodological construction examined.

**Keywords** Interdisciplinary research · Research methodology · Settlement · Baja California · San Quintin Valley

M. L. Coubès (✉) · L. Velasco
El Colegio de la Frontera Norte, Tijuana, BC, Mexico
e-mail: mcoubes@colef.mx

C. Zlolniski
University of Texas, Arlington, TX, USA

L. Rivera-Sánchez and F. Lozano-Ascencio (eds.), *The Practice of Research on Migration and Mobilities*, SpringerBriefs in Environment, Security, Development and Peace 14, DOI:10.1007/978-3-319-02693-0_2, The Author(s) 2014

## 2.1 Introduction

This chapter discusses the methodological experience in a multi- and interdisciplinary study on the settlement process of laborers and families in San Quintin Valley since the 1980s.[1] Located in the state of Baja California, Mexico, some 300 km south of the US border, San Quintin Valley is one of the most economically dynamic rural regions of northwestern Mexico, thanks to its specialized export-oriented agricultural production of fresh vegetables for the US and Canadian markets. Since the 1970s, growth in the horticulture export sector has fostered an increasing demand for field workers in the region, leading to a gradual but solid transformation in labor composition from migratory laborers residing in camp settlements and in constant movement, to laborers settled in *colonias*–subdivisions of land lots where settlers have built their own homes—with more stable employment opportunities. We refer to this residential shift from camps to *colonias* as settlement, with important implications for family and labor life and for the constitution of the local and regional community.

At the regional level, settlement has led to notable demographic consequences, including the population growth registered in recent decades. Between 1990 and 2010, the population of the San Quintin Valley more than doubled, jumping from 38,151 to 92,177 inhabitants.[2] Given the new pattern of residence in *colonias*, the traditional agricultural camps where farm workers were generally located have decreased in size, and some have disappeared. In their place, a large number of recently forming *colonias* have been emerging, with agricultural workers and their families building their own housing, creating new forms of employment, developing new local communities, and gradually establishing roots in the region. Residential settlement, however, did not lead to the end of migratory mobility in the region; on the contrary, it fostered new forms of geographic mobility and migratory patterns. This process of mobility-settlement-mobility is characteristic of the border region between Mexico and the United States, reflecting a global phenomenon of simultaneous human migrations and settlement processes.

With the objective of studying residence and mobility as constitutive aspects of this settlement experience, we decided from the outset to apply an interdisciplinary approach that would allow us to capture the richness and complexity of this process, which has profoundly transformed the region in the last decades. Methodologically, the interdisciplinary and teamwork approach promised better conditions than an approach based on a single discipline to confront the challenge of achieving a comprehensive understanding of settlement and its consequences.

---

[1] The study presented is part of a larger project "Migración, Trabajo Agrícola y Etnicidad" (Migration, Farm Labor, and Ethnicity) conducted in Baja California funded by Conacyt and El Colef in Mexico. Ethnographic research was also funded by grants from the Wenner-Gren Foundation and the National Science Foundation.

[2] Elaboration of the El Colef-Conacyt project, based on the General Censuses of Population and Housing, 1990 to 2010.

Welcome to San Quintin Valley, Baja California, Mexico. *Source* Photo by Abbdel Camargo who granted permission to reproduce this photo

Mayordomía handing over in Nuevo San Juan Copala, San Quintin Valley, Baja California, Mexico. *Source* Photo by Abbdel Camargo who granted permission to reproduce this photo

With the purpose of giving an account of the new residential forms and the changes in migratory flows to the region, we decided to combine three disciplinary approaches: demography for studying the interactions between demographic and residential dynamics; sociology for studying the collective action associated with new residences and its consequences in the social integration processes; and anthropology for documenting this process from the perspective of the laborers and families who are the protagonists of settlement.

Following Smelser (2003), we define interdisciplinarity as the collaboration and synergy among researchers from distinct disciplines who converge with different focuses, concepts, and perspectives in the comprehension of a determined social phenomenon. From this perspective, our intention is to go beyond the mere sum of empirical results arising from diverse disciplines and methods. We aim to pursue interdisciplinary dialogue that can lead to a critical review and formulation of new concepts and theories pertinent to the research topic.

Fortunately, we are not starting from zero in this undertaking. The academic literature covering the epistemological and theoretical basis upon which interdisciplinary research is conducted is of great value. Examples in interdisciplinary research can be found in fields such as international migration, ethnic, and gender studies, which have all developed on the basis of cross-disciplinary fertilization. Yet there is scarce reflection and discussion about the praxis of interdisciplinary research and the challenges that collaboration across disciplines entails. We specifically refer to the praxis of interdisciplinary research as process, the different stages an interdisciplinary project involves, the set of challenges each stage presents, and the research strategies available to respond to them.

The objective of this chapter is to contribute to reflection on this matter based on our experience of interdisciplinary collaboration in the study of the above referred settlement process in the San Quintin Valley. Generally, scholars who form part of a research team possess experience around a specific theme and have studied a particular discipline, developing a certain degree of dominion of theoretical knowledge and specialization in determined methodologies and techniques. Yet at the same time, this specialization often becomes a straitjacket, inhibiting interaction and the generation of shared knowledge among researchers with distinct themes and disciplines when they take part in joint projects, as is our case.[3] Throughout the project, we realized that interdisciplinarity required a certain degree of disciplinary defocalization in order to facilitate comprehension of the logics of reasoning, basic variables and parameters, theoretical assumptions, and methodologies employed by other 'specialists'.

The argument we present here is that interdisciplinary research implies both specialization and defocalization, with the crossing of disciplinary borders. Each of these logics dominates in a different way in the conceptualization phase and in methodological construction. Thus we view interdisciplinary research as a process made up of distinct phases including: (1) conceptual design of the project, (2) selection of study methods and techniques, (3) collection of data and information, (4) analysis and interpretation, and (5) write up and presentation of results. Distinct possibilities exist in each of these phases, as well as challenges, advantages, and disadvantages for the interdisciplinary encounter, compelling the

[3] In our research team, each member has not only a different disciplinary education, but also specializes in different areas of knowledge. The sociologist, Laura Velasco, focuses on studies of migration and identity processes, particularly of indigenous populations from Oaxaca migrating to destinations along the northwestern Mexican and southwestern US border regions. The demographer, Marie Laure Coubès, has studied employment along the northern Mexican border, particularly gender differences in labor markets and labor trajectories. The anthropologist, Christian Zlolniski, specializes in issues of labor and migration, particularly with respect to Mexican immigrant workers and communities in the United States.

research team to make some strategic decisions. We believe that a discussion of the challenges that each of these stages entails is a necessary step for researchers who aspire to overcome the disciplinary barriers that often prevent truly interdisciplinary teamwork.

In this chapter we present only the first two phases of our research. The first section addresses the conceptual design of our study, its objectives, disciplinary approaches, hypotheses, and levels of analysis. We discuss the experience of developing concepts that resonate across different disciplines, and how we built upon the theoretical corpus of each of them. In the second section, we describe the project's methodological design and the research techniques selected to respond to the multidisciplinary construction of the project.

## 2.2 Conceptual Design: The Study of Settlement from an Interdisciplinary Perspective

Our initial interest was to understand the transformations occurring in the region during the last two decades, particularly the process of residential settlement of thousands of laborers and their families in the region. This phenomenon contrasted with the image of San Quintin—still present in the literature of the 1990s—as a region of seasonal migrants. One of our first challenges then was to conceptualize the various aspects that characterize this residential settlement process. We defined settlement as a demographic and social process through which a high proportion of agricultural workers made this region their place of residence, changing from seasonal migrants to residents with ties and a sense of belonging to a local and regional community without implying the end of their geographic mobility.

In order to understand how residential settlement emerged, we also considered other transformations in the larger region's economy. The San Quintin Valley's recent history presents a clear illustration of how the articulation between global and regional forces has fostered formidable economic and demographic growth in this arid region which, prior to the 1980s, was scarcely populated. Growing demand for horticultural products in the US market, as well as the flow of capital south of the border and the relocation of numerous export-agriculture sector consortiums to the San Quintin region have contributed to sparking this region's soaring economic growth.

In this context, our aim was to study the new residential and mobility patterns that such macro-structural transformations have engendered, and the ways in which individuals and collectives respond and frame their options for action. Statistical and qualitative data indicate that a large segment of the region's inhabitants have experienced residential change from camps for laborers residing in the area only temporarily, to low-income *colonias*. For example, the proportion of agricultural laborers residing in camps during the high season dropped from two-thirds to one-third between 1989 and 1999 (INI/PRONJAG, cited by Velasco

2002, p. 71), and in the 1990s 20 new *colonias* were create.[4] These changes have been accompanied by social differentiation in labor and ethnic terms. A large number of the new settlers are no longer as vulnerable to the changing agricultural seasons, since agricultural employment has extended throughout more months during the year. In addition, population growth has fostered the development of employment possibilities in other sectors such as services and regional commerce, contributing to the increasing diversification of the region's labor markets. There has also been increasing ethnic differentiation of the migrants arriving in the San Quintin Valley, including Mixtecs, Triquis, Zapotecs, and Purépechas, as well as mestizo workers who come from states such as Sonora and participate at a different point in the production process.

In the context of these changes, we seek to examine the residential and mobility dimensions associated with settlement from an interdisciplinary articulation at both the conceptual and methodological levels. We begin with the premise that settlement should be addressed as a diachronic process that develops in stages over time, involving important transformations at both the macro level in the region's demographic structure and in meso–implications for the families and domestic units that are the subject of settlement. With the objective of capturing these distinct levels, our proposal consists of combining different approaches from various disciplines with regard to the concept of settlement.

Specifically we approach the settlement experience in the San Quintin Valley from two different and complimentary angles: as a colonization endeavor, and as a social integration process. In one of its primary meanings, the concept of settlement has been used by historians and human geographers to refer to the process of colonization of scarcely populated areas by new settlers who migrate from other regions and who contribute to its economic development. In this sense, the concept of settlement is closely linked to the idea of settlers as *pioneer agents* who contribute to opening up, populating, and developing new regions in bordering/ peripheral locations which, due to their geographic, climatic, or political characteristics, had been scarcely developed. These pioneer agents may establish themselves in previously uninhabited territories or may join settlements already established by earlier inhabitants.

The notion of colonization as the organizer of settlement has been developed by geographers, who have proposed a theoretical model of urban systems resulting from this process (Whebell 1969). The settlement resulting from colonization is represented by the corridor model, which serves as a transportation axis that shapes residential settlement along this axis. In this sense, the history of San Quintin's development includes various elements of this corridor model. San Quintin is located in a long plain area, connected to the cities of the north by the trans-peninsular highway. This transportation axis has played a key role in the development and distribution of its main settlement points and the expansion of its economic relations with cities in the north as well as in California. Settlement in

[4] Elaboration of the El Colef-Conacyt project based on Observación de colonias.

this region is thus organized in different staggered locations located along the highway axis. The economy, almost exclusively oriented toward exportation, is also an important element of this colonization model.

The concept of colonization also has a long tradition in studies about the history of economic development in the southwestern United States and its border region with Mexico since the mid-nineteeth century. For example, some historians have used this concept to outline the slow colonization process in the state of Baja California. The first projects to develop large-scale commercial agriculture in the peninsula took place in the late nineteeth century during the Porfiriato regime spearheaded by various national and foreign companies; however, in the San Quintin Valley these projects failed (Piñera 2006; Taylor 2011). On the threshold of the twentieth century, Mexicali emerged as the first and largest agricultural enclave in Baja California in the Colorado River Delta (Deasy and Gerhard 1944, p. 584). This development reflected a broader historic process through which the Mexican state began to promote large agricultural irrigation projects, especially for cotton production, along the country's northern border.

The San Quintin Valley, however, can be seen as a case of late colonization in one of the northern Mexico border regions which had remained outside of the border's economic development, was scarcely inhabited, and where the state had a weak presence. As such it shares similar traits with, and also offers important contrasts to, the previous experiences of colonization in Mexicali and other northern border regions. In all the cases, colonization was a result of export-oriented commercial agriculture development projects first around cotton in the first half of the twentieth century, and then around vegetable production beginning in the 1970s. Thus it was not until the 1970s when the San Quintin Valley began to take off economically and demographically, stimulated by the development of export agriculture, especially tomato production. This growth was also facilitated by the construction of the trans-peninsular highway connecting the region to the Tijuana-San Diego border. In this undertaking, the Mexican state sought to develop this border region with the objectives of providing sources of employment, populating the region, and fomenting the export-agriculture industry by seizing upon the natural advantages of geographic proximity with the US market.[5]

Unlike the large irrigation projects constructed in Mexicali and other regions of northern Mexico, however, state investment in infrastructure in the San Quintin Valley was scarce. The initiative for promoting the agro-export sector was left in the hands of private investors, particularly US companies, through commercial alliances with local producers. In this sense, the state makes its appearance late in the region's history, most visibly in the 1980s, both to bring order to the massive population process unleashed by economic growth and to mediate labor disputes between producers and laborers in a climate marked by high levels of social

[5] For a discussion of the growth of the export-oriented horticultural industry in Mexico and its role in fomenting massive forms of labor migration and flexible employment, see Lara Flores (2010) and Lara Flores and de Grammont (2011).

inequality and conflict. The state then became a central actor in the distribution of lands for *colonias* in which agricultural workers and their families gradually settled, the regularization of property rights, the installation of certain basic services and infrastructure for these recently-formed *colonias*, and the development of assistance programs for alleviating the problems related to poverty, hygiene, and public health that began to ravage the indigenous agricultural worker population.

In short, the San Quintin Valley illustrates a case of late economic development directly linked to the globalization process of the export-agriculture sector (Zlolniski 2010). As such, it poses a number of questions: How did the transition from agricultural camps to *colonias* take place in this colonization endeavor? How has the demographic and ethnic profile of the Valley's population transformed? And how have the new settlers developed a sense of belonging and community in this region? To answer these questions we felt we needed to look beyond the concept of colonization explained above to capture the social mechanisms by which individuals and collective groups set up roots in the region and mobilize to advance their rights as settlers. Next we turn our attention to a second approach to settlement that addresses the economic, social, and political dimensions of this process.

### *2.2.1 Socio-Economic and Political Integration*

The concept of settlement also has a long-standing tradition in sociology and social anthropology. In these disciplines, this concept is often used to refer to the mechanisms, strategies, and collective actions through which new inhabitants, generally immigrants, attempt to incorporate and integrate within a new social and political context. In the field of migration studies, the notion of settlement as incorporation within the receiving society is a tool that has been used widely. Particularly in the studies on Mexican migration to rural California in the 1980s, the concept of settlement was used to distinguish between migrants (sojourners) and settlers (Chávez 1988, p. 105; Cornelius 1992, p. 187), pointing out an important change in the living conditions and the vital orientation of migrants once they achieve a stable residence.

While recognizing the contribution of these studies to the documentation of the settlement experience of Mexican immigrants in California, it is important to challenge the dichotomy implied in the distinction between these two types of immigrants. Viewing settlement from the biographic perspective of the individual or the family, the new residence does not necessarily inhibit the mobility of the individual or other family members. Instead it may actually facilitate or foment geographic and migratory mobility. According to Rouse (1992, p. 43), while a process of stability for some members of the family exists, this same condition extends to others the possibility of continuing in movement, developing a type of bifocality in the residential settlement process that combines with the establishment of trans-territorial or transnational circuits. This simultaneous and multiple reality has been recognized as one of the premises of the transnational migration model, exhibiting the intermingling of integration practices in the new places of residence with those of transnational or translocal linkage, as well as the coexistence of links with places of origin and other locations in the migratory circuits at the family and community levels (see Levitt et al. 2003, p. 571).[6] In this perspective, family life is not limited to the local sphere, but may take on a trans-territorial or transnational tone, depending on the places in which family members are located. This creates a situation in which what happens in one region, such as California or Oaxaca, has implications for individuals residing in other regions, such as San Quintin.[7]

In our theoretical model on settlement there is then a conceptual connection between mobility and residential establishment by formerly migrant workers. Mobility is at the origin, since the process of demographic growth in the region was in large extent the result of the arrival of the pioneer settlers and thousands of workers and their families. But once these migrants settled, establishing residence in the region, new forms of mobility and migration appeared. This makes the San Quintin Valley a point of both arrival and departure, in which internal and international migration intersect.

Thus both residential stability and geographic mobility reflect the above-mentioned bifocality. Placing this phenomenon in historic and social perspective, we decided to conceptualize settlement not only as the development of a rural region inhabited by businesspeople, ranchers, and laborers, but also characterized by the emergence of new regional actors, new forms of identity, and new processes for establishing roots linked to the significant changes in forms of residence.[8] Hence in the San Quintin Valley (Velasco 2005), like in some agricultural regions in Oregon made up of immigrant workers (Stephen 2005), associative forms with more institutional life achieve viability once the residential settlement process has been placed into action. The grassroots organizations and political organizations thus become constitutive agents of the settlement process and therefore of the region itself. In addition, in the San Quintin case, the fact that the residential settlement process is produced in a region that until recently was scarcely populated, with little infrastructure and weak state institution presence, poses new questions about the collective forms and political strategies used by settlers to secure access to basic public services in their communities (i.e. water, electricity, schools, health), and strive for their rights as residents.

In sum, from the start of our project we sought to integrate two complementary dimensions of settlement–colonization and social integration—to describe and analyze the recent residential settlement process in San Quintin Valley in all its

[6] In this sense it is important to recognize the work carried out by academics such as Juan Vicente Palerm (2010, 2002, p. 255) and Travis Du Bry (2007, pp. 15–18), who elaborate more diverse typologies of agricultural workers in rural populations of California using the criteria of length of stay, place of birth, and time and radius of mobility.

[7] According to Peter Schmitt-Egner (2002), regions are always part of a larger spatial unit that translates into distinct borders and vertical connections in a national or transnational context.

[8] For a discussion of the symbolic identity in the formation of regions, see Giménez (2009).

richness and complexity. As such, our project is focused on two different but complementary spheres of settlement. The first sphere refers to the transformation of the patterns of residence and mobility of the agricultural laborer population, and the second is focused on how these changes affect the demographic structure of the region, the structure and social organization of families, and the content and orientation of collective actions by the new residents.

With this goal in mind, we approach settlement from a multidisciplinary perspective. We employ demography to document the transformation of mobility, in terms of the diversification of its temporality and rhythm, and the changes in the places of origin and destination. Demography can also be used to explore the transformation of residence in terms of its type and localization and the interactions between the two dimensions. From an anthropological perspective, we focus on the strategies and social resources used by families to access lands and build their own housing, and the economic strategies that serve to reinforce their residential settlement. The collective strategies of social and political movements led by the new inhabitants in the process of residential change are addressed by sociology, through the sociological intervention method described further below, and by ethnographic research; both approaches are focused on the reconstruction of collective actions carried out during the settlement process.

Having outlined the objectives and conceptual design of our project, in the next section we turn to the research methods and techniques we constructed to study the different dimensions of settlement presented above. In this section we also discuss the opportunities and limitations encountered in interdisciplinary collaboration during the phase of designing the study's methods and techniques.

## 2.3 Methodological Strategy and Research Techniques

### *2.3.1 Articulation Between Conceptual Scheme and Methodological Strategy*

A common methodological strategy in interdisciplinary projects consists of combining research methods and techniques originating from different disciplines into a common methodological instrument that integrates the virtues and strengths of each discipline. Such is the case in migration studies that combine quantitative and qualitative methods with the objective to guarantee both representativity and the richness and depth of results. An example of this approach is the now classic study carried out by Douglas Massey and his collaborators on the migration process of urban and rural communities of western Mexico to the United States, and the role performed by the migrants' social networks in that process (Massey et al. 1987). One of this study's most original methodological contributions was the use of an ethno-survey that combined the goal for representative quantitative findings with the qualitative richness and depth endowed by the ethnographic method. Its authors defined the ethno-survey as the result of interdisciplinary collaboration between ethnography, sociology, and demography; in other words, a methodological marriage between ethnography and the survey with the objective of obtaining high degrees of both representativity and depth in the study of migration as a social process (Massey et al. 1987, p. 12).

In contrast, after an initial phase of interdisciplinary collaboration in the project's conceptual formulation, the design of the research methods and techniques in our study was marked by disciplinary specialization in which the particularities of demographic, sociological, and anthropological methods were preserved. This research strategy, which seeks to maintain the distinction and rigor of diverse research techniques with the purpose of maximizing the specialization and experience of each team member, was adopted based on both heuristic and pragmatic reasons.

In heuristic terms, in order to address the study of settlement in its double dimension of residence and mobility, we used a combination of quantitative and qualitative methods from demography, sociology, and anthropology. This approach could give an account of both dimensions, the first at the macro-level of the region, and the second at the meso-level of the family and social organizations involved in this process.

These are highly-differentiated levels of analysis difficult to capture by a single methodological technique or instrument. As we can observe in Table 2.1, the methodological work consisted of empirically constructing the concepts of mobility and residence that characterize the experience of settlement in the region, combining the two theoretical perspectives of colonization and social integration described before. Each of these approaches allows us to address different levels of analysis. The colonization approach conceptualizes the phenomena of mobility and residence at the region's macro-historic level. At this level, demography's methodological arsenal appears to be the most appropriate, supported by the region's oral history, which can be contributed by cultural anthropology and sociology through biographical or testimonial interviews with the pioneer inhabitants.

The second level of analysis is meso and is composed of observation of the same residential and mobility phenomena but in analytical units such as the family and social organizations. The conceptual focus of social integration provides explanatory tools for this level. Here, the methodological contribution from each of the disciplines is complemented in both phenomena and in the analytical units, with greater complementarity existing here than at the macro level.

In pragmatic terms, we decided to take advantage of the specialization of each of the team members in certain research methods and techniques in order to delve deeper into the demographic and social processes of residence and mobility. With this approach, we aimed to complement, rather than integrate, the specific methods employed from demography, anthropology, and sociology, and to develop a dialogue among these disciplines as the basis for analysis and interpretation of the empirical results obtained through these methods. It is in this dialogue that we locate both the potentialities and challenges of interdisciplinary work.

**Table 2.1** Theoretical and methodological multidisciplinary approach

| | Theoretical focuses | Analytical levels and units | Dimensions | Disciplinary perspectives | Methods | Indicators or observable characteristics |
|---|---|---|---|---|---|---|
| Settlement | Colonization | Macro: region | Mobility | Demography aggregated data | Chronological history of population censuses (1960–2000) | - Total population<br>- Distribution among administrative delegations |
| | | | Residence | Demography aggregated data | 1990–2000 censuses | - Characteristics of housing<br>- Socio-demographic characteristics of the population |
| | | | | Oral history | Biographical interviews | - Meaningful passages and events<br>- Memory tropes<br>- Leading characters<br>- Historic story lines |
| | Integration | Meso: family | Mobility | Sociology | Biographical interviews | - Logic and reasons behind mobility<br>- Dynamics of mobility |
| | | | | Anthropology | Ethnography | - Family strategies employed to organize mobility |
| | | | | Demography individual data | Biographical survey (EBIMRE) | - Temporality of mobility<br>- Duration, frequency<br>- Origins/destinations |
| | | | Residence | Demography individual data | EBIMRE | - Type of residence<br>- Localization of residence<br>- Residential trajectories |
| | | | | Anthropology | Ethnography | - Family strategies to obtain land and establish residence |
| | | Meso: social organizations | Residence | Anthropology<br>Sociology | Ethnography Interviews<br>Sociological intervention. Biographical interviews | - Collective strategies to obtain lands<br>- Residential strategies<br>- Agents, interests, resources, and power relations<br>- Mobilization events<br>- Symbols of regional identity<br>- Collective identifications<br>- Local attributions |

*Source* the authors

Below we present the connection between the previously described conceptual design and the methods and techniques employed in our study. In the presentation of methods and techniques we advance some results that were fundamental in the alignment of the method in the research process. In other words, the research instruments were refined on the basis of some of the preliminary results.

### *2.3.2 Settlements as a Colonization Process: Macro Level*

To analyze the San Quintin region at the macro level, we defined a demographic methodological approach based on analysis of aggregated data from the different population censuses. Because the San Quintin region does not correspond to a single administrative entity, the greatest challenge in this documentary technique consisted of making the INEGI data at the localities level coincide with the regional unit of analysis defined by our project.[9] This recompilation facilitated reconstruction of the chronological history of the region's population since 1960, illustrating the exponential demographic growth that transformed an almost barren region with a small number of pioneer outposts (with fewer than 4,000 inhabitants in 1960) to a semi-rural area by the year 2010 with 92,177 inhabitants distributed in numerous localities of varying sizes. The greater availability of census data beginning in 1990 allowed us to study the transformation of the population's residential patterns, particularly between 1990 and 2000. Several indicators were constructed in relation to the socio-demographic characteristics of the population (sex, age, educational level, economically-active population, etc.) and of the housing at the beginning and the end of the 1990s, a decade of profound transformations in the region. The decline in the male-to-female index (from 105.4 to 102.5 %) and in the economic activity rate (from 55 to 49 %) speaks to the process of family settlement during the 1990s. The residential transformation toward greater access to services and better housing conditions is also documented. For example, the percentage of housing with electricity increased from 63 to 83 %, while that of homes with dirt floors decreased from 24 to 15 %.

In addition, some qualitative techniques such as collecting life histories of pioneer settlers were implemented by the sociologist and the anthropologist with the objective of documenting the region's colonization process from an oral history perspective.

---

[9] We define the region as composed of four delegations of the Ensenada municipality (Punta Colonet, Camalú, Vicente Guerrero, and San Quintin).

## 2.4 Settlement as a Social Integration Process: Family, Community and Social Actors

### *2.4.1 Demography of Residence and Mobility*

To obtain quantitative information on both the residence and mobility dimensions at the meso level of the family, a specific survey was developed to compile information at the individual and household levels. To document the change process (from camps to *colonias*), this was a retrospective survey aimed at providing information on the trajectory of the individuals. Called the Biographical Survey on Residential Mobility and Employment in San Quintin (*Encuesta Biográfica de Movilidad Residencial y de Empleo en San Quintín*—EBIMRE), it was applied between May and June 2005. The survey questionnaire consisted of two parts: one section compiled information on all members of a household at the time of the interview, and a second section recorded an individual biography with information on the entire life of a member of the couple who heads the household (head of household or spouse).

Given the scarcity of data on the San Quintin region, the decision was made to develop the survey using probabilistic sampling, with the purpose of obtaining results that could be generalized to the population as a whole. The sample design for a region like San Quintin required various adjustments. Population distribution within the region indicates a pattern of wide dispersion among differently sized localities. For example, in 2000 43 % of the population lived in localities with fewer than 2,500 inhabitants. To take into consideration this population dispersion, it was important to include the highest number of population centers possible, but this could only be achieved if a more reduced geographical area was considered. Thus we limited the survey area to the two most highly populated administrative delegations (75 % of the population is concentrated in this southern part of the region, corresponding to the Vicente Guerrero and San Quintin delegations), and we included all localities with more than 1,000 inhabitants in the sampling frame. Among these localities, we distinguished between *colonias* and labor camps. In the first, we constructed the sampling frame in both individual homes and collective homes, or tenement rooms. Based on this frame, we selected the 900 homes in which we would carry out the survey. In the camp localities, we used a specific sampling process, taking into account that the sample selection could not be random since we needed the owner's authorization for access to these camps. Within the authorized camps, a random selection was made of the 120 rooms/housing units in which the interviews were carried out. The objective of this small sample was to obtain information on family structures in this residential universe that would allow comparisons to be made with those of the residents of *colonias*.[10]

---

[10] The EBIMRE's household section documents family organization, including household tructure and domestic economy. In comparison with the camps, family organization in the

The EBIMRE was applied by local interviewers contracted for the project, the majority of whom were employees of the *Programa Nacional con Jornaleros Agrícolas* (PRONJAG) under Mexico's *Secretaría de Desarrollo Social* (SEDESOL). Their strong familiarity with the various *colonias* in the region allowed us to obtain a good response rate (the survey's non-response rate was 9 % in *colonias*). The survey was designed to document and analyze the settlement process of agricultural workers in the area, based on the trajectories of mobility, residence, employment, and family. The trajectories compile a large number of events from the different dimensions of the life histories of heads of households or spouses. This questionnaire design is based on international experience in the field of biographical methods in demography, including some innovations for gathering information on seasonal mobility (Coubès 2005).

Regarding mobility, the biographical survey describes the different migratory movements of the head of household or spouse, according to two seasonal scales. The first is the annual scale for primary migrations, while the second is a more precise scale of the residential system organized in months, used for seasonal movements. These two registries allow the construction of various indicators around the seasonality, duration, and frequency of mobility as well as the origin and destination of movements. In regards to the residence, the EBIMRE collects information on the type of residence (camp, tenement room, *colonia*) of the head of household/spouse since their arrival in San Quintin. This information allows the reconstruction of the residential trajectory in San Quintin, and is analyzed with classification methods based on duration and type of transition, including a direct move from camp to colony, an intermediate phase of tenement housing, or other variations. In addition, the survey facilitates observation of this residence trajectory in relation to both the labor trajectory and family trajectory, serving to analyze interactions between residential transition and labor and family changes. The EBIMRE survey allows the generalization of its results based on a probabilistic sampling characteristic of quantitative methods and, at the same time, a deeper look at life trajectories based on the registry's precision.

Although the methodological instrument used is particular to demography, the questionnaire design benefited from interdisciplinary teamwork. Prior to construction of the survey, both the team's anthropologist and sociologist conducted an inquiry with male and female inhabitants of different ages on the logics and dynamics of mobility, through ethnography and in-depth interviews with a biographical perspective. Both methods provided us with first-hand information on the logics of geographic mobility, which might be family or labor motivated and characterized by different directions and diverse purposes. In addition, because the EBIMRE was designed from the start with a multi-thematic vocation that would reach across several of the aspects associated with residential settlement

(Footnote 10 continued)
colonias presents differences that we suggest are results of the settlement process, including the reconstitution of the nuclear family and the diversification of labor opportunities among household members.

experience, it favored the participation of all team members contributing their particular experiences from their own fields of knowledge and specialization. The design and wording of the questions in the questionnaire reflected the field research experience from the exploratory ethnographic and biographic interview. Construction of the questions also benefited greatly from pilot fieldwork, as for example adapting the wording of some of the questions to the folk expressions used by the region's inhabitants.

Once the design was concluded, the labor of testing the survey in the field also benefited from teamwork. For example, while the team's demographer conducted the interview, the anthropologist or sociologist observed and took notes on what happened in the interviewer-interviewee interaction, and the reactions and doubts expressed by the latter. The objective was to use these observations to adjust the type and order of the questions, as well as the way in which some of the questions were stated. Because the survey is a rather widely-used instrument in the social sciences, and there is generally a certain familiarity with this type of instrument in many disciplines, interdisciplinary work using surveys seems to be rather manageable. Despite this collaboration, given the technical complexity of the biographic survey as a highly specialized instrument, the team's demographer had the final responsibility for its design in order to guarantee its rigor.

### 2.4.2 Ethnographic Approach

To document the residential and mobility aspects of the settlement process, the anthropologist in the team carried out field work in several *colonias* in San Quintin Valley. The design of the ethnographic work addressed two differentiated areas of settlement. In the first, the domestic group was adopted as the unit of analysis with the goal of understanding the economic and social strategies that allow the act of settlement and the residential transition from camps to *colonias*. While the survey reflects the structure and demographic composition of households, the ethnographic work promoted observation of the dynamics within household groups that facilitate settlement. The ethnographic study employed two primary techniques: in-depth interviews, and participant observation. The in-depth interviews helped to document the transition process from camps to *colonias* with a high degree of detail, as well as the family strategies that make it possible for rural laborers to obtain plots of land and build their own housing. In both the interviews and participant observation, special emphasis was placed on understanding the impact of residential settlement on the division of labor by gender and age within the family, the way in which production and reproduction activities are reorganized as consequences of this process, and how workers themselves evaluate the impact of settlement on their lives.

In contrast to the survey, the household interviews were not based on random sampling, but were chosen to illustrate the diversity of residential and mobility patterns. The goal was to obtain a diachronic perspective and a wealth of detailed information to complement and illustrate the results obtained by the EBIMRE. Household interviews allowed the collection of precise data on family budget including income and expenses, division of labor by gender and age, housing investment strategies, education, and other spheres related to the residential settlement experience. In addition, life histories of both men and women heads of households allowed precise documentation of the trajectories through which they settled in the region, their labor histories before and after settlement, and the diverse ways by which they developed a sense of belonging in their new communities. These interviews and life stories also gathered information about the migration trajectories of household members prior to and after residential settlement, including the motives that drove them to migrate to the United States after settling down in San Quintín. In so doing, this information allowed us to analyze the dynamic connections between settlement and geographical mobility mentioned earlier in this chapter.

The second arena of ethnographic field research focused on the role performed by both government agencies and private institutions at the local level to facilitate and regulate the residential settlement of families in the *colonias* studied. In each of the selected *colonias*, the anthropologist documented the state governmental programs implemented to support this process, as well as the roles played by churches, NGOs, and other institutions. The hypothesis that underlies this approach is that settlement is a complex process that goes beyond settlers themselves, involving a variety of other actors and institutional resources that constitute the social and political framework within which the settlement experience of workers and families must be situated and analyzed.

Three San Quintin Valley *colonias* were chosen for the ethnographic work, including one mostly inhabited by Triqui indigenous immigrants, one by Zapotecs, and a third with a more ethnically heterogeneous population of mestizos and indigenous people. With a population of just over 1,900 inhabitants, this last colony includes not only rural laborers but also merchants, drivers, independent contractors, among others, illustrating the occupational mobility processes and socioeconomic differentiation that result from the settlement process. For its part, the Triqui colony has a population of close to 1,200 and it is poorer in economic terms and more homogenous in its ethnic profile. Nonetheless, its inhabitants have developed some of the most effective organizations to negotiate with the state government for access to basic resources, making it possible to study the way in which ethnic identity is mobilized as a political resource to strengthen settlement and establish roots in the region.

### *2.4.3 Sociological Intervention and Biographical Interviews*

As mentioned above, an important dimension of the concept of settlement as social and political process refers to the collective actors that participate in this process.[11] The focus on these associative forms enriched the hypothesis on residential settlement as a complex phenomenon that involves a variety of social actors and collective resources that are mobilized beyond the domestic group. It also allowed for the documentation of the obstacles these groups and organizations encounter and the strategies they deploy to face these challenges.

This hypothesis on the role of collective action to advance settlement was tested from the sociological standpoint through the sociological intervention method (Touraine 1981), a method predicated on the recognition of the capacity of social actors to reflect upon themselves and their collective actions. One of the method's initial tasks is to define the social movement that is the object of study. This research defined social movement as the set of grassroots and political organizations active in the region. The method involves three phases. In the first, members of the social movement under study debate among themselves to define the unity of the movement. In the second, this group meets with allies and adversaries to discuss the movement's agenda. And in the third, the researcher presents the systematization of findings from the first two phases for discussion within the original group-members of the movement.

For this project, a methodological adjustment was made by introducing a preliminary phase for defining the subject of the movement and reconstructing the context of the social actors to delimit the collective field of action. In the end, four phases were implemented, taking place between 2004 and 2005. In each of the research phases, the residential settlement process emerged as a central theme. In the first phase, encompassing the arduous work of biographical interviews with the leaders and activists of organizations, the objective was to construct the universe of organizations and the agenda for discussion in workshops. As this universe was slowly constructed, it progressively broke away from our initial assumptions regarding the leadership role of the traditional labor-oriented organizations with high visibility in the movements in the region during the 1980s. This research phase was also characterized by the ethnographic findings of the team's anthropologist, who revealed the importance of small colony committees or settler groups as relevant actors in residential settlement formed on the basis of relations among those originating from the same region. Finally, the universe was definitively constituted by leaders and activists from fourteen organizations that each defended its declared interests, such as labor, ethnic-political, and residential interests. The biographical interviews made it possible to reconstruct a chronology of mobilizations in relation to lands, assistance for housing construction, and installation of public services.

[11] A detailed description can be found in Velasco (2011).

In-depth interviews with different inhabitants of the region had already brought to light the role played by collective action in the process of leaving the camps and becoming established in *colonias*. Later in the interviews with leaders and activists conducted during the course of fieldwork, we began to delineate the various possible collective strategies for achieving such residential change. As a result of these interviews, we found varying types of residential settlement agents, whose profiles were considered for the construction of the sample of activists invited to the sociological intervention workshops.

This phase was fundamental not only because it allowed us to identify a certain social unity in terms of class and ethnicity of organizations, but also because it allowed us to define the social actors with whom these organizations were contending, either in alliances or in disputes. Those other actors were part of the context for the collective action of these organizations, and for this reason in-depth interviews were also carried out with journalists, governmental functionaries, church members, and agricultural and service-sector business people.

The following phases of the method's application were carried out through three workshop sessions, which as a whole sought to reveal the unity, conflict, and identity of the movement. The struggle for residence surfaced as a central theme. For example, in the first workshop session, similar experiences in mobilizing for lands and services emerged as a line of collective identity among participating activists and leaders.

The reconstruction of mobilizations identified a turning point between the labor mobilizations of the 1980s and the residential movements that began in the late 1980s and gained full force in the 1990s. When land was seized, broad-based mobilizations appeared with different strategies and residential agents. When housing was built and installations were completed, collective action fragmented further, depending more on small committees that were formed in the new residential nuclei. The committees immediately acquired status in the administrative structure of the territorial organization in the nascent region, specifically the *colonias* and delegations. This was how the colony committees emerged, and their mission was to act as intermediaries for the new settlers in their demands for the legalization of plots and provision of services. The importance of residence in the definition of the social movement's unity around the residents' identity guided the decision to incorporate the residential allies and adversaries in the following workshop session.

In the workshop's second session, when the study group compared its viewpoints with those of allies and adversaries, the issues of land legalization and services emerged once again. In this area of dispute, governmental functionaries had displaced the businesspeople and yellow unions who were the antagonists in the mobilizations during the 1980s. In the final workshop session, the initial group had grown, and some allies—such as leaders of transportation associations—had come to form part of the nucleus group. In this session, the researcher presented a systematization of the discussions into a few hypotheses on the central issues of unity, conflict, and the field of relations in regional and global contexts. Participants in this phase were the members of the first workshop who made up the target group, evaluating and critiquing the systematization and hypotheses presented by the researcher.

The units of analysis in this last methodological approach were the social organizations, including those based on ethnicity, class, or residential factors. The sociological intervention method demands not only solid knowledge of the theory that underlies this focus but also its rigorous application according to its particular guidelines. For this reason, the workshops were conducted under the strict supervision of the project's sociologist, although she benefited from the work as a team during the discussion around both the planning and logistics of the instrument's application. As mentioned above, the results obtained through this method were complemented by ethnographic work carried out in the *colonias* which served to document the manner in which collective action operates at the local level in the political dispute for access to resources in the *colonias*, and through which new settlers seek to consolidate and legitimize their establishment in the region.

## 2.5 Conclusion

Interdisciplinary work poses important theoretical and methodological challenges that require strategic decisions on how to build conceptual bridges to respond to them. This problem is further complicated when trying to study topics that have traditionally been located in a particular academic discipline with limited dialogue with others. In such cases, multidisciplinary research is different than work in areas such as migration studies and ethnic studies, which by nature are interdisciplinary and have a long history of collaboration among disciplines. In this chapter, we have described the experience of the study of the settlement process in the San Quintin Valley—in its double aspects of colonization and social integration—that confronted the challenge of a sparse tradition of interdisciplinary dialogue centered on the notion of settlement. In this context, our challenge has consisted, to a large degree, in building conceptual bridges, developing a theoretical focus, and designing methodological approaches that, in the analysis of the results obtained, will allow us to establish a fluid interdisciplinary dialogue.

In this chapter we have aimed at opening up the 'black box' of interdisciplinary collaboration as research praxis. From this perspective we propose that the praxis of interdisciplinary research can be seen as a process that consists of different stages. Each stage poses a distinct set of challenges but also presents opportunities to enhance dialogue across disciplines, requiring different approaches and research strategies. As we have explained, rather than a unique integrated interdisciplinary approach, our study has used diverse degrees and forms of collaboration among the participant disciplines of anthropology, demography, and sociology, depending on the particular phase of the project. The project's conceptual design was characterized by a high degree of synergy in teamwork, particularly when integrating the perspectives of colonization and social integration in order to study the settlement of thousands of indigenous and non-indigenous laborers and their families over the past decades in this arid region of Baja California. This approach was based on the notion that an interdisciplinary project has to combine and integrate conceptual tools from various disciplines from the onset in its theoretical design to ensure that the later phases of analysis and write up can capitalize on the heuristic potential offered by cross-disciplinary research. This interdisciplinary dialogue was essential when defining the project's macro and meso units of analysis along with the models of residence and mobility, which are the nucleus of our study.

A different approach was taken on the next phase of methodological design during which, as explained above, there were different degrees of interdisciplinary collaboration. The biographical survey was designed and implemented following the canon of this demographic research tool to ensure its rigor, although interdisciplinary synergy of the project's participants facilitated a certain amount of border-crossing among disciplines. Likewise, the ethnographic field research and the sociological intervention workshops were each developed individually by the anthropologist and sociologist in the team respectively, and even though some degree of teamwork was involved, interdisciplinary dialogue was scarce. This limitation can be explained by both the desire to preserve the rigor of these methods as well as our own disciplinary identities, which at times complicates the interdisciplinary endeavor. Nonetheless, our collective work and interdisciplinary perspective functioned as self-critiquing mechanisms and often served to question the methodological and practical assumptions of our respective disciplinary specializations.

Although our study integrates quantitative and qualitative methods, our methodological strategy differs then from the strategy of other interdisciplinary projects that seek disciplinary integration in the design and implementation of methods. In our case, we opted for a different epistemological strategy that seeks to maintain the distinction and rigor of each of our own disciplinary methods. Neither of these two interdisciplinary research strategies is superior a *priori*. Rather, the criteria that should serve as guides when determining the most adequate methodological approach are the nature of the topic to be studied and the specific objectives pursued by each project.

Our experience in this project shows that the challenge of interdisciplinary research consists of resolving the tension between, on the one hand, specialization—which guarantees rigor in methods and techniques—and on the other, defocalization and the crossing of disciplinary borders. The objective is not to constantly work to resolve this tension. Instead, according to the different phases of research, disciplinary specialization and defocalization from individual disciplines can alternately come into play. It is in this back-and-forth between poles that teamwork experience and interdisciplinary work are constructed. We believe the heuristic value of interdisciplinary work depends in large part on maintaining the rigor of the research techniques employed. From this perspective, the division of labor among the different disciplines should not be seen as an obstacle but rather as a necessary phase from which one transits to interdisciplinary dialogue.

The challenges presented by interdisciplinary research do not end in the phase of methodological design and implementation. Rather, these challenges persist and pose new dilemmas in the next stages of analysis and writing up the results. How should results obtained through methodologies anchored in different disciplines be presented and integrated? How should the tensions and contrasts between quantitative and qualitative data and information be resolved? And, what is the best way to modulate the different disciplinary voices when writing up the results of the study? In our case, at the present time, we are confronting and learning to address the dilemmas involved in these two last phases of our interdisciplinary project.

## References

Cornelius, Wayne, 1992: From sojourners to settlers: the changing profile of migration to the US, in: Bustamante, Jorge A.; Reynolds, Clark W.; Hinojosa Ojeda Raúl A. (Eds.): *U.S. Mexico relations. Labor markets interdependence* (Stanford: Stanford University Press).

Coubès, Marie-Laure, 2005: La collecte des systèmes résidentiels dans une enquête biographique: un exemple de questionnaire auprès de travailleurs agricoles de San Quintin (Basse Californie, Mexique), Paper presented at the XXV International Population Conference, Tours, 18–23 July 2005.

Chavez, Leo, 1988: Settlers and Sojourners: The case of Mexicans in the United States, in: *Human Organization*, 47,2.

Deasy, George F, Gerhard, Peter, 1944: Settlements in Baja California: 1768–1930, in: *Geographical Review*, 34,4: 574–586.

Du Bry, Travis Anthony, 2007: *Immigrants, Settlers, and Laborers: The Socioeconomic Transformation of a Farming Community* (New York: LFB Scholarly Publishing).

Giménez, Gilberto, 2009: Identidades sociales, México, Conaculta/Instituto Mexiquense de la Cultura, in: Hondagneu-Sotelo, Pierrette (Ed.), 1994: *Gendered Transitions: Mexican Experiences of Immigration* (Berkeley: University of California Press).

Lara Flores, Sara María, 2010: Los 'encadenamientos migratorios' en regiones de agricultura intensiva de exportación en México, in: Lara Flores, Sara María (Ed.): *Migraciones de trabajo y movilidad territorial* (México, Conacyt-Porrúa): 251–279.

Lara Flores, Sara María; de Grammont, Hubert C., 2011: Reestructuraciones productivas y encadenamientos migratorios en las hortalizas sinaloenses, in: Lara Flores, Sara María (Ed.): *Los encadenamientos migratorios en espacios de agricultura intensive* (México, El Colegio Mexiquense—Miguel Ángel Porrúa): 33–78.

Levitt, Peggy; De Wind, Josh; Vertovec, Steven, 2003: International perspectives on Transnational Migration: An introduction, in: *International Migration Review*, 37,3 (Fall).

Massey, Douglas S.; Alarcon, Rafael; Durand, Jorge; Gonzalez, Humberto, 1987: *Return to Aztlan: The Social Process of International Migration from Western Mexico* (Berkeley: University of California Press).

Palerm, Juan Vicente, 2002: Immigrant and Migrant Farmworkers in the Santa Maria Valley, in: Vélez-Ibáñez, Carlos; Sampaio, Anna (Eds.): *Transnational Latina/o Communities. Politics, Processes and Cultures* (Lanham: Rowman and Littlefield).

Palerm Viqueira, Juan Vicente, 2010: De Colonias a Comunidades: La Evolución De Los Asentamientos Mexicanos en la California Rural, in: Lara Flores, Sara María (Ed.): *Migraciones de Trabajo y Movilidad Territorial* (México: Conacyt/Porrúa).

Piñera Ramírez, David, 2006: *Los orígenes de las poblaciones de Baja California, Factores externos, nacionales y locales* (Mexicali: Universidad Autónoma de Baja California).

Rouse, Roger, 1992: "Making Sense of Settlement: Class Transformation, Cultural Struggle and Transnationalism among Mexican Migrants in the United States", in: Basch, Lucila; Glick Schiller, Nina; Blanc-Szanton, Cristina: "Toward a transnational perspective on migration. Race, Class, Ethnicity and Nationalism Reconsidered", in: *Annals of the New York Academy of Sciences*, 645 (6 July): 25–52.

Smelser, Neil, 2003: On Comparative Analysis, Interdisciplinarity and Internationalization in Sociology, in: *International Sociology*, 18,4 (December): 643–657.

Schmitt-Egner, Peter, 2002: The Concept of 'Region'. Theoretical and Methodological Notes on its Reconstruction, in: *European Integration*, 24,3: 179–200.

Taylor Hansen, Lawrence Douglas, 2011: Baja California, ¿el cuerno de la abundancia? Inversiones estadounidenses y desarrollo económico en el norte de la península, en el Porfiriato, in: Gómez Estrada, José Alfredo; Almaraz Alvarado, Araceli (Eds.): *Inversiones, colonización y desarrollo económico en el noroeste de México, 1870*–1940 (Mexicali: Universidad Autónoma de Baja California–Tijuana: El Colegio de la Frontera Norte.

Velasco Ortiz, Laura, 2002: *El regreso de la comunidad: Migración indígena y agentes étnicos. Los mixtecos en la frontera México-Estados Unidos* (Mexico: El Colegio de Méxic–Tijuana: El Colegio de la Frontera Norte. Mexico.

Velasco Ortiz, Laura, 2005: *Mixtec Transnational Identity* (Tucson: The University of Arizona Press).

Velasco, Laura, 2005: Organizational Experiences and Female Participation among Indigenous Oaxaqueños in Baja California, in: Fox, Jonathan; Rivera Salgado, Gaspar (Eds.): *Indigenous Mexican Migrants in the United States* (La Jolla: Center for US Mexican Studies, UCSD).

Velasco, Laura, 2011: Identidad regional y actores: una experiencia de intervención sociológica en el Valle de San Quintín, Baja California, in: *Región y Sociedad*, México, El Colegio de Sonora, 23,51: 43–70.

Stephen, Lynn, 2005: Mixtec farmworkers in Oregon: linking labor and ethnicity through farmworker unions and hometown associations, in: Fox, Jonathan; Rivera Salgado, Gaspar (Eds.): *Indigenous Mexican Migrants in the United States* (La Jolla: Center for US Mexican Studies, UCSD).

Touraine, Alain, 1981: *The Voice and the Eye: An analysis of social movements* (Cambridge: Cambridge University Press).

Whebell, C.F.J., 1969: Corridors: A Theory of Urban Systems, in: *Annals of the Association of American Geographers*, 59,1 (March): 1–26.

Zlolniski, Christian, 2010: Economic Globalization and Shifting Capital-Labor Relations in Baja California's Export-Oriented Agriculture, in: Durrenberger, Paul; Reichart, Karaleah (Eds.): *The Anthropology of Unions* (Boulder: University Press of Colorado): 157–188.

Public demonstrations for better labor conditions in domestic service in Hempstead, Long Island, New York, 2007. *Source* The photograph was taken by Marina Ariza who granted permission to reproduce it

# Chapter 3
# A Comparative Approach to Global Domestic Service in Two Cities: Methodological Notes

**Marina Ariza**

**Abstract** From a pedagogical approach, this chapter has two objectives: (1) to highlight the usefulness of comparative analysis as a tool for social research in the study of migration; (2) to describe the way this methodological strategy is to be applied in a concrete field of enquiry (global domestic service) as specified in a research project by the author. Comparative analysis has been the preferred methodological option when a small number of cases are being observed. It is based on a series of assumptions and procedures to assure the validity of any inferences made. In the case of migration studies, it offers the advantage of minimizing methodological nationalism. A comparative approach to the study of international domestic service in two countries helps to capture the global nature of this burgeoning female labor market and to identify the institutional and labor regime particularities of each context of reception.

**Keywords** Comparison · Methodological · Global domestic service · Female migration

## 3.1 Introduction

In the increasingly abundant field of international migration studies, researchers have frequently pointed to the need to conduct comparative studies (Castles 2001; Schuerkens 2005). Many of the numerous studies carried out in recent years have been focused on very specific analysis of case studies in a particular country or for a particular ethnic group. This analysis is generally rich in details and local

M. Ariza (✉)
Institute of Social Research (Instituto de Investigaciones Sociales),
Mexico's National Autonomous University (Universidad Nacional Autónoma de México),
Coyoacán, Mexico
e-mail: ariza@unam.mx

L. Rivera-Sánchez and F. Lozano-Ascencio (eds.), *The Practice of Research on Migration and Mobilities*, SpringerBriefs in Environment, Security, Development and Peace 14,
DOI:10.1007/978-3-319-02693-0_3, The Author(s) 2014 

aspects, but has little heuristic potential for an understanding of similar processes beyond particular national or ethnic borders. Comparative studies are posed as one of the ways to avoid 'methodological nationalism, and as an alternative for understanding some of the profound repercussions—*social transformations*—which the new *era* of migration has brought (Wimmer and Glick Schiller 2003; Vertovec 2004).[1]

Both within the sociological tradition and in the more restricted sphere of migration studies, comparative analyses are part of an old academic tradition. What is methodologically challenging is to engage in this type of analysis in the current conditions created by economic globalization and the emergence of transnationality. From its modest analytical perspective, the research project on which this chapter is based is one of the comparative efforts attempting to increase our knowledge of the relation between international female migration and labor insertion in the context of the social transformations associated with globalization. This research project studies two migration flows of women from two different countries (the Dominican Republic and Mexico) to two urban destinations that attract a significant Latin American population (Madrid, Spain and New York City, U.S.A.), and analyzes the labor insertion of a group of these female migrants engaged in paid domestic work as a feminized labor market. The chapter contains three sections: In the first I will describe the main methodological strategy of the project: the comparative perspective, underscoring its centrality in sociological analysis in general. In the second section I will discuss the pertinence of this approach in the analysis of the relation between female migration and labor markets in the context of globalization. In the third and last section I will specify the theoretical and methodological assumptions that guided this inquiry process, indicating their advantages and limitations.[2]

## 3.2 The Comparative Perspective as an Analytical Strategy

With the aim of providing an adequate context of reference, I will now present some of the central assumptions of comparison as an analytical strategy and as a methodological resource.

---

[1] Representing an intermediate position between the *hyperglobalizers* and *skeptics*, between those who subscribe to the idea that globalization constitutes a new era in the history of humanity and those who emphasize its continuity with prior stages, the *transformationalists* maintain that the series of inter-related changes provoked by globalization (technological, cultural, migration, etc.) has reached unprecedented levels, affecting practically all societies in one way or another (Castles 2001).

[2] The project on which this chapter is based, "Migration and female labor markets in the context of globalization: a comparative perspective (*Migración y mercados de trabajo femeninos en el contexto de la globalización. Una perspectiva comparativa*)" was supported by Mexico's National Autonomous University (*Universidad Nacional Autónoma de México),* through the PAPIIT (IN 300006) program.

### 3.2.1 Definitions and Assumptions

Comparison, in its most straightforward sense, is a cognitive resource that is inherent to all processes of understanding. As pointed out by Smelser (2003), even the simple effort of describing any observed event involves an exercise of drawing comparisons: a given object has a certain characteristic precisely because it does not have another. We establish the identity of an event—a sunny day, for example, in relation to its opposite, a rainy day, on the basis of a comparison of the features that make it similar or different from one or the other. This use of comparison is different from what predominates in social sciences, in which comparison is used as a tool to assist in producing scientific knowledge, in a way that is more or less explicit or implicit, systematic or lax (Bechhofer and Paterson 2000). On the basis of comparison, it is possible to systematize the distinctive features of phenomena observed, with the aim of establishing regularities, whether or not the latter are characterized by a causal determination. In the strictest sense, comparison is one of the three methods used in social sciences, together with the statistical or experimental method and case studies (Colino 2007). When a research study does not use comparison in a systematic, explicit manner, it cannot claim to be based on the comparative method, as such, but instead on an implicit, lax use of comparison as a cognitive resource in and of itself.

In order to offer an idea of the contemporary and central nature of comparative analysis in sociology, it is necessary only to remember the decisive role it played at the time the field was established. It is now common to paraphrase the statement made by Durkheim (1981, p. 137), that "the comparative method is the only one in sociology". Meanwhile, according to Weber (1973, p. 118), "comparison… intervenes as a means of imputation… as one of the most important means, which is not even remotely used sufficiently". The ideal type, the most notable methodological tool from Weberian sociology, lies precisely in systematic comparison as a means of causal imputation. In the interest of simplification, one might say that from these two classical social scientists emanate two of the most important traditions in comparative analysis: that which visualizes it as an imperfect equivalent to the experimental method, and that which conceives it as a genuine means, an heuristic resource *per se*. What Durkheim said in this regard is totally eloquent:

> we have only one way to demonstrate that a given phenomenon is the cause of another [and it is] to compare the cases in which they are simultaneously present or absent, to see if the variations they present in these different combinations of circumstances indicate that one depends on the other. When it is possible to produce them artificially at the will of the observer, the method is experimentation, clearly stated…when the production of facts is not possible… the method used is one of 'indirect experimentation, or the comparative method' (Durkheim 1981, p. 137).

From Weber's perspective, in contrast, comparison is not an alternative or lower-ranking analytical strategy in response to the impossibility of manipulating social facts, but rather, it is the method of analysis that best coincides with the historic, contingent nature of social processes. It is important to clarify that while both authors turn to comparison as a means for causal imputation, they do so on the basis of diametrically opposed notions of causality. While Durkheim subscribes to the idea of causality based on the logic of determination, Weber does so from the logic of possibility (Ariza 1994).[3] In the latter case we can acknowledge a number of likely courses for a single event, although only from a logical point of view. The initial association between causal imputation and comparative analysis will constitute a long-lasting legacy for sociological classics—and it has only been challenged in recent years by the more interpretative approaches to social processes.

Having acquired legitimacy since the very beginnings of sociology, the comparative method has conserved a preeminent place in the discipline's scientific practice. In the second half of the twentieth century, there were at least two moments when it received special attention: between the late 1960s and the early 1970s, due to the work of Lijphart (1971; Collier 1993); and from the mid-1980s to the present time, with the comprehensive reformulation proposed by Ragin (1987, 2006, 2008).

In the most frequent meaning given to the comparative method, it is defined as the description and explanation of similar and different (primarily the latter) conditions and results between large social units, usually regions, nations, societies and cultures (Smelser 2003, p. 645), or as the systematic observations of data extracted from two or more macro-social entities, or at various moments in the history of a society, in order to analyze their similarities and differences and inquire into the causes (Colino 2007, p. 1). It is worth taking a moment to examine the underlying assumptions of this definition. The first refers to the inclusion of *only a few cases*, with at least two being necessary. Traditionally, the comparative method was proposed as the option of preference in situations in which the researcher came up against a small N (Lijphart 1971; Collier 1993). Confronting the impossibility of using conventional statistical methods for evaluating the correlations between processes, rigorous comparison was proposed as an alternative means of control, similar to the experimental method (see Durkheim supra), to arrive at valid inferences in the research process.[4] However, this initial position has been gradually changing.

---

[3] From the logic of determination, constructed on the basis of a mechanicistic model of social processes along the lines of Newtonian physics, it is impossible to acknowledge the plurality of causes, since among other things, the following must be considered: (a) all social processes are necessarily determined; (b) all determinations are necessarily causal; (c) when there is a cause, there is an effect; (d) the effect can only assume the shape and intensity imprinted by the cause, etc… (Ariza 1994). In a passage frequently cited, Durkheim vehemently opposes the idea of the plurality of causes as sustained by J.S. Mill, stating the following: "This supposed axiom of the plurality of causes is, in fact, a negation of the principle of causality… an effect can maintain this relation only with a single cause, since it can only express a single nature" (1981, p. 139).

[4] This is a conception shared by Przeworski and Teune (1970), when they define it as an approach in which a form of control is exercised, similar to that used in experimentation, and as a form of inquiry in which more than one level of analysis is possible.

A second assumption is the *controlled, careful nature of comparison*, which is fundamentally important. Determining the mode capable of achieving it has been controversial. The most emphatically suggested precept is to assure the comparability of cases under comparison, guaranteeing a significant degree of similarity among them, a prescription that has also, nonetheless, been the object of discussion. One of the most well-known proposals was made by Przeworski and Teune (1970), who focused their attention on the most appropriate type of research design for resolving the problems of bias and inference inherent in the selection of a small number of cases. These authors distinguish between two types of designs, depending on the degree of similarity among the variables thought to have causal force: the *most similar systems* and *most different systems*, based, in turn, on two of the logical methods proposed by J. S. Mill (1974, cited by Collier 1993, p. 111): *agreement* and *disagreement*, or concordance and difference. The *most similar systems*, also referred to as *concomitant variation*, contemplate a series of shared inter-systemic factors that serve as elements of control, and a reduced set of dissimilar or unknown variables that will constitute the inter-systemic differences. With a reduced number of dissimilar independent variables, it would in principle be possible to better isolate the role played by each one of them, although this would not resolve the problem of over-determination, one of the most serious limitations of studies focused on a small number of cases which I will briefly discuss in the next section. The *most different systems*, in contrast, are based on the selection of a small number of very different cases (in relation to the dependent variable) on the basis of which an analyst describes similar processes of change. This latter option was considered the most ideal by Przeworski and Teune (1970), contrasting with the habitual norm in comparative method practice, most frequently focused on assuring a significant degree of similarity among independent variables, with the aim of *controlling* the causal effect of the few variables that differ from each other.

Given that the validity of scientific inference depends on the careful exercise of comparison, it is vitally important to achieve an adequate comparison of the similarities and differences among the cases under study. This is why Smelser (2003) assigns a decisive role to the *systematization of the context of comparison*. From his perspective, systematization refers both to the selection of comparable indicators and to the level of explanations formulated in order to account for the similarities and divergences. In both cases the equivalence in the independent variables thought to have causal force is necessary, as well as in the indexes used and the explanations proposed. The selection of two analogous contexts of reception as a central element of the methodological design in which this study is based (two cities in two developed countries, with a significant amount of Latin American immigration, aged demographic structures, tertiarized economies and a significant demand for female labor force in low-level service sectors), aims at fulfilling the function of equivalence to which Smelser refers.

According to Przeworski and Teune, comparability depends on the level of generality of the language used to express observations. Comparative research refers to situations in which inquiry is conducted from different levels (of observation and/or analysis): it may examine patterns of relation within systems (at the intra-systemic level); the systems themselves (systemic level), or both, according to the research design (1970, p. 10, 50).[5]

The last of the basic assumptions underlying the comparative method is that its application makes it possible to arrive at causal explanations of the processes under study. While it is true that the aim of providing causal explanations is at the very core of the comparative method, as conceived by Durkheim and Weber, there is discussion around the type of causality and its scope.[6] Positions fluctuate between those who point out that it is possible to establish causal regularities that are general but different, depending on the level of analysis (macro, meso or micro) (Goldthorpe 2000, cited by Mills et al. 2006, p. 624); those who speak of 'causal mechanism or a 'causal effect in reference to non-legal forms of regularity (that do not follow laws), with varying levels of determination (Alexander and Bennett 2004); and those who appeal to contextually conditioned causalities, in contrast to the additive model of linear causality underlying most variable oriented analysis (Ragin 1987, 2006).[7]

In summary, the explicit use of comparison as a method of analysis and causal inference has constituted part of the repertoire of social sciences since their beginnings. It has been the preferred methodological option when only a small number of cases are being observed, and it is based on a series of assumptions and procedures aimed at assuring the validity of the inferences, which include the systematization of the context of comparison and the careful, controlled nature of comparison. Although one line of thought originating from Durkheim and the positivist derivation of sociology considers it to be a residual, alternative method that, in a way, ranks below the experimental method, there is another line of thought emerging from Weberian sociology that proposes it as the methodological resource par excellence in social sciences, with inherent validity and heuristic potential.

### *3.2.2 Limitations and Advantages*

Among the limitations of comparative analysis more frequently addressed are worth mentioning the small number of cases, the selection of those to be compared, and the equivalence of indicators.[8]

---

[5] According to Przeworski and Teune, a research study in which there are multiple levels of observation, but reflections are limited to a single level, does not constitute a comparative analysis,.

[6] More relativist positions within the social sciences challenge the assumption asserting that the object of comparison is not to achieve causal explanations but only to *interpret* the differences encountered.

[7] For a detailed discussion of these aspects, see Ragin (1987, 2006, 2008).

[8] Others refer to the levels of analysis, the problem of causality, and the decision of whether to orient research toward cases or variables. Entering into these aspects would exceed the purpose of this paper (see Collier 1993; Mills et al. 2006).

The most significant problem associated with the restricted number of cases is the risk of over-determination.[9] In this circumstance, the selection of empirical situations may be predetermined by the theoretical interests of the researcher, disproportionately favoring a situation in which the findings tend toward the direction anticipated by theory. This is perhaps the most serious objection raised against the use of the comparative method, and even authors as important as Weber are not exempt. In this regard, Alexander (1990, p. 39) suggests that since there were other social contexts, such as the modern Italian primitive city-states, in which capitalists manifested a strong entrepreneurial impetus, the renowned association proposed by Weber between the spirit of capitalism and British entrepreneurs from the seventeenth and eighteenth centuries—based on a limited number of cases—could have been over-determined by its theoretical reference to the Protestant ethic. As underscored by the same author, the decision of which empirical events to select in relation to the problem of theoretical interest is an aspect subject to discussion in practically all research efforts.

A limited number of cases makes it difficult to eliminate rival explanatory hypotheses, since there is an excessive number of independent variables that converge and compete with each other in the explanation of the process under study. Usually the theoretical determination of the selection of cases tends to give preference to entities most emblematic of the phenomenon, those most clearly expressing their singularity, although not the most frequent or representative from a statistical viewpoint. No matter how this is framed, the consideration of which cases to select for comparison does not tend to be self evident, unless the comparison is limited to differences between countries. Phrasing again Przeworski and Teune (1970, supra), what are the criteria that should guide case selection in a comparative approach: major similarities or major differences? Neither methodological design is exempt from problems.

There have been various responses to the limitations that arise from a limited number of cases. Presenting them here would extend beyond this chapter's objectives. It is worth stating, however, that some researchers have attempted to increase the number of cases as a means of reducing the explanatory variables considered; while others, on the contrary, insist in the relevance of studying a small numbers of cases. In one of the most vigorous defenses of small-N studies, Ragin (1987, p. 51, 2006) refutes Smelser by stating that the very nature of the comparative method makes a limited number of cases a necessity with enormous

[9] Due to the type of methodological design chosen for this study, we will focus on qualitative analysis, necessarily restricted to a small number of cases. There are, however, countless numbers of research studies in which comparisons are made on the basis of sample populations, involving considerable numbers of cases. In these situations comparative analysis may involve at least two problems: (1) superficiality, due to the restricted number of explanatory variables in relation to the number of cases included in the comparison; and (2) the existence of many irrelevant cases that, exhibiting values close to zero in dependent and independent variables, will lead to a spurious confirmation of the anticipated relation. In other words, an elevated number of cases carries the risk of some of them being irrelevant from a theoretical point of view, and allowing an artificial rejection of the null hypothesis (see Mills et al. 2006; Ragin 2006).

heuristic advantages. Only in this way, the author states, is it possible to achieve theoretically significant comparisons of empirical situations understood as totalities, comparisons in which all the logical possibilities of combinations are exhaustively examined.[10]

Another problem inherent in comparative analysis refers to the *difficulties in achieving equivalence between indicators*, also a very important issue. There is no doubt that this limitation has had a long-lasting effect on the range of possibilities for comparisons since contexts that are very dissimilar in many regards (cultural, levels of development, etc.) bring up serious questioning as to the construction of standard, interchangeable indicators. One might think, for example, of synthetic measures of well-being that include—in the same indicator—rates of maternal mortality or rates of literacy in countries as dissimilar as Tanzania and Sweden. Ideally, the process should be preceded by a theoretical discussion on the meaning of what is to be measured and compared, and by the application of ad hoc questionnaires that include complex measures of the dimensions to be evaluated. As already underscored here, in accordance with Smelser (2003), equivalence should involve not only the construction of empirical indicators in relation to the dependent variable, but also those postulated as causal or independent variables.[11] In other words, when different contexts are compared, the variables selected as explanatory variables should have similar meanings. Given these difficulties, one of the proposals by Smelser is to multiply the number of indicators oriented toward measuring the same phenomenon.

In contrast to these difficulties, among the various virtues of the comparative method, one can mention, in line with Ragin (1987), the combinatorial and contextual (non-linear, non-probabilistic) nature of causality. Since social processes are examined as significant totalities and not broken up into a set of variables with a measurement of the isolated effect of each variable on the dependent one—outside the context—the comparative analysis of a small number of cases makes it possible to outline an all-encompassing (although necessarily contingent and provisional) description of the situations under study. Far from approaching a causal connection through the examination of the concomitant variation between empirical indicators (correlation between variables), a rather static search for symmetry (Ragin 1987), the comparative analysis within qualitative methodologies is aimed at searching for the set of particular conditions that must be combined in order to produce the effect in question, such conditions are combined in a variable manner and are always contingent. Although not all qualitative comparative effort has to follow the particular methodology developed by Ragin and colleagues (QCA), their systematic reflection of the potentiality of comparative analysis in small-N studies—in general—is very illuminating (Ariza and Gandini 2012).

[10] Other advantages mentioned are that the reduced number of cases allows for making 'dense' descriptions (Geertz 1973), and avoids the theoretical emptying of concepts (Sartori 1970, cited by Collier 1993).

[11] Perhaps it is worth pointing out that in research studies based on most similar designs the equivalence function is fulfilled by the contexts of reference.

Lastly, the preference for extreme cases of observed processes, frequently classified as irregular or deviations from the average whenever the statistical recurrence is prioritized, can be identified as another virtue of the comparative method based on a small number of cases. The orientation toward extreme or emblematic situations makes it possible to prevent singularity or exceptions from being overshadowed by statistical frequency. From an analytical viewpoint, extreme cases represent a theoretical limit that allows to maximize the differences between possible and real situations, facilitating causal imputation. An analogous exercise in the logical realm takes place when, for example, ideal types in the Weberian sense are constructed. In these cases, typological construction (thus, the connotation of *ideal*) models the means-ends relation under analysis (for example, charismatic domination), the analytical limit for conducting comparisons with empirical cases as de facto realities.

### *3.2.3 Comparative Analysis and Migration*

There are at least three advantages offered by a comparative analysis of migration process: (1) minimizing the risk of tautological statements; (2) reducing the tension between the micro and macro levels of analysis; (3) combating methodological nationalism by contributing to a transnational understanding of the current migration process and of the social transformation associated with it (Green 1994, 2002; Wimmer and Glick Schiller 2003; Popkin 2005; Ghorra-Gobin 1998). I will briefly focus on each one of them.

As emphasized by Green (1994, p. 11), echoing the self-critical reflection offered by Brettell (1981), analysis that is focused on the observation of a single community of migrants frequently falls into the making of tautological statements. This happens, for example, when findings tend to be interpreted as part of the uniqueness of the group under study, with the resulting risk of leading to culturalist explanations.[12] Introducing a second or third group in the analysis, or examining the same collective in another context, allows for the relativization of statements, and at the same time, the distinguishing of the specific from the general, effectively responding to individual factors in relation to the characteristics of the group or the socioeconomic structure of the receiving country. Thus, the comparative method opens up the possibility of moving away from culturalist explanations, although it does not, of course, guarantee they will be avoided.[13] It is likely that the basis for this tautological reasoning lies in the presumption of equivalence between ethnic

[12] As pointed out by Brettell (1981, p. 46, cited by Green 1994, p. 11), "One chooses a community to find or prove'community.' The assumptions become the conclusion."

[13] The same thing can happen when comparison is used in a certain way at the level of nation-states, particularly when, in an analogous reflection, all the differences found are immediately attributed to the contrasting profiles of the two nations, and consequently analysis ends up confirming the initial assumptions (Green 1994, p. 5).

community, identity and culture, inherent in the predominant paradigm in ethnicity studies within the field of migration studies, as mentioned by Wimmer. According to this author, what has predominated in migration and ethnicity studies is an analytical paradigm based on Herderian proto-nationalist modes of classification,[14] which assume a principle of equivalence between culture, community and ethnic group, and tend to conceive of ethnicity as a cultural expression that is objectively defined, instead of subjectively constructed. This equivalence, Wimmer emphasizes, constitutes an alleged tactic of the assimilationist paradigm, an analytical framework par excellence in migration studies in the United States. What Wimmer proposes instead is the *formation of ethnic groups*, also referred to as the *formation of boundaries* (Wimmer 2007, p. 13).[15]

In addition to minimizing the risk of tautological imputation, comparative analysis of migration induces a more general level of reflection that makes it possible to integrate the cases observed into a shared concept, in an analytical category with a higher degree of abstraction, encompassing the different groups included in the comparison. In other words, this allows for a principle of classification of what is observed at a 'supra-monographic level of reflection' (Green 2002, cited by Odgers 2002). This is similar to, for example, the conceptual exercise that allows for integrating shrimp and lobster in the more general category of crustaceans. In epistemological terms, comparison leads to a process of classification that discriminates between similar and different, with distribution into more general categories, on the basis of which constant (or invariant) aspects of the phenomenon in question can be derived (Ghorra-Gobin 1998). Even when all classification schemes are arbitrary, in some way, categorization fulfills a central role in the knowledge process, to the extent that it occurs logically prior to specifying: in order to specify a list, it is necessary to know beforehand the order, species or type to which that which will be listed belongs (Velasco 2008).

Located at an intermediate level of reflection that is at least supra-individual, the comparative method helps to reduce tension between the micro and macro levels in migration analysis: the broader the scope of the first, the greater the specificity of the second (Green 2002, cited by Odgers 2002). Thus, for example, a carefully contextualized examination such as that carried out by Bloemraad (2005) of the

[14] Johann Gottfried Herder, a philosopher from the eighteenth century, maintained a perspective of the social world as constituted by a multitude of nations and ethnic groups in which each nation represented a particular manifestation of human capacity to be cultivated, analogous to the capacities of species in the natural world. In this tradition of thought, ethnic groups and nations constitute total social phenomena, made up of three isomorphic aspects: (1) a community that maintains its unity on the basis of the strong links among its members; (2) an identity built around a feeling of a common destiny and historic continuity; and (3) a unique vision of the world established through the (Wimmer 2007, p. 3).

[15] The author draws attention to the need to 'de-ethnicize' designs for migration research, to be able to report both the emergence of ethnic groups and their absence. From the perspective of the formation of ethnic groups as she proposes, the selection of *non*-ethnic units of observation is important, to facilitate evaluating whether group boundaries are actually formed and where they are formed, before assuming that they exist (see Wimmer 2007).

differences in the number of Portuguese naturalized in Canada and in the United States, with a gradual expansion to include more observation groups, made it possible to precisely clarify both the weight of micro factors (refuting the affirmation that differences in the number of Portuguese naturalized responded to the particularities distinguishing the different groups of immigrants), with respect to macro structural factors (emphasizing the role of government support, in this case from the Canadian government, in promoting political participation by immigrants), and to introduce new explanatory factors of the differences initially observed in the number of persons naturalized.[16] For Bloemraad (2005), creative comparisons in migration studies can reinforce the information available, by favoring an exhaustive assessment of the logical implications contained in a hypothetical proposal.

Finally, as already pointed out, the comparative method has been proposed during recent years as one of the ways to confront what is referred to as methodological nationalism in the field of migration studies. According to Wimmer and Glick Schiller (2003) and Popkin (2005), this has been the dominant epistemic structure in social sciences during the past twentieth century, at least since the post-war period. As such, it constitutes the naturalization of the nation-state as the unquestioned reference point for social processes, overshadowing society with state, and overshadowing national interest with state interest.[17] For the authors cited above, the most eloquent manifestation of methodological nationalism in theoretical studies has been the non-perception of the bias that the nationalist focus induces in the reflection process; and in the case of empirical studies, the particular preference for the nation-state as the unit of analysis (Wimmer 2007; Glick Schiller 2003).

If the point of departure of a research is the idea that social events taking place within national borders are essentially different than those taking place outside those borders, the limits of the nation-state define the scope of the units of analysis and obstruct an understanding of the transnational nature of social processes (Wimmer and Glick Schiller 2003; Ariza and Portes 2010). If such processes, including migration, refer increasingly to a multiplicity of spatial loci (from the local to the transnational), comparative studies may constitute one of the ways for overcoming methodological nationalism, as long as the analytical exercise transcends the nation-state as the main point of reference for the processes examined, although it will continue to be included.[18]

---

[16] In the authors' words: "By tracing immigrants' stories of their political incorporation upward, to the assistance provided by community organizations, I could link micro-level dynamics with the larger structural argument about institutional differences" (Bloemraad 2005, p. 17).

[17] It appears, as mentioned by Green (1994, p. 3) in the article quoted several times here, that there were voices that warned of the dangers of nationalist tendencies in social sciences early on. Thus, already in the early twentieth century, Henri Pirenne made a fervent call in favor of the comparative method as a means to liberate social sciences from nationalist prejudices—which he thought had been inherited from nineteenth century romanticism.

[18] As pointed out by Green (1994, p. 3): "Through a comparative method…we can explore the universalism inherent in certain processes while understanding the diversity of both their representations and realities".

Methodological nationalism is also expressed in the tendency toward the homogenization of social processes. A clear example of this is the attempt to place all Latin American migrants in the category of *Hispanics*. In this way the particular cultural features of each group are erased, by labeling them as only part of a shared category—constructed by the state—that is contrary to *nationals*, or those who by their own law form part of the nation-state. It is precisely the nation-state the parameter on the basis of which criteria for inclusion/exclusion, for belonging and for accessing the benefits of citizenship, are defined.[19]

## 3.3 The Comparative Perspective in the Study of Female Migration and Labor Markets: The Case of Global Domestic Service

In this Sect. 3.3.1, I will highlight the way in which the use of the comparative analysis strategy is proposed for this research study. As a framework of reference, I will first briefly describe some antecedents of the relation between female migration and domestic service.

### *3.3.1 Female Migration and Domestic Service: The Continuity of a Structural Relationship*

Historically, domestic service has been the most important form of female employment in Latin America (Kuznesof 1993). Its significance in women's labor profile diminished throughout the twentieth century as levels of schooling among the female population increased and women's labor opportunities in skilled manual and non-manual segments of the tertiary sector were diversified. In the case of Mexico, for example, domestic workers represented an average of no less than a third of the total female economically active population between 1895 and 1940. This single occupation accounted for approximately 30 or 35 % of female workers during approximately 45 years (Ariza 1998).[20]

There has been a structural link in historic terms between internal female migration as a social process and domestic service as a labor market, because of

---

[19] As emphasized by Centeno (2010, p. 213), from a migration angle, the state is the institution that certifies the right of individuals to enjoy the prerogatives that define an exclusive sub-group of individuals—of citizens—as being the ones that belong. It is precisely with the advent of the state in its modern form that the "illegality" of migration emerges as a social problem. The author draws attention to the recent nature of the phenomenon in historic terms, since it was not until the late nineteenth century and early tweentieth century that state control over migration became a crucial element in sovereignty (Centeno 2010, p. 213).

[20] It was necessary for 100 years to pass before this occupation dropped to second place in the labor profile of Mexican women, around 1980, according to Suárez (1989).

the over-representation of migrants in the universe of domestic workers. This link can be traced to more general relations between internal female migration, female economic participation and development, since it was through migration and insertion in domestic service, to a significant degree, that a considerable portion of the female population was incorporated into remunerated extra-domestic activity in the expanding urban centers during the most dynamic years of internal migration in Latin America, approximately from 1940 to 1970 (Ariza 2000).

Among the many changes occurring in the context of globalization and the profound reorientation of production in Latin American economies since the mid-1980s, we find an uncommon increase in international migration. According to Martínez Pizarro (2003, p. 19), the percentage of women is higher than that of men in the total number of migrants in the world's two main regions of immigration: Europe and the United States. As in the major internal migration flows during the past century, current international female migration is significantly associated with domestic service as a labor market—, which can now be observed internationally. Countless women turn to this area of work, as they migrate from Latin America, Asia, Africa and Eastern Europe to cities in the European Community, the Middle East and the United States (Ehrenreich and Russell Hochschild 2003, pp. 276–280; Ariza 2004).[21]

The internationalization of domestic service in the context of globalization is associated with a series of structural processes that have existed for a longer period of time. From the side of labor demand stand: (a) the growth of low-level non-manual segments of the services sector (hostels, restaurants, housekeeping) associated with a tendency toward the polarization of the job structure accompanying the expansion of the tertiary sector in so-called *global* cities (Sassen-Koob 1995); (b) the reformulation of the welfare state; (c) demographic aging process; and (d) the growing female economic participation. These last three factors are directly linked to what has been referred to as the *care system crisis* (Zimmerman et al. 2006).[22] In terms of labor supply, the outstanding processes include: (a) profound

[21] Specialists on this topic have been able to sketch out maps with the primary routes of this international female migration toward markets that, like domestic service, have been reactivated in the context of globalization. Thus, women from southern Asia (Indonesia, the Philippines, Thailand, India and Sri Lanka) migrate to the Persian Gulf (Saudi Arabia and Kuwait), Italy, Spain and Greece. Women from Africa (Nigeria, Ethiopia and Morocco) move to Spain, Italy and Greece. Mexican and Central American women migrate to the United States and Canada, and enter into domestic service as well as other poorly remunerated activities in the tertiary sector. Caribbean women, including women from the Dominican Republic, migrate to the United States, Spain, Italy, Switzerland, Belgium and Germany, among other countries (see Ehrenreich and Russell Hochschild 2003, pp. 276–280; Ariza 2004).

[22] The most obvious expressions of this crisis are *care deficits* and the *commodification* of care work. The first concept refers to the shortage or insufficient supply of remunerated services for meeting the needs of caring for members of a family, as well as the lack of care provided by relatives in the restricted context of the family world. Commodification refers to the fact that in first world countries, care work (or reproductive work in its simplest sense) is becoming the object of increasing organization, as it is turned into activities and services that can be bought and sold (Zimmerman et al., 2006, p. 20).

social and economic erosion causing constant economic ups and downs in recent decades in the sending countries of the migrant labor force, making monetary remittances a factor of structural micro and macro equilibrium (at the household level); and (b) the consolidation of migration in the social imaginary as the alternative for social mobility par excellence for a considerable segment of the population. The corrosive effects of recent economic policies on the stability of third-world countries, and the dismantling of precarious social welfare systems, has led to the growing economic dependence of households on the international work of migrant women These international female migration flows will form part of what are being identified as counter-geographies of globalization, survival circuits—made up of the most disadvantaged individuals and constituting the dark side of globalization (Salazar Parreñas 2001; Sassen 2002). There is no doubt that a catalyzing element between labor supply and labor demand originates in the unprecedented conditions of labor mobility and communication promoted by the globalizing environment.

It is therefore evident that domestic service is an element of continuity in the relation between female migration and labor markets at different moments in history, and this is true whether we are speaking of internal or international migration. For this reason we have given it priority in our analytical proposal for this project, as a key aspect for understanding the particularities imprinted on the relation between female migration and labor markets by the globalizing context. In both cases—internal and international migration—domestic service continues to exist due to the convergence of a number of long-term structural factors (development, tertiarization, feminization, globalization) that favor the supply and demand of the female labor force in low-level manual segments of the services sector, as well as specific contextual and historic factors. At the national level and during the years in which the import substitution model was on the rise in most Latin American societies, the demand for domestic workers was supplied primarily by the local, often rural, labor force characterized by very low levels of schooling. However, we find that at the international level and in the context of some of the most important first-world metropolises, a diverse mosaic of nationalities provides the labor required for carrying out the reproduction tasks characterizing this activity.[23] In contrast with internal migration, part of this labor force often has high levels of schooling. This is notoriously the case with, for example, Eastern

[23] Which aspects are included in paid domestic service is, in itself, a matter of controversy. The unspecific nature of the tasks involved, the fact that this work is carried out in the private sphere, and the predominant informal nature of the occupation all make it difficult to establish clear limits. As emphasized by some authors, efforts such as those by the International Labor Organization (ILO) to delimit the tasks encompassed in the occupation tend to trail far behind reality (Andersen 2000, p. 15). Cleaning, preparing food and caring for others—usually children but also the elderly—are currently some of the daily tasks of immigrant women inserted in this occupation (Andersen 2000, p. 15). It is in this broad sense that paid domestic service is being referred to in this study.

European immigrants in the city of Madrid. It also occurs, although to a much lesser degree, among Latin American immigrants. I will now focus on presenting the comparative strategy proposed in this research project.

### *3.3.2 The Comparative Approach Selected*

Based on an examination of the labor insertion of two groups of immigrant women in domestic service, specifically Dominican Republic women in Madrid, and Mexican women in New York City, this research study is aimed at learning about the relation between female labor markets and migration in the context of globalization. The study is based primarily on qualitative methodology, although complementary quantitative information is generated from population censuses and surveys. Placing more priority on qualitative methods[24] than on quantitative ones responds to a series of inter-related factors. The first factor is the irregular or undocumented nature, from a legal point of view, of the population under study.[25] It is difficult to gain access to this population, particularly Mexican women in United States since a high percentage of them are under-represented in official statistics. The second factor refers to the limitations presented by standardized quantitative sources of information (censuses and surveys) when broken down for the level of analysis required, difficulties that are even more pronounced in the case of the female migrant worker population and for the specific occupation under study here: domestic service. A final aspect refers to the suitability that qualitative-type field work—focused on the geographical terrain and using direct informants—represents for the research objectives. An evaluation of the labor insertion and the characterization of domestic service as a highly informal, secondary labor market that places a significant percentage of the immigrant labor force in irregular conditions, could not be easily achieved to a satisfactory degree with the general statistical indicators that can be constructed on the basis of the questions contained in survey questionnaires and the available population censuses.

The *unit of analysis* is the link between migration and domestic service as a particular labor market—the mode in which both processes reinforce each other. The *unit of observation* is composed of the migrant women interviewed in both cities (Madrid and New York City), belonging to each of the two national groups mentioned (Dominican and Mexican women) and incorporated into the labor force

---

[24] Using the definition provided by Denzin and Lincoln (2003: 4, 5), we understand qualitative research as a situated activity that locates the observer in the world and consists of a series of interpretative, material practices that make the world visible…Among other things, it assumes a naturalist, interpretative approach to the reality being studied (Bechhofer and Paterson 2000; Ariza and Velasco 2012).

[25] Dominicans in Madrid and Mexicans in New York have a diametrically opposed migratory status, with low percentages of irregularity among the former (approximately 23.6 %) and extremely high percentages among the latter (around 60 %) (Domingo and Martínez 2006; Passel and D́Vera Cohn 2009).

as domestic workers. Between the two units—of analysis and observation—there is a conceptual hiatus that contains implications for the inquiry process.[26] In our case, the main implication is that the labor market as a process is not limited to the worker as an active agent in that market, but includes employers (or those creating the demand for the labor force) and the diverse institutional factors that intervene in labor relations, such as the current labor framework and the presence of labor organizations. In this research study, these aspects are supplied through indirect information obtained from the women interviewed, from key informants and from the specialized literature.

The decision to conduct an international comparative analysis lies precisely in the global nature that domestic service has come to acquire, as a feminized labor market, its internationalization in the context of the profound socioeconomic changes during recent decades in both sending and receiving countries. From our viewpoint, in order to comprehend the global nature of this market, it is necessary to move beyond the reference of a single country. Through the inclusion of more than one country we are taking note of the international nature of this labor market, prioritizing in that way the global economic link over the national perspective and visualizing the country in question as one of many manifestations of the overall phenomenon being studied.

However, while the intention of the comparative strategy is to serve as a way for capturing the global or general aspects characterizing the process, it is also a means for defining the specificity of domestic service as a labor market in each of the two countries and cities observed, identifying the particularities imprinted by each urban and national context. The key concept here is *contexts of reception* (Portes and Rumbaut 1990, p. 85). As we know, this concept constitutes a matrix of analysis for understanding the modes of incorporation of migrants into the receiving society defining a set of probable courses depending on the characteristics of the national political attitude toward migration (greater or lesser opening), the labor market framework (positive or negative discrimination) and the type of ethnic community (working, professional or non-existent class) in each context (Portes and Rumbaut 1990, p. 85).

In the case of this research study, aspects acquiring special relevance include those related to migration policy as well as institutional factors that regulate labor relations and have an impact on the way in which immigrant women are inserted into paid domestic service, since the analytical objective is not the social incorporation of Dominican or Mexican immigrants into Madrid or New York societies, but rather, their labor insertion into this occupation. In this comparative exercise,

[26] Ragin (1987, p. 9) calls attention to the underlying ambiguity of the notion of the unit of analysis, sometimes identified simply with data, and at other times in theoretical terms. This ambiguity increases in the case of comparative studies, in which analysis is usually carried out at one level (individual, for example), while the explanation comes from another (macro-social). Ragin proposes differentiating between the unit of observation (referring to the collection of data) and the unit of explanation, used to explain the pattern observed on the basis of the results.

the particular labor market is the constant, not immigrant groups *per se*, and this yields some advantages from an analytical point of view.[27] For example, New York City typologically represents a context of reception most notably characterized by the *passive acceptance*[28] of migration, together with a discourse that criminalizes immigrants and a labor market governed by the purest principles of liberalism. In contrast, Madrid combines: a state policy that encourages immigration for certain labor niches, through the establishment of immigration and strong barriers of entry to those labor niches reserved for nationals as well as a *passive* acceptance of migration flows from the South, the contingent nature of the status of legal residence (Calavita 2006), and an increasingly xenophobic climate that current economic crisis has strengthened (Ioé and OIM 2012). Other differences stem from the type of welfare state predominating in each of these societies (liberal versus corporate, Esping-Andersen 1990),[29] and the major obstacles placed by the United States on legalization of immigrants. The latter signifies an enormous potential mass of a captive undocumented labor force, given the magnitude of the international immigration to that country. A common factor is that in both cities domestic service is subjected to a regimen of exception in which it is exempt from complying with the general stipulations regulating other labor activities.

The selection of countries for this study responds to academic aspects related to the importance of migration flows and the personal history of the primary researcher.[30] The United States and Spain are the primary places of destination for immigrants from Mexico and the Dominican Republic, respectively. Selecting the migration flow from Mexico does not require a justification, since its long history and massive nature, together with Mexico's close geographical proximity to the United States, make it a highly relevant case.

In the case of the Dominican Republic, Spain's emergence as the second most important international destination of migration is related to the process of

[27] Green (1994) proposes the analysis of an economic sector at a particular moment in time, as a way of avoiding the limitations of what are referred to as "divergent" or "convergent" comparative analyses, typically focused on ethnic groups.

[28] In line with the concept developed by Portes and Rumbaut (1990, pp. 85–86), we find that exclusion, passive acceptance and active promotion are the three most common government responses to foreigners. Among these three, passive acceptance corresponds to a situation in which access to the country is tolerated explicitly or implicitly, without any other additional effort to impede or stimulate this phenomenon.

[29] The recent economic measures developed by the Spanish government since the 2008 crisis aimed at reaching fiscal equilibrium, may in some way bring closer the two welfare systems.

[30] The research group is composed of five members: the main researcher, an academic with a Master's in Regional Development, and two students. The main researcher is a sociologist (with undergraduate and doctorate degrees in this field), who studied demography at the Latin American Center for Demography (*Centro Latinoamericano de Demografía*—CELADE). She has been working for 18 years at the Institute for Social Research at Mexico's National Autonomous University (UNAM), having worked as a researcher at the Institute of Population and Development Studies of the Dominican Republic (PROFAMILIA) between 1987 and 1991. Her primary lines of research have been migration (especially female migration), labor markets, gender, family, sociodemographic processes (including urbanization) and methodological reflection.

diversification of migration experienced in this country since the mid-1980s.[31] The rhythm in which immigration to Spain increased between 1990 and 2007 was truly significant. Official statistics indicate a total of 6,640 legal immigrants in 1991. Eight years later, this number had increased by four times, reaching a total of 26,854 legal immigrants, excluding undocumented immigrants (Báez 2001). Figures from the municipal registries (in which there is no distinction between legal and undocumented immigrants) indicated a total of 37,380 Dominicans residing in Spain in the year 2002; 65, 119 in 2007; and 89,813 in 2012, 57.9.2 % of which were women (INE 2003, 2008, p. 212). The migration flow from the Dominican Republic continues to be feminized, and the main niche in which female immigrants are inserted is domestic service. Dominican migrants have experienced a relative diversification in recent years, and male migration has increased alongside processes of family reunification. One of the unexpected effects of the current economic crisis has been to place domestic service as the first occupation for foreign female population, whether communitarian or extra communitarian (Foro 2010).

The contrast between countries originates not only from differences in international migration flows, migration policies and the size of their economies, but also from differences in family structures. Here we have the assumption that similar economic processes (labor insertion of international migrant women in a feminized activity) can bring differentiated consequences for those participating in them, depending on the conditions imposed by each context of reception (Europe and Madrid versus the United States and New York City), whether or not international female migration is predominant (Dominican Republic versus Mexico), and the sociodemographic characteristics distinguishing migration flows, including pre-existing family structures (high levels of marriage dissolution, extended family households, and female heads of households in the Dominican Republic, versus high marriage stability, lower levels of extended family households, and medium levels of female heads of households in Mexico, among other aspects (see Ariza et al. 1994; Ariza and Oliveira 1997, 2004a, b).[32]

[31] New York is the most important place of destination for emigration from the Dominican Republic, and Spain is the second. The year in which the international migration of Dominicans to Spain began to increase coincides with the approval of the US Immigration Reform and Control Act (1986), which established new barriers to the international flow of immigrants. In contrast, at the same time and up to 1993, the Spanish government did not place restrictions on Dominicans entering its territory, and in fact they could enter without a visa.

[32] One of the clear consequences from processes of globalization and transnationality affecting family structure is the tendency toward the *fragmentation* of family units and the dispersion of residential spaces (Guarnizo 1997). In those families in which spatial dispersion is expressed in the absence of the mother in homes, regressive effects have been detected on the teaching–learning processes of children and the opportunities for personal growth and development in low-level socioeconomic contexts. The absence of mothers appears to have a stronger destabilizing effect on families than the absence of fathers. In contrast to the effects on intra-family dynamics from male emigration, when mothers are the ones who emigrate, the fathers do not assume domestic roles but rather delegate responsibility for the care and attention to their children to other relatives (Gregorio Gil 1995; Ariza 2012).

Consequently, the flow of Dominicans to Spain represents an invaluable opportunity to observe: (1) an independent female migration flow; (2) a labor market—domestic service—that absorbs the majority of this flow; and (3) a European immigration context through the perspective of the Spanish society. At the same time the migration flow from Mexico to the United States offers a point of contrast in which: (1) most women enter the migration flow by following male family members (independent female migration is not the dominant pattern)[33]; (2) domestic service is one of the sectors through which female worker enter to US labor market; and (3) we can observe the nature of the United States as a context of reception.

In an effort toward specification, we can say that, in line with the typology described by Przeworski and Teune (1970) mentioned above, the research design we are using is close to the *most similar systems*, to the extent that there is a significant degree of similarity in most of the variables postulated as causal: the type of economy (tertiarized), the strong demand for the female migrant labor force to engage in reproduction work, sociodemographic characteristics (aging societies), and the importance of the international migration from Latin America. Such research design, also referred to as *concomitant variation*, contemplates a series of common inter-systemic factors that serve as elements of control,[34] and a reduced set of dissimilar or unknown variables, that will constitute the inter-systemic differences. In our case the dissimilar aspects come from the particular migration policy in each country, the type of welfare state, and some local characteristics of the labor markets, which would be expected to generate differences between domestic service in one place of destination and another (dependent variable). Thus, while the inter-systemic similarities offer a homogenous basis for reflection, the differences provide the necessary contrasting factors for understanding the nature of domestic service in Madrid (Dominican migrant women) and New York City (Mexican migrant women).[35] By maximizing the shared aspects between systems, the differences observed can be expected to respond to a small number of factors, achieving this way the objectives of generality, parsimony and precision that are pursued by all scientific effort (Ibidem). This inquiry

[33] However after they have reached their destinations, they have a high probability of becoming part of the economically active population (see Cerrutti and Massey 2001).

[34] If we had opted for using the *most different* design, this would have required the causal factors contemplated (countries' level of development, type of economy, degree of aging, relative importance of immigration) to be highly dissimilar, and even so, for the result to be the same.

[35] Of course, the degree of homogeneity or heterogeneity observed is relative and is defined by the researcher. At one extreme, we are all equal because we all belong to the human race, and at an intermediate point, we are irreducibly different because we belong to different races. The degree of homogeneity or heterogeneity will depend on the level of analysis we are engaged in and actually constitutes the scale in which we are conducting our reflection. A scientist can play freely with these relative factors or degrees of homo/heterogeneity, interchanging them and reformulating the level of generality in which the comparison is made, as long as the place from which comparison begins is explicitly identified.

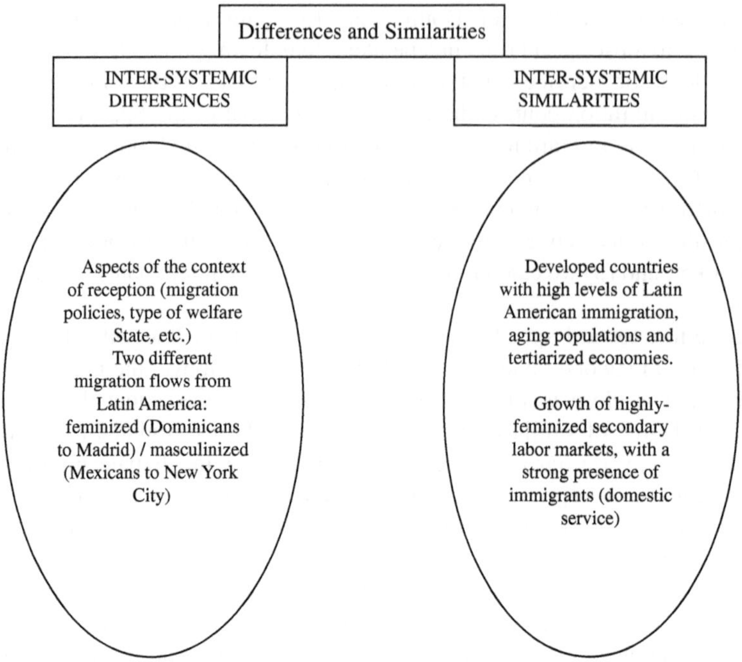


**Fig. 3.1** Basis of comparison. *Source* The author

process is not, however, free from the problems accompanying analysis of a small number of cases (small N), as suggested before. The most important of these problems is the lack of independent variables that might exert causal force on the phenomenon in question, due to the reduced number of situations (cases) that are observed.

Figure 3.1 illustrates the type of comparative design we have selected. The inter-systemic similarities are due to: (1) countries involved are developed economies with a predominance of the tertiary sector and aging demographic structures; (2) the growth or reactivation of feminized secondary labor markets, such as domestic service and care work in general, with an important presence of an immigrant labor force; and (3) period of reference and year of observation.

In contrast, the inter-systemic differences refer to: (1) the characteristics that differentiate some aspects of the contexts of reception represented by the two countries primarily due to their migration policies, labor market regulations and the type of welfare state; (2) the two migration flows selected, specifically Dominican women and Mexican women, characterized by contrasting internal compositions (migration status, irregular/regular, or naturalized in the case of Spain, and undocumented, resident or citizen, in the case of the United States), the degree of feminization of their migration flows and other aspects (independent or associational

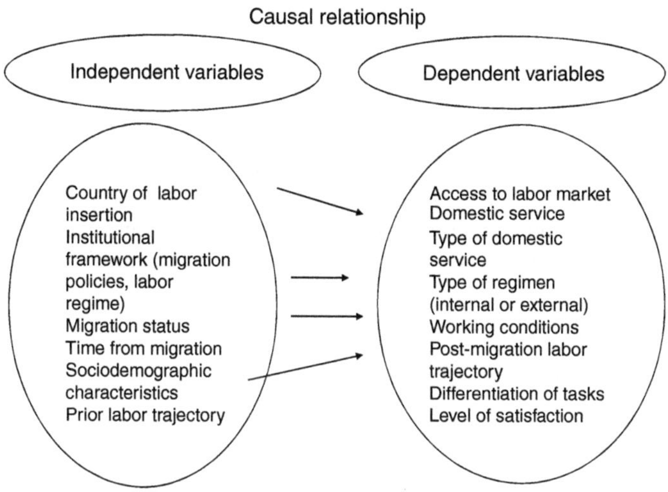


**Fig. 3.2** Causal relationship. *Source* The author

migration)[36]; lastly, (3) the dissimilar family structures in the two sending countries, Mexico and the Dominican Republic, as previously emphasized here.

The relation between inter-systemic differences and similarities can also be viewed in terms of explained or explanatory (dependent or independent) variables. While similarity between the systemic factors serves as an element of control, the inter-systemic differences provide the explanatory variables (independent variables) of the process under study (Przeworski and Teune 1970). In our case this refers to the characteristics of domestic service as a labor market in each of the cities and countries selected. Although analysis is conducted at the systemic level, this does not prevent references to intra-systemic processes from being made if necessary. This back-and-forth between the different spheres of reflection speaks about the dynamic, dialectic nature of all efforts in scientific inquiry. The relation between the two types of variables—dependent and independent—can be outlined graphically in the following way:

As summarized in Fig. 3.2, we can expect to find differences in the way domestic work is carried out in terms of the conditions in which women enter the job in each context of reception (through private intermediary agencies, informal networks, through the state or by non-governmental organizations), the modalities acquired by the activity (whether in private homes or elsewhere), the tasks fulfilled (whether or not they include caring for the elderly, for children, cleaning, or a combination of tasks); the degree of overlapping among tasks, labor conditions (intensity of workday, absence of benefits, income), and the level of personal satisfaction, among other aspects.

[36] The search for heterogeneity, a common practice in qualitative analysis, was one criterion that explicitly guided the selection of the women interviewed.

## 3.4 Methodological Proposal: Axis, Levels of Analysis and Data Construction

In Sect. 3.4.1, I will describe the axis and levels of analysis prioritized in this research study, as well as the way in which data is constructed. I will identify three axis and three levels of analysis. There is not necessarily a specific correspondence between *axis* and *levels*, since any of the levels of analysis can serve as an explanatory element for what takes place in any of the three prioritized axis of analysis.

### *3.4.1 Axis and Levels of Analyses*

#### 3.4.1.1 Analytical Axis 1: The Migration Process

This is a crucial dimension for analysis in our research, since it is proposed as the analytical link that makes it possible to understand the relation between the internationalization of domestic service and globalization. One of the distinctive characteristics of this labor market is the relative inelasticity of the demand (Orlansky and Dubrovsky 1977). To the degree that a significant portion of domestic reproduction tasks remain *invisibilized* in the private sphere, conceptualized as 'not work' and as a 'natural' space for females, there will invariably be a potential demand for a labor force to carry out these tasks. The abundant availability of low-skilled female workers willing to enter into this and other labor markets provided through migration is clearly one of the decisive factors explaining its expansion.

From a macro-structural viewpoint based on this axis of analysis, our study explores the characteristics of the migration process, its history and evolution, and the particular traits it has acquired in recent years. It considers women's place in this process, and especially the significant and, in some cases, increasing feminization of international migration. At the micro level, our study looks at the moments in which migration emerges as a life-defining option in the personal histories of the women workers interviewed, the concrete way in which they migrated, the type of networks, and the subjective perceptions associated with the experience of migration. In the intermediate meso analysis, in contrast, attention is directed toward reflecting upon the way in which the abundance of the immigrant labor force from countries in the South has contributed to the reactivation of this old labor market.

#### 3.4.1.2 Analytical Axis 2: Labor Insertion

This is a central dimension of analysis around which other dimensions revolve.[37] The idea is to produce an X-ray of women's labor insertion in this market, on the basis of information collected during in-depth interviews. The information describes: (1) access to the labor market, or in other words, the means through which insertion was achieved (networks, the state, or private hiring agencies); (2) labor conditions: income, stability, benefits, workday, type of hiring contract if applicable, workload, breaks, vacation; (3) pre and post-migration labor trajectory; (4) the degree of personal satisfaction with the activity, and expectations for leaving or remaining in this sector in the medium term.

From a macro level of reflection, the idea is to consider the structural aspects that explain the expansion of domestic service in the context of globalization, both generally and in the particular case of these two urban contexts and countries of reception analyzed. This activity is evaluated in terms of its historic continuity and also the unique characteristics it has acquired as a response to the enormous demand for *proximity services*[38] in some of the most important cities in the western world since the end of the twentieth century. The factors that explain the proliferation of proximity services include: population's aging, growing female economic participation, changes in the realm of family world (dissolution, increase in one-parent households, progressive tendency toward geographic dispersion), and the welfare state crisis (Parella Rubio 2003, p. 12).[39]

#### 3.4.1.3 Analytical Axis 3: The Family World as Mediation

In contrast, family structure as an analytical axis has a relatively secondary function with respect to the other two areas. This area is understood as a conditioning factor that can make it possible to comprehend both women's migration history and their current labor situation. This is not only because of the intrinsic relation between family networks and migration, but also due to the way in which the family situation conditions female economic participation. From a macro

---

[37] As emphasized by Parella Rubio (2003), the relevance of analyzing the immigrants economic incorporation into the host society lies in its centrality for defining the social position they occupy, and thus, the range of opportunities opened or closed to them.

[38] Also referred to as "daily living services," they include six different areas, with the first two focused on remunerated activities carried out to satisfy the needs of individuals and their families, and services provided to homes (Torns 1997, cited by Parella Rubio 2003, pp. 12, 252). Some of these services are linked to people (elderly, persons with illnesses, children), and others refer more to tasks traditionally considered to be domestic services, such as cleaning and food preparation. The other four areas, according to the European Commission, are: new information and communication technologies, assistance provided to young people experiencing difficulties, mediation and consultation services in conflict resolution, and job risk prevention (Parella Rubio 2003, p. 252).

[39] The reduction in the state's social spending accompanying the reformulation of the social security scheme impacts the care provided to the elderly, one of the tasks most frequently assigned to Latin American female immigrants working in domestic service in Spain.

viewpoint, the contrasting family structures in the Dominican Republic and Mexico within the Latin American context are used as a starting point. Indirectly, these differences in family structure patterns are related to the aggregated tendencies in international migration in both countries: in one case (Mexico) migration is predominantly male and more family dependent; in the other (Dominican Republic) migration is more female and relatively independent. These differences are also related to the ways in which female workers enter the labor market. Prior research has documented an increasing number of female heads of households in the universe of Dominican immigrants, partially attributed to the incentive provided by the labor demand (Oso 1998). We can expect to find tangible signs of some of these differences in the life histories of the migrant women interviewed—which constitute the micro level within this axis of analysis.[40] With the objective of capturing the relation between family structure and migration, this study explores the changes in household composition associated with migration, at both the pre and post-migration stages.

As explained earlier, in addition to these analytical axis, there are three levels of analysis: macro, meso and micro-structural. In the first level, the globalizing context and migration play a crucial role as long-term social processes that provide a framework for the labor market to be observed. This level of analysis is based on a conception of migration that is defocalized from the individual migrant, and visualized as a partial consequence of the economic expansionism of central countries in the context of the economic integration promoted by globalization (Portes and Rambaut 1990; Sassen 2000).

This process of expansion and subordinated integration of peripheral countries has been accompanied by a profound deterioration in their social structures and an intensification of social inequality. Together with these aspects, consideration is given to the mediation of another series of factors, some of which are demographic (family structure, aging population) and institutional (migration policy, labor frameworks).

At the *meso level*, priority is given to the urban contexts that both cities and both countries represent from a labor point of view, and also in terms of their migration policies and labor markets. As we have emphasized, each of these two countries (Spain and the United States) and their cities (Madrid and New York)—in virtue of their histories, their place in the international division of labor, their idiosyncratic characteristics, their migration policies and regulatory frameworks—make up a particular *context of reception* (Portes and Böröcz 1989; Portes and Rumbaut 1990), with the capacity to impact the way in which such labor markets function and therefore, the social condition of migrant women.

[40] Recognizing that aggregate patterns (average statistical values) conceal variability (or dispersion), we would expect to also find cases that are discrepant with the general tendencies in family dynamics at the level of individual interviews—cases that are illustrative of the diversity of the process.

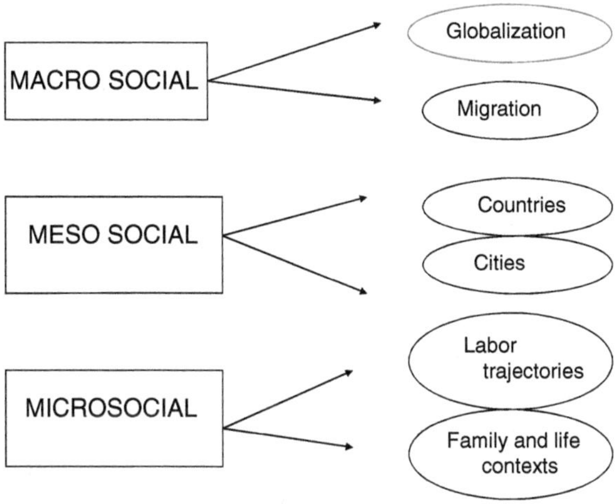


**Fig. 3.3** Levels of analysis

Lastly, in *micro-social* level of reflection, analysis is focused on the working and life trajectories histories of the migrant women interviewed. Two important dimensions are identified: the socio-structural and the socio-symbolic, from which complementary analysis of the information gathered are developed. Based on the first, qualitative information is treated at an objectivist level, with the aim of contrasting the pre and post-migration labor histories of a set of women who vary on a series of central aspects looking for common patterns. From the socio-symbolic approach, the subjective aspects contained in the interview guide are highlighted: perceptions of the labor situation, level of personal satisfaction, assessment of migration, sense of belonging, expectations for returning (Fig. 3.3). At this level of reflection, the life histories are the framework of reference that provides meaning to the labor trajectory followed and the perceptions associated to it.

### 3.4.2 Data Construction: Field Work and Systemization of Information

Field work[41] encompasses four phases that correspond to the different possibilities of origin and reception in the two female migration flows observed—Dominican women to Madrid and Mexican women to the United States—with a particular approach depending on whether it takes place in the sending or receiving country.

[41] Field work is understood as a type of research that takes place in the context in which things occur, as opposed to research that takes place far from the context (Bechhofer and Paterson 2000).

For the receiving countries and cities a more intensive field work was designed, based on a series of in-depth interviews with women working in paid domestic service, interviews with key informants and an undetermined number of informal conversations with individuals in the ethnic community within each of these cities. A quota was designed for the in-depth interviews, in order to make the selection of the population as heterogeneous as possible, in terms of sociodemographic characteristics (age, schooling, marital status, maternity, migration status, rural or urban origin, etc.) and type of labor insertion in domestic service (internal/external; care/cleaning). The idea was not only to prevent the construction of information from being confined to a very particular sub-group within the universe of reference, given the networks through which we gained access to the population, but also to allow for enough diversity. A semi-structured guide was used for the interviews. Within a flexible framework of interaction, the objective was to gather systematic information in relation to the three primary analytical dimensions in the study: migration, labor insertion and family structure.

In the sending countries, Mexico and the Dominican Republic, ethnographic tours were conducted in the primary localities of origin of the women previously interviewed in Madrid or New York City. In those localities researchers interviewed key informants (local authorities, priests, teachers, social organizations, cooperatives) and had informal conversations with inhabitants. In all cases the project's main researcher personally conducted the interviews, with the exception of the ethnographic visits to the sending localities in Mexico, where other members of the research team also participated. Throughout the four phases of field work, a total of 50 in-depth interviews were conducted in the cities of destination, together with over 40 semi-structured interviews with key informants, inhabitants of localities and members of migrants' families in both sending and receiving locations.

As already explained, the data was constructed following two paths: (1) by obtaining aggregated figures based on the available statistical information (secondary sources: surveys, census)[42]; and (2) by directly obtaining information from female migrant workers in the various modalities of domestic service in the two cities and countries selected (primary sources), as well as from key informants and informal contacts.

There are specific procedures for the systematization of information in each of these two paths. The quantitative approach is well known, and it is only necessary to adhere to technical and methodological principles—which are practically universal—through which information is addressed at this level of aggregation. In the case of a qualitative approach, there are no guidelines or specific, uniform

[42] The quantitative sources used in the case of Spain are the National Census and the municipal registry; and for the United States, the Population Census, the Current Population Survey and the American Community Survey.

standards for the systematization of information, which instead depends in many cases on the researcher's academic tradition (anthropological, sociological, linguistic), in addition to a considerable dose of personal creativity (Denzin and Lincoln 2003; Ariza and Velasco 2012).[43]

Focusing on a point that combines objectivist and constructivist approaches to the qualitative information obtained, analytical matrices were developed for systematically comparing the relevant information for the main analytical dimensions of this research: migration, labor and family structure. Each life history provided characteristics of the current labor insertion, and a detailed sequence of the pre and post-migration labor trajectory, as well as the changes occurring in the household's composition and structure before and after migration in order to address the whole migration experience. This specific, objectivist approach to the working history will be complemented with interpretative, constructivist narration on the life history and the most subjective aspects included in the interview guide: the meaning attributed to the migration experience, the notion of belonging (here or there, or here and there), and a self-assessment of the labor activity carried out.

## 3.5 Final Considerations

Our presentation of the way in which this study proposes the use of the comparative method in analyzing the labor insertion of two groups of Latina workers in domestic service in the cities of Madrid (Dominican women) and New York City (Mexican women), was preceded by some clarifications regarding the permanence of the comparative method in social sciences in general, and its pertinence in the particular case of migration studies.

It was made clear that not only has the systematic use of comparison been among the main methodological resources employed in sociology since this field of study was created, but this method has some important advantages when we engage in studying the complexity of migration processes. As we have indicated, the use of the comparative method can represent a way to avoid at least two of the most frequent problems encountered in the analysis of migration: (1) the tendency to essentialize the characteristics observed in a collective of immigrants, as if they were idiosyncratic—and therefore irreducible—aspects of the culture to which

[43] Citing Becker (1998), Denzin and Lincoln (2003, p. 6) describe the qualitative researcher as "a bricoleur or maker of quilts who uses the tools of his or her methodological trade, deploying whatever strategies, methods and empirical materials are at hand. If new tools have to be invented, or pieced together, then the researcher will do this. The choices as to which interpretative practices to employ are not necessarily set in advance. The decision around which research practice to use depends on the questions formulated, and the questions depend, in turn, on the context, what is available, and what the researcher can manage to achieve".

they belong, leading to culturalist reasonings of a tautological nature; and (2) the inclination to give the nation-state a central position in the understanding of migration processes, by emphasizing it as a unit of analysis. The contrasting exercise implied in the use of comparison as a methodological strategy may allow for relativizing both the characteristics deemed as exclusive to a particular collective, and the position of the nation-state within more inclusive social processes. Of course, the use of comparison does not guarantee that these limitations will be overcome, however it does point to the path in this direction. In general, to the extent that in the comparative method it is necessary to refer to several intertwined levels of reflection (macro, meso and micro), a more complex understanding of migration as a social process is facilitated.

In order to take full advantage of its heuristic capacities, the use of the comparative method requires the fulfillment of some basic precepts, including: (1) the careful selection of cases; (2) systematic comparison of differences and similarities; and (3) the need for equivalence among indicators. In our study of the labor insertion of female immigrant workers in domestic service, the two cases compared (Madrid and New York) were selected by using a set of connected factors including the criteria of major cities in countries with a high level of international immigration, especially from Latin America, with tertiarized economies, aging demographic structures and a significant demand for female labor force for care work, cleaning and domestic work (reproduction activities). The systematic comparison of the differences and similarities that both contexts of reception represent, can lead to an understanding of the explanatory factors behind the differences observed in the labor insertion, and in general, in the condition for female immigrant workers in this labor market. For a comparison like the one proposed here, to be productive, it is vitally important that the indicators compared refer to the same aspect; in other words, that they are equivalent, since it is imperative that the factors to which causal force is attributed, as explanatory variables, have similar meanings.

While such analysis makes it possible to learn about the ins and outs of the functioning of a highly feminized labor market with a significant presence of immigrant labor force in the cities selected, while revealing some of the causal factors behind the differences observed, it suffers from the limitations inherent to small-N studies. Nonetheless, to the extent that all research involves a compromise in which some points are won but others are lost, we believe that the lesser capacity for generalization implicit in the study of these two cases is widely compensated through two factors: first, the advantages gained in the specificity of knowledge attained with regard to a secondary, feminized, highly precarious labor market in the context of globalization; and secondly, the attempt to move toward a more complex, contextual causal type of explanation.

## References

Alexander, J., 1990: "La centralidad de los clásicos", in: Giddens, Anthony; Turner, Jonathan et al. (Eds.): *La teoría social, hoy* (Mexico, D.F.: CONACULTA—Alianza Editorial): 22–20.

Andersen, Bridget, 2000: *Doing the dirty work? The global politics of domestic labour* (London—New York: Zed).

Alexander L. George; Bennett, A., 2004: *Case Studies and Theory Development Cases in the Social Sciences* (Cambridge, MA—London: MIT Press): 126–149.

Ariza, Marina, 1994: "La causalidad como lógica de determinación en las ciencias sociales", in: *Anthropos*, No. 45 (Suplementos): 80–85.

Ariza, Marina; González de la Rocha, Mercedes; de Oliveira, Orlandina, 1994: "Características, estrategias y dinámicas familiares en México, América Latina y el Caribe", prepared for the Population and Quality of Life Independent Commission (unpublished).

Ariza, Marina; de Oliveira, Orlandina, 1997: "Formación y dinámica familiar en México, Centroamérica y el Caribe", in: *Ibero-Amerikanisches Archiv*, Neue Folge, 23, 1–2: 27–44.

Ariza, Marina, 1998: "Los cambios en las ocupaciones de las mujeres: auge y declive del servicio doméstico", in: *Universidad de México*, Revista de la Universidad Nacional Autónoma de México, Special Edition No. I [Mexico City]: 7–11.

Ariza, Marina, 2000: *Ya no soy la que dejé atrás... Mujeres migrantes en República Dominicana* (Mexico City, Universidad Nacional Autónoma de México, Instituto de Investigaciones Sociales and Plaza y Valdés).

Ariza, Marina, 2004: "Obreras, sirvientas y prostitutas. Globalización, familia y mercados de trabajo en República Dominicana", in: *Estudios Sociológicos*, Revista del Centro de Estudios Sociológicos de El Colegio de México, 2, 64 (January).

Ariza, Marina; de Oliveira, Orlandina, 2004a: "Familias, pobreza y necesidades de políticas públicas en México y Centroamérica", text prepared for the Reunión de Expertos sobre Familia, CEPAL, Santiago de Chile, 28–29 October.

Ariza, Marina; de Oliveira, Orlandina (Eds.), 2004b: *Imágenes de la familia en el cambio de siglo*, Colección México: Los Escenarios del Nuevo Siglo (Mexico D.F.: Universidad Nacional Autónoma de México, Instituto de Investigaciones Sociales).

Ariza, Marina; Portes. Alejandro. 2010: *El país transnacional: Migración mexicana y cambio social a través de la frontera* (Mexico City, D.F.: Universidad Nacional Autónoma de México, Instituto de Investigaciones Sociales—Editorial Porrúa—Instituto Nacional de Migración).

Ariza, Marina; Velasco, Laura, 2012: *Métodos cualitativos y su aplicación empírica: por los caminos de la investigación sobre migración internacional* (México, D.F.: Universidad Nacional Autónoma de México, Instituto de Investigaciones Sociales; Tijuana B.C.: El Colegio de la Frontera Norte).

Ariza, Marina; Gandini, Luciana, 2012: "El análisis comparativo cualitativo como estrategia metodológica", in: Ariza, Marina; Velasco, Laura (Eds.): *Métodos cualitativos y su aplicación empírica: por los caminos de la investigación sobre migración internacional* (México, D.F.: Universidad Nacional Autónoma de México, Instituto de Investigaciones Sociales; Tijuana B.C.: El Colegio de la Frontera Norte): 412–443.

Ariza, Marina, 2012: "Vida familiar transnacional en inmigrantes de México y República Dominicana en dos contextos de recepción", in: *Si Somos Americanos. Revista de Estudios Transfronterizos* [Chile], 12, 1: 17–47.

Báez Evertsz, Carlos J., 2001: "La inmigración dominicana en España", in: Álvarez Pastor, Pedro; Báez Evertsz, C. J.; Esteban, N. (Eds.): *La Inmigración Dominicana en el Tercer Milenio* (Madrid: Editorial Betania): 53–96.

Bechhofer, Frank; Paterson, Lindsay, 2000: *Principles of Research Design in the Social Sciences* (London—New York: Routledge).

Becker, H. S., 1998: *Tricks of the Trade: How to Think about Your Research While You're Doing It* (Chicago: University of Chicago Press).

Bloemraad, Irene, 2005: "Of Puzzles and Serendipity: Doing Research with Cross-National Comparison and Mixed Methods", in: De Sipio, Louis; Kossoudji, Sherrie; García y Griego, M. (Eds.): *Research Method Choices in Interdisciplinary Contexts: War Stories of New Scholars* (New York: SSRC Books): 35–49.

Brettell, Caroline, 1981: "Is the Ethnic Community Inevitable? A Comparison of the Settlement Patterns of Portuguese Immigrants in Toronto and Paris", in: *The Journal of Ethnic Studies*, 9.

Calavita, Kitty, 2006: "Contradicciones estructurales de la política de inmigración: los casos de la Europa del Sur y de los Estados Unidos", in: *Revista Española de Investigaciones Sociológicas* (October–December): 195–212.

Campbell, Donald; Stanley. Julian, 1973: *Diseños experimentales y cuasi experimentales en la investigación social* (Buenos Aires: Amorrortu Editores).

Castles, Stephen, 2001: "Studying Social Transformation", in: *International Political Science Review*, 22,1: 13–32.

Centeno, Miguel Á., 2010: "Leviatanes y coyotes: migración y stado", in: Ariza, Marina; Portes, Alejandro (Eds.): *El país transnacional. Migración mexicana y cambio social a través de la frontera* (Mexico City: Universidad Nacional Autónoma de México, Instituto de Investigaciones Sociales—Editorial Porrúa—Instituto Nacional de Migración): 205–230.

Cerrutti, Marcela; Massey, Douglas, 2001: "On the Auspices of Female Migration from Mexico to the United States", in: *Demography*, 38, 2 (May): 187–200.

Colectivo Ioé; Organización Mundial de las Migraciones, 2012: *Impacto de la crisis sobre la población inmigrante* (Madrid: Colectivo Ioé).

Colino, César, 2007: "Método comparativo", in: *Diccionario crítico de las ciencias sociales* (Madrid—Mexico, D.F.: Editorial Plaza y Valdés).

Collier, David, 1993: "The Comparative Method", in: Finifter, Ada W. (Ed.): *Political Science: the State of the Discipline II* (Washington D.C.: American Political Science Association): 105–119.

Denzin, Norman K.; Lincoln, Yvonna S. (Eds.), 2003: *Collecting and Interpreting Qualitative Materials* (Thousand Oaks, CA: Sage).

Domingo ÍValls, Andreu; Martínez, Rosana, 2006: "La población latinoamericana censada en España en el año 2001: un retrato sociodemográfico", in: *Notas de Población*, 81: 99–127.

Durkheim, Emile, 1981: *Las reglas del método sociológico* (Buenos Aires: Editorial Pléyade).

Ehrenreich, Barbara; Russell Hochschild, Arlie (Eds.), 2003: *Global Women: Nannies, Maids, and Sex Workers in the New Economy* (New York: Henry Holt and Co.).

Esping-Andersen, Gosta, 1990: *The Three Worlds of the Welfare Capitalism* (Princeton, NJ: Princeton University Press).

Foner, Nancy, 2005: *In a New Land: A Comparative View of Immigration* (New York: New York University Press).

Foro para la integración social de los inmigrantes, 2010: "La evolución del empleo de la población trabajadora extranjera en España: de la bonanza a la crisis", in: *Informe anual sobre la situación de la integración social de los inmigrantes y refugiados en 2010* (Madrid: Ministerio de Trabajo e Inmigración).

Geertz, Clifford, 1973: "Thick Description: Toward an Interpretative Theory of Culture", in: Geertz, Clifford (Ed.): *The Interpretation of Culture* (New York: Basic Books).

Ghorra-Gobin, Cynthia, 1998: "The Comparative Social Science Approach. Outline for a Debate on Methods and Objectives Based on Three MOST Projects Carried Out by International Networks of Researchers", in: *Management of Social Transformation-MOST*, Discussion Paper No. 40 (Paris: UNESCO).

Goldthorpe, J.H., 2000: *On Sociology: Numbers, Narratives and the Integration of Research and Theory* (Oxford: Oxford University Press).

Green, Nancy, 1994: "The Comparative Method and Poststructural Structuralism: New Perspectives for Migration Studies", in: *Journal of American Ethnic History*, 13, 4 (Summer): 3–22.

Green, Nancy, 2002: *Repenser les migrations* (Paris: Presses Universitaires de France).

Gregorio Gil, Carmen, 1995. "La migración rural dominicana a España y su impacto en el sistema de estratificación de género. Problemas de género, migración y desarrollo", in: *Género y Sociedad*, 3,1: 67–94.

Guarnizo, Luis Eduardo, 1997: "The Emergence of a Transnational Social Formation and the Mirage of Return Migration Among Dominican Transmigrants", in: *Identities*, 42, 2: 281–322.

Hondagneu-Sotelo, Pierrette, 2001: *Doméstica: Immigrant Workers Cleaning and Caring in the Shadows of Affluence* (Los Angeles—Berkeley, CA: University of California Press).

Kuznesof, Elizabeth, 1993: "Historia del servicio doméstico en la América Hispana (1492–1980)", in: Chaney, E.; García Castro, M. (Eds.): *Muchacha, cachifa, criada, empleada, empregadinha, sirvienta y… nada más: trabajadoras domésticas en América Latina y el Caribe* (Caracas: Nueva Sociedad): 25–40.

Instituto Nacional de Estadística, 2003: *Los extranjeros residentes en España, 1998–2002, Explotación estadística del padrón municipal* (Madrid: Instituto Nacional de Estadística).

Instituto Nacional de Estadística, 2012: "Padrón Continuo de Población"; at: http://www.ine.es/jaxi/tabla.do (March 22, 2013).

Instituto Nacional de Estadística, 2007: "Padrón Municipal de España"; at: http://www.ine.es/prensa/np457.pdf (February 17, 2008).

Instituto Nacional de Estadística, at: www.ine.es (May 24, 2008).

Liphart, Arend, 1971: "Comparative Politics and Comparative Method", in: *American Political Science Review*, 65: 682–693.

Martínez Pizarro, Jorge, 2003: *El mapa de América Latina y El Caribe, las mujeres y el género*, Serie Población y Desarrollo 44 (Santiago de Chile: United Nations, CEPAL, September).

Mill, J.S. [1843], 1974: *A System of Logic* (Toronto, University of Toronto Press).

Mills, Melinda; van Bunt, Gerhard G.; de Bruijn, Jeanne, 2006: "Comparative Research. Persistent Problems and Promising Solutions", in: *International Sociology*, 21, 5 (September): 619–631.

Odgers, Olga 2002: "Review of Nancy Green: 'Repenser les migrations'", in: *Migraciones Internacionales*, 1, 3 (July–December) [Tijuana, Mexico: El Colegio de la Frontera Norte]: 170–173.

Orlansky, Dora; Dubrovsky, Silvia, 1977): *La mujer migrante como transferencia de fuerza de trabajo femenina hacia Buenos Aires* (Santiago de Chile: FLACSO).

Oso, Laura, 1998: *La migración hacia España de mujeres jefas de hogar* (Madrid: Ministerio del Trabajo y Asuntos Sociales, Instituto de la Mujer).

Parella Rubio, Sonia, 2003: *Mujer, inmigrante y trabajadora. La triple discriminación* (Barcelona: Anthropos).

Passel, Jeffrey S.; Cohn, D'Vera, 2009: "A Portrait of Unauthorized Immigrants in the United States" (Washington, DC: Pew Hispanic Center): at: http://pewhispanic.org/files/reports/107.pdf (10 October 2011).

Popkin, Erick, 2005: "The Emergence of Pan-Mayan Ethnicity in the Guatemalan Transnational Community Linking Santa Eulalia and Los Angeles", in: *Current Sociology*, 53, 4: 675–706.

Portes, Alejandro; Borocz, J., 1989: "Contemporary Immigration: Theoretical Perspectives on its Determinants and Modes of Incorporation", in: *Internacional Migration Review*, 23, 3 (Fall): 606–630.

Portes, Alejandro; Rumbaut, Rubén G., 1990: *Immigrant America: A Portrait* (Los Angeles, CA: University of California Press).

Przeworski, Adam; Teune, Henry, 1970: *The Logic of Comparative Social Inquiry* (New York: Wiley-Interscience).

Ragin, Charles, 1987: *The Comparative. Method. Moving Beyond Qualitative and Quantitative Strategies* (Berkeley—Los Angeles, CA: University of California Press).

Ragin, Charles; Becker, Howard (Eds.), 1992: *What is a Case. Exploring the Foundations of Social Inquiry* (Cambridge: Cambridge University Press).

Ragin, Charles, 2006: "How to Lure Analytic Social Science out of the Doldrums", in: *International Sociology*, 21,5 (September): 633–646.

Ragin, Charles, 2008: *Redesigning Social Inquiry* (Oxford: Oxford University, Economic and Social Research Council's Research Methods Festival, Saint Catherine's College).

Salazar Parreñas. Rachel, 2001: *Servants of Globalization. Women, Migration and Domestic work*, (Stanford, CA: Stanford University Press).

Sartori, Giovanni, 1970: "Concept Misinformation in Comparative Politics", in: *American Politial Science Review*, 64: 1033–1053.

Sassen-Koob, Saskia, 1995: "Immigration and Local Labor Markets", in: Portes, A. (Ed.): *The Economic Sociology of Immigration. Essays on Networks, Ethnicity and Entrepreneurship* (New York: Russel Sage Foundation).

Sassen, Saskia, 2000: "Women's Burden: Counter-geographies of Globalization and the Feminization of Survival", in: *Journal of International Affairs*, 53,2 (Spring): 503–524.

Sassen, Saskia, 2002: "Global Cities and Survival Circuits", in: Ehrenreich, Barbara; Russell Hochschild, Arlie (Eds.): *Global Women: Nannies, Maids, and Sex Workers in the New Economy* (New York: Henry Holt and Company, A Metropolitan/Owl Book): 254–274.

Schruerkens, Ulrike, 2005: "Transnational Migration and Social Transformation: A Theoretical Perspective", in: *Current Sociology*, 53,4: 535–553.

Smelser, Neil, 2003: "On Comparative Analysis, Interdisciplinarity and Internationalization in Sociology", in: *International Sociology*, 18,4 (December): 643–657.

Suárez, Estela, 1989: "La fuerza de trabajo femenina en el sector servicios", in: Cooper, J. et al. (Eds.): *Fuerza de trabajo femenina urbana en México*, Vol. 1 (Mexico City: Universidad Nacional Autónoma de México, Coordinación de Humanidades—Miguel Angel Porrúa Editores): 493–537.

Torns, T., 1997: "Los servicios de proximidad, ¿un yacimiento de empleo?", in: *Revista de Treball Social*, No. 147: 40–47.

Velasco, José Luis, 2008: "Algunos antecedentes del análisis comparativo cualitativo", Uni-versidad Nacional Autónoma de México, Instituto de Investigaciones Sociales, Seminario de Discusión, unpublished.

Vertovec, Steven, 2004: "Migrant transnationalism and modes of transformation", in: *International Migration Review*, 38,3: 970–1001.

Weber, Max, 1973: *Ensayos sobre metodología sociológica* (Buenos Aires: Amorrortu editores).

Wimmer, A.; Glick Schiller, Nina, 2003: "Methodological Nationalism, the Social Sciences, and the Study of Migration: An Essay in Historical Epistemology", in: *International Migration Review*, 37, 3: 576–610.

Wimmer, Andrea, 2007: *How (not) to Think about Ethnicity in Immigrant Societies: A Boundary Making Perspective*, Working Paper No. 44 (Oxford: University of Oxford, ESRC Centre on Migration, Policy and Society).

Zimmerman, Mary K.; Litt, J. S.; Bosee, C. E., 2006: *Global Dimensions of Gender and Carework* (Stanford, CA: Stanford Social Sciences).

Private Agency for domestic service employment. Plaza Callao, Madrid, 2006.*Source* Photograph by Marina Ariza who granted permission to reproduce it

Project Presentation and Community Consultation in Apartado, Antioquia, Colombia, 2005. *Source* Photos by Pilar Riaño Alcalá and Marta I. Villa Martínez who granted permission

# Chapter 4
# Forced Migration of Colombians: A Relational Perspective

**Pilar Riaño-Alcalá and Marta I. Villa-Martínez**

**Abstract** This chapter examines the research process and the methodological and ethical challenges of a comparative study of the forced migration of Colombians in three national contexts: Colombia, Ecuador and Canada. During the years in which this research study was carried out (2005–2009), Colombia was the country with the second highest rate of internal displacement in the world and the primary source of persons from the region seeking refuge. The chapter discusses the insights and questions that emerge from examining the dynamics of fear in the displacement and integration processes of forced migrants and the various social and political locations used by internally displaced persons and refugees in their interactions with local societies and a host of local, national and international institutions. It discusses the challenges the research team encountered in the attempt to construct differentiated typologies of forced migration, which risked missing the complexities of the phenomenon and the continuities between different forms of migration. The chapter highlights the research potential of a relational comparative perspective that reconstructs fields of relations and variations between the experiences of internally displaced persons and persons living in refugee situations. Our analysis of the forced migration experiences of displaced persons and refugees in a number of sites revealed a host of factors that impact on forced migration and integration processes and the links between local, internal, regional and international migration movements.

**Keywords** Forced migration · Internal displacement · Refugee experience · Fear · Colombia · Ecuador and Canada

P. Riaño-Alcalá (✉)
University of British Columbia, Vancouver, BC, Canada
e-mail: pilar.riano@ubc.ca

M. I. Villa-Martínez
Corporación Región, Medellín, Colombia
e-mail: marvima2012@gmail.com

L. Rivera-Sánchez and F. Lozano-Ascencio (eds.), *The Practice of Research on Migration and Mobilities*, SpringerBriefs in Environment, Security, Development and Peace 14, DOI:10.1007/978-3-319-02693-0_4, The Author(s) 2014

In this article we reflect upon the experience and methodological challenges of a research study on the forced migration of Colombians in three national contexts: Colombia, Ecuador and Canada. Colombia has been the epicenter of historic, complex processes of human mobility, and since the second half of the 1980s, of intense migration flows including predominantly forced internal displacements and cross-border refuge. These flows are related to the intensification and territorial expansion of an armed conflict that has lasted over a half century and has involved multiple agents (paramilitary groups, guerrillas, army, drug trafficking) as well as economic, territorial, regional and political dynamics. Our research study examined how social fears affect the reconstruction of social worlds and the local integration of those who leave their homes, cross internal and external borders and establish themselves temporarily or more permanently in another place of residence.[1] We addressed the phenomenon of forced migration from a qualitative focus, that is, as a significant, complex and multidimensional phenomenon. The analysis revolved around the *experience* of persons in displacement and refugee situations. In this context the comparative exercise sought to highlight continuities and variations in the experiences of mobility and the local integration of persons in displacement and refugee situations—based on field research conducted in nine different sites, three in each of the countries mentioned above.

Methodology is understood in this article as the means and practices used to acquire and organize knowledge regarding a specific social problem or dynamic—in our case, forced migration—but also the means and practices on the basis of which research relations are constructed and social and intellectual responsibilities are defined in relation to the social dynamics studied and the individuals who are experiencing forced migration (Denzin and Lincoln 2008; Schrartz and Walker 1995). This chapter examines the methodological strategy used in our research with the aim of illustrating the way in which analysis was constructed, the questions that arose in the research process, and some tensions and challenges faced in research work.

---

[1] Participating in the study were nine researchers from different disciplines (sociologists, anthropologists, historians, political scientists and psychologists) associated with *Corporación Región* in Colombia, FLACSO in Ecuador, and the University of British Colombia (UBC) in Canada. Marta Villa from *Corporación Región* and Pilar Riaño have been working in the area of urban conflict and violence in Colombia for more than 15 years and have previously collaborated on other research projects. The current project was formulated by these two researchers in collaboration with Ana Maria Jaramillo, sociologist and historian, and Amparo Sánchez, anthropologist and philosopher, from *Corporación Región*. In Colombia, the team was formed by Marta Villa, Ana Maria Jaramillo and Amparo Sánchez. In Ecuador, the team was composed of Fredy Rivera, sociologist and FLACSO professor; Hernando Ortega, an anthropologist studying for his Master's degree in anthropology at FLACSO; and Paulina Larreategui, a lawyer specializing in refugee issues, and studying for her Master's degree in international relations at FLACSO. In Canada the team consisted of Pilar Riaño, anthropologist and UBC professor; Marta Colorado, psychologist; Patricia Diaz, doctoral candidate in political thought at the University of York; and Amantina Osorio, doctoral candidate in anthropology at the University of Montreal.

In order to develop a reflexive, critical perspective of the methodological process, we approach methodology as a dynamic, simultaneous process consisting of the construction of the research problem, the methods used in that construction, and its critique (Bourdieu and Wacquant 1995, p. 30). Here, we acknowledge the contradiction confronted when attempting a systematic description of the research process that tends to lend coherence and unity to a process that, to the contrary, is characterized as iterative—returning over and over to questions involving research, information and modes of comprehension and analysis—and not unfolding in a linear manner (Gershon 2008; Maxwell 2005).

The chapter is divided into three parts. In the first part, we describe the reasons that led us to introduce a human mobility perspective to the study and research we had been conducting on violence and conflict in Colombia. In this section we briefly characterize the research problem and specify what we are referring to when we speak of internal displacement and refuge as migration modalities. In the second part we address the research process and dialectics, initially presenting the analytic focus of the research and its unit of analysis. In the third part we focus on the challenges that emerge in a comparative exercise, and the ways in which we questioned and at times became entangled in the construction of differentiated categories and typologies of forced migration. We explain in this section the reformulations that led us to prioritize and recuperate the comparative exercise in its relational sense—in other words, comparison as a perspective that reconstructs nodes of relations, highlights continuities, and identifies variations and contrasts in and between the experiences of internally displaced persons and persons living in refugee situations.

## 4.1 Explanatory Contexts

The research trajectory of the team that formulated this project had been previously concentrated on the analysis of urban violence and problems such as narcotraffic, drugs and urban violence (Salazar and Jaramillo 1994), political conflict and culture (Jaramillo et al. 1998); memory and conflict (Riaño 2006) and urban fears (Villa et al. 2003, Jaramillo et al. 2004). With our research on forced migration, we continued to analyze the dynamics of violence and conflict in Colombia, particularly in its human dimension. However, we introduced an analytical perspective that investigates violence and conflict from the perspective of human mobility. Our intention was to further explore conflict in a way that reveals its impacts, movements and geographies as a *historic, space–time* process (between a sending area, transit areas and receiving areas) characterized by the *crossing of territorial, geopolitical and cultural borders*.

As we addressed the study of variations in the experience of forced migration from an analytical focus on fear and mobility, we attempted to analyze the impact of conflict and violence on the social worlds of those affected by them. We also aimed to deepen our understanding of the ways in which forced mobility and migration processes are linked to broader global migration processes. In this way our research dialogues with studies on violence (to enhance the complexity of analysis and conceptualizations of conflict and war in contemporary societies) as well as with migration studies (to underscore the influence of wars and violence on contemporary migrations). To better understand the research strategy and methodological design we have used, in the following section we offer a brief characterization of the phenomenon of forced migration within and from Colombia.

### *4.1.1 Colombia: Displacement and Refuge*

During the years in which we conducted this research study (2005–2009), Colombia was the country with the second highest rate of internal displacement. In 2007, 50 % of all the world's displaced persons were concentrated in Colombia, Sudan and Iraq (Norwegian Refugee Council 2008). The phenomenon of internal displacement in Colombia is characterized by its prolonged duration and by its distribution throughout the entire national territory: forced displacements have taken place in 87 % of its municipalities, and displaced persons have been received in 71 % of its municipalities (*Conferencia Episcopal* and CODHES 2006). As 2009, the necessary conditions for displaced Colombians to return to their places of origin were insufficient, and therefore their return did not represent a long-lasting solution for re-establishing their rights or protecting the factors that placed their lives in danger.[2]

Alongside the problem of internal displacement, Colombia has been the primary source of persons from the region seeking refuge since the end of the 1990s (ACNUR 2006). According to figures reported by the United Nations High Commissioner for Refugees (UNHCR) office, Colombia was one of the three main places of origin for the world's refugees in 2008, following Afghanistan and Iraq (UNHCR 2008). It is calculated that nearly a half million Colombians[3] crossed national borders and lived in a refugee situation in other countries since the period from the mid-1990s (when a significant increase was registered in the number of requests for asylum made by Colombians) to 2007 (US Committee for Refugees 2005; UNHCR 2008).

The phenomenon of Colombians seeking refuge in other countries has unique characteristics. Colombians in general do not live in refugee camps. After crossing national borders, and sometimes continental borders, some live in towns and cities in the countries where they request asylum and receive humanitarian protection.

---

[2] According to the global panorama described annually by the Norwegian Refugee Council (2008), Colombia is the country with the worst conditions in the world for guaranteeing the return to one's place of origin as a long-lasting solution.

[3] Calculations vary between 453,300 (US Committee for Refugees 2005) and 552,000 Colombians (UNHCR 2008).

There are others who fled the country but do not seek institutional protection out of fear or because they are unaware of this possibility. Ecuador and Canada are among the main countries that receive Colombians seeking international protection (Rivera et al. 2007; Riaño et al. 2007). Ecuador is the country where the most Colombians are living in refugee situations, both at the continental level and internationally,[4] and by 2006, Canada became the country with the second largest number of Colombians whose refugee status has been acknowledged (Riaño et al. 2007). Nevertheless, in the case of Colombians receiving humanitarian protection from Canada over 55 % of them were resettled directly from Colombia (Riaño and Díaz 2007), and consequently, when they requested asylum they did not pass through refugee camps, nor were they outside the country, as stipulated by the Geneva Convention. In the case of Ecuador, a high percentage of Colombians who flee to that country do so without knowing that their situation makes them eligible for receiving international humanitarian protection (Rivera et al. 2007; Servicio Jesuita a Refugiados 2006). Those who access the route to protection are not in refugee camps, and a small percentage have accessed humanitarian care in temporary shelters.

While we distinguish between the analysis of migration processes we characterize as 'forced' and those identified as 'economic' or 'voluntary', we do recognize the gray areas between them and the difficulty in rigidly separating them. There is increasing literature that emphasizes the connections between migration and asylum, and recognizes that migrants and those who request refuge have multiple reasons for emigrating, and that it is not easy to separate economic reasons from those corresponding to human rights violations (ACNUR 2007; Castles 2003; Diaz 2008). It is also important, along these lines, to underscore the links between forced migration and global migration processes, and the tendency registered since the end of the Cold War toward an intensification of the stratification of the migration system. Crosby (2006), Nolin (2006) and Nyers (2006) examine the inequalities in power and access to resources that distinguish the relation between individuals, migration flows and the capacity for transboundary migration mobility in the context of globalization. They conclude that displaced and undocumented persons, those living in poverty and those lacking access to transnational networks are in an unequal, vulnerable position. The differences and the gray line between economic migration and forced migration are associated with this process of unequal power and stratification. The latter can be found in the migration policies of countries from the North, such as Canada, structured to attract a certain type of immigrant (skilled, professional, young and educated), and in their policies on human protection. These policies are used as a mechanism for selecting and attracting immigrants with a certain profile—who, it is believed, will be able to successfully integrate into society in labor and social terms (Riaño and Díaz 2007)—or as an unacknowledged mechanism for fulfilling the need for an

---

[4] UNHCR estimates that close to 250,000 Colombians are in need of international protection in Ecuador (Bilsborrow and CEPAR 2006).

unskilled labor force (Castles 2003). In Latin America, studies on dictatorships and exile have noted the singularity of the exile experience and the many relations between exile and migration (Roniger 2012). Delgado and Márquez (2010) and Gzesh (2008) have proposed to extend the notion of forced migration to describe the human rights violations characterizing several forms of economic migration.

### 4.1.2 Process and Dialectics: Research, Methodological Design and Central Concepts

There are three central assumptions that situate our research in the literature on violence and mobility and the debates on the singularity of *circumstances* (the vulnerability of rights) and *experience* for forced emigrants: (1) Internal displacement and refuge are migration modalities under coercion[5] and therefore phenomena that can be characterized within a specific migration modality: forced migration; (2) these modalities of forced migration can be analyzed from a relational perspective that points to their variations and similarities; and (3) the forced migration experience has a unique nature due to the circumstances that lead to the decision to migrate and to the modes in which individuals in displacement or refugee situations seek incorporation into a new society. In relation to these three assumptions, the analytical focus of our research was constructed around the relation between fear, violence and human mobility.

Although our research was carried out in three countries, it was not defined as a national level study. In each country and after initial fieldwork and consultation with experts, workers and local community leaders, we selected three sites that would allow us to document different types and modalities of forced migration. In the selection process we considered sites in which a significant proportion of persons in displacement/refuge situations are concentrated, and that illustrate specific modalities of migration or specific historic dynamics and contexts of integration or exclusion, and of recognition or denial of displaced/refugee status.

Thus, in Ecuador, for example it was decided to include Quito, the country's capital and the city in which the greatest number of Colombians are concentrated; San Lorenzo, a border town with historic ties of cultural and commercial exchange with Colombia, and characterized by very few infrastructure resources, low human development indexes and very little coverage in terms of access to basic social services; and Ibarra, a mid-sized city with a history of Colombians migrating and establishing themselves, and characterized by more institutional resources for humanitarian attention, because of its proximity to the border.

---

[5] Coercion, according to Penz (2006), is the restriction of possibilities for an individual's choices and decisions, by another individual or individuals, however this does not necessarily involve the total absence of alternatives or possibilities for making decisions.

In Canada our research was conducted in Vancouver, the country's third largest city, with the greatest concentration of Colombian population along the country's Pacific Coast; London, a mid-sized city in the province of Ontario, with the greatest proportion of Colombians in Canada, and where most of the Colombians who live there made a refugee claim at the US–Canadian border; and Sherbrooke, in the French speaking province of Quebec, with a high concentration of Colombian refugee population, and one of only two Canadian cities with a municipal policy that welcomes immigrants.

Our definition of the scale and site of research progressed differently in Colombia due to regional contrasts and differences in the country, both in terms of the geopolitics of war as well as political, cultural and displacement dynamics. In this case, our research was concentrated in a specific region, the Antioquia Department, since it is one of the departments with the highest rates of expelling and receiving displaced persons, and it is a region we have considerable knowledge regarding the dynamics of war and social conflicts. In this department the city of Medellin and the Urabá and Eastern Antioquia sub-regions are those that have most directly suffered from displacement and war. Therefore in the selection of places for our study, we combined the criteria for region and locality.

The consideration of aspects such as the migration history in each locality, socioeconomic characteristics that facilitated or obstructed the settlement and incorporation of displaced persons and refugees in the local society and economy, and the analysis of public policies designed to address this population, were important in understanding the similarities and differences in the experiences of forced emigrants.[6]

## 4.2 Experience as a Unit of Analysis

Located at the center of our methodological focus were the persons in displacement or refugee situations. We analyzed their experiences in a historical context (a multipolar, prolonged war lasting more than a half century) and within specific space–time axis (places of displacement and exile, migration routes, relations established, places of temporary or permanent settlement). The concept of *experience* is used in refugee studies (Ager 1999) to denote the human consequences—personal, social, economic, cultural and political—of forced migration. Experience is produced in the intertwining of the internal, subjective experiences of fear, migration and uprootedness, and the impact from social, political and economic forces and contexts shaping forced migration and local integration processes (Brettell 2000).

[6] These results are presented in the publication of three documents, one for each country, on the forced migration of Colombians (see Villa et al. 2007; Rivera et al. 2007; Riaño et al. 2007).

In our references to displaced persons and refugees, we followed a form of categorization from international and national systems for humanitarian protection, or in other words, the forced migration regime.[7] Nevertheless, from the beginning, our field research revealed the problematic boundaries in these categorizations. On one hand this was because of the difficulties in establishing a clear differentiation between forced migrants and other types of migrants who are neither institutionally recognized nor do they self-identify under these categories. On the other hand, it was because of the ways in which people who find themselves in situations of displacement and refuge recreate, appropriate or reject these categories.

In Medellin, for example, a group of displaced persons together with a non-governmental organization proposed in 2005 that the internally displaced should be recognized as internal refugees, given the lack of protection from the government and the need to call for stronger international solidarity. This proposal to be recognized as refugees puts in question precisely the element that establishes the difference between displaced persons and refugees in the framework of the international forced migration regime: the State's responsibility to guarantee protection for persons within national borders and the international community's obligation to provide protection for persons outside the borders of the country of their nationality. As noted by Daniel (2002), the distinction between the internally displaced and refugees leads us to once again consider the role of the nation-state in the transformation of the 'refugee' or 'displaced' into a discursive fact and a recognized category. Without the construction of nations and clearly-defined national borders, the distinction between these two modalities of forced migration would be irrelevant.

---

[7] A *refugee* according to the 1951 Geneva Convention is a person who "owing to well-founded fear of being persecuted for reasons of race, religion, nationality, membership of a particular social group or political opinion, is outside the country of her/his nationality and is unable, or owing to such fear, is unwilling to avail herself/himself of the protection of her/his country; or, who, not having a nationality and being outside the country of her/his former habitual residence as a result of such events, is unable or, owing to such fears, is unwilling to return to it." (UNHCR) Office of the High Commissioner for Human Rights, "Convention on Refugee Status" [in Spanish] at: http://www.unhchr.ch/spanish/html/menu3/b/o_c_ref_sp.htm. This definition of a refugee has been expanded upon through regional declarations and national legislation in various countries. The Cartagena Declaration, a non-binding instrument supported by many of the region's countries, expands the definition of persons in need of protection and incorporates analysis of the existing objective situations in a given country, catalogued as generalized violence, foreign aggression, internal conflicts, massive violations of rights and other situations that have disturbed public order. Internally displaced persons, according to the "Guiding Principles on Internal Displacement" are "persons or groups of persons who have been forced or obliged to flee or to leave their homes or places of habitual residence, in particular as a result of or in order to avoid the effects of armed conflict, situations of generalized violence, violations of human rights or natural or human-made disasters, and who have not crossed an internationally recognized State border." (Guiding Principles on Internal Displacement, [in Spanish] at: http://www.hchr.org.co/documentoseinformes/documentos/html/pactos/principios_rectores_desplazamientos_internos.html).

Colombians in Ecuador who have been denied refugee status demand to be recognized as refugees, remain in Ecuador as 'undocumented' (Bilsborrow and CEPAR 2006), and self-identify as 'negados' (denied) to emphasize the institutional rejection they face—UNHCR does not even recognize them as persons of interest and they cannot access UNHCR services directly or through its operating agencies. In fact, it is a result of the way they view themselves that they responded to the call for participating in this study. In Canada, in contrast, Colombians who have been recognized as Government Assisted refugees tended to avoid referring to themselves as refugees, because they feared they will be perceived as defenseless victims or they will be labeled as ideologically aligned with one of the groups involved in the conflict. Others call themselves 'exiles' to emphasize the political dimension of their forced migration and identify themselves as the 'true' refugees (those who suffer political persecution as a result of their ideological positions and their human rights work) in contrast to those they consider to be 'false' refugees (those who do not directly suffer persecution or who used/abused the refugee system in order to emigrate).

Consequently, in the course of our research, we decided to use descriptors such as persons in displacement or refugee situations (what Liisa Malkki (1995) conceptualizes as 'refugeeness') to emphasize that there are negotiations and different ways of relating to one another, and to strategically use terms such as 'displaced' or 'refugee' within specific social contexts and settings (Stepputat and Sørensen 2001). Thus, these terms are not assumed to be categories of identity or descriptors of experience per se, but are rather viewed from the perspective of anthropologist Elizabeth Colson (2003), who emphasizes that displacement and refuge are structuring events in peoples' experiences, and are accompanied by processes of resignification of individual experience and identity.

The acknowledgement of unclear boundaries between types of migration (forced, economic, voluntary) and the different ways that people position themselves poses some challenges in terms of conceptualization, both in the characterization of the scope of the phenomenon of forced migration and its singularity in relation to other forms of migration. This also presented a challenge for the definition of the research sample, specifically the criteria used for inviting and selecting participants. Here, we opted for extending an open invitation to displaced persons and refugees—without establishing a definition of exactly who is a displaced person or a refugee. Those who responded to this invitation considered themselves as refugees and/or displaced independently from whether they were officially recognized as such. Thus, for example, in Ecuador the application for refugee status had been rejected for 24 % of the 68 participants in the study, and 14 % were still awaiting decisions on their applications. In Colombia approximately 13 % of the 140 persons participating in the research had not formally follow the process to be recognized by the government as an internally displaced person.

The research teams in the three countries used the same research design and the same methodological tools. Information was collected through individual, in-depth interviews and memory workshops with displaced persons and refugees. In the interviews, the interviewees were invited to reconstruct their social networks and the key moments in their journey of displacement, refuge and settlement. In all, 54 persons were interviewed in the three countries.

The workshops with displaced persons and refugees included a series of activities carried out in a group format and under the guidance of a facilitator.[8] The purpose of the workshops was to reconstruct the experiences of forced migration and arrival in another social environment through a variety of verbal and visual methods (for example, oral history, place and network mapping, and image making,) and interactive methodology. The workshops traced migration routes, experiences arriving in a new society, the memories with which this experience is associated, the challenges and difficulties encountered, the networks of support, and the fears experienced during displacement and in the new environment. In each of the nine localities, one workshop was conducted with men, one with women and in some cases, one with young people. In all, 21 workshops were conducted (7 in Colombia, 7 in Ecuador and 7 in Canada), with participation by 244 displaced persons and refugees (120 women, 124 men).

While the interviews and workshops were the primary methods for collecting information, they were conducted as part of broader fieldwork and *participant observation*. In each country *relevant public policies were analyzed* in the areas of protection, attention and reintegration, with the goal of complementing, analyzing and contextualizing information from the field. In each locality we also held one or two *discussion groups* (8 in all) with service providers from governmental and non-governmental organizations, with policy makers and with local residents. The aim was to explore images and representations of displaced persons and refugees that circulate among the receiving populations, including governmental and non-governmental organizations providing services to displaced persons/refugees and the management and staff in these organizations. For the purpose of complementing documentary analysis, 22 interviews were conducted with functionaries and service operators, and in Colombia six workshops were held with functionaries and service operators.

## 4.3 Methodological and Conceptual Constructions in Research Work

When we approached forced migration as a form of displacement regulated by the coercion exerted by an external agent and the fear experienced by the victim, fear was revealed as a powerful analytical axis for exploring the ways in which displaced persons and refugees live their migration journeys and reconstruct their social worlds. Clues regarding the potential of fear as analytical tool emerged from two previous studies conducted by Marta Villa, Ana María Jaramillo and Amparo

[8] For a description of this research methodology, see Riaño (2005, 2008).

Sánchez addressing fear, violence and displacement in Medellin (Villa et al. 2003), and by Pilar Riaño on youth, memory and violence in Medellin (Riaño 2006). From the first study we learned about the ways in which a geography and phenomenology of fear marks the relationship between the internally displaced persons and the responses from the societies where they arrive in search of protection. From the last study we learned about the historicity of fears and the ongoing re-elaboration of the maps of fear, legends and narratives of rural origin in urban mythologies (ghosts, satanic figures, or possessed bodies). These narratives represented social strategies for confronting the tangible fears created by conflict and displacement, and ways to express the social tensions resulting from war and forced migration.

In the context of forced migration, fear is a factor that shapes migrants' experiences. It is an emotion that causes them to flee, that accompanies the migration journey, and that impacts the possibilities for reconstructing their social worlds. Mármora (1990) emphasizes the importance of the sending and receiving contexts in the decision to migrate, and maintains that in the case of forced migration, it is the sending context (in Colombia, the generalized situation of violence, fear and threats) that has the most impact on the decision to migrate, while in the case of economic migration, the characteristics of the receiving context (the opportunities it offers) have the greatest impact on this decision. Fear is also the element used to define a refugee. According to the Geneva Convention of 1951, a refugee is someone who "owing to *well-founded fear* of being persecuted for reasons of race, religion, nationality, membership of a particular social group or political opinion, is outside the country of his nationality and is unable or, *owing to such fear*, is unwilling to avail himself of the protection of that country" (italics used by authors for emphasis) (UNHCR 2010: 16).

As Nyers (2006) pointed out, this definition divides a refugee into a rational being who exercises the human capacity of reasoning—which is implicit in the phrase "owing to *well-founded* fear of being persecuted"—and an emotional being who flees in response to the sensation of fear. Nyers argues that from the perspective of what is contained in the Convention, the construction of a refugee as a fearful being constitutes the essence of what defines a refugee as such. In other words, on the basis of a 'subjective' emotion like fear, an attempt is made to construct a universal and 'objective' definition of refugeeness. In the case of forced displacement, the same rationality is used to place priority on recognizing 'objective' situations that lead to displacement. Colombian legislation, for example, defines displaced persons as "those who have been forced to migrate within national territory, abandoning their locality of residence or usual economic activities, since their lives, physical integrity, security or individual liberties have been violated, or are directly threatened" (Law 387/97). The country's Constitutional Court, however, has maintained that displacement is not only the result of de facto situations, but is especially the result of fear and terror, and thus the latter become, in fact, significant reasons for seeking institutional protection (*Sentence Su1150*).

When reference is made to *forced* migration, the element of restriction is emphasized, specifically the way in which these forms of human mobility respond to external pressure and take place under *coercion*—since those who suffer a threat or attack on their lives and belongings are fearful of and are escaping a generalized atmosphere of terror. These individuals face a reduced field of options and cannot freely make decisions regarding whether or not they will remain in their usual place of residence, and maintain their usual means of livelihood, and decisions regarding their response to threats or danger, and the way in which displacement and migration are organized (Penz 2006). When forced displacement takes place in the context of an armed conflict, individuals are coerced by agents or institutions that use violence in the form of threats, attacks, symbolic violence, bodily harm, and the destruction of the environment or means of livelihood, and such coercion leads directly or indirectly to the displacement of individuals or communities (Penz 2006).

The act of being displaced under coercion involves, therefore, a series of material and economic losses, accompanied by breakdowns in the community's social fabric, means of livelihood and cultural and symbolic repertoires. Consequently, the experiences of displaced persons and refugees tend to be framed by *involuntary* processes in which they are uprooted from the referents of place, mobility and belonging that articulate their everyday worlds. This takes place even for those whose personal and family histories have been marked by processes of migration mobility, border colonization and mobile livelihood practices (Stepputat and Sørensen 2001). In the migration process, the uprooting of individuals is caused by and takes place in very different contexts and for very different people, but in the specific context of migration under coercion, uprooting and displacement to other social environments is a feeling that structures the experience (Colson 2003). This is especially true when forced displacement involves a process of exile—a loss or interruption in the relationship with or possession of the land in which roots and a sense of place have been established (Restrepo 2008).

The field research we conducted allowed us to develop a characterization of fear as an expelling factor and as a mediating element in the relationship between displaced persons/refugees and receiving societies. It also allowed us to identify the modes in which migration under violent coercion by an external actor brings a singularity to the experience, to the routes taken and resources to which individuals have access during the migration process and in the settlement and incorporation processes. The histories and narratives shared by displaced persons and refugees in the three countries indicate that fear does not disappear when they flee to another city or another country and/or when they are granted protection within a humanitarian system. This continuation of fear means that not only the traumatic events and experiences of terror are embodied, as corporal, narrative memories, but also the difficulties in accessing humanitarian protection systems, the fragility of the mechanisms created for their settlement and integration, and the precarious responses they find in the places where they arrive. A comparative perspective of the experiences of each group of displaced persons and refugees in each locality, however, allows us to describe and further explore this generalization, and to sketch out some of the variations in line with factors such as the type of borders they crossed, their legal status, the routes taken, whether or not there is conflict in the places where they arrive, and the attitudes and perceptions of the receiving society in relation to displaced persons and refugees. We will now look at this more closely.

In the case of internal displacement in the Urabá Antioquia and Eastern Antioquia regions of Colombia, what we documented was predominantly intra-regional displacement. This is a form of displacement in which persons were displaced from rural areas and villages to a larger municipality within the same region (Urabá Antioquia or Eastern Antioquia), or to Medellin, the department capital. In their interactions with members of paramilitary groups, guerrillas or government armed forces, the inhabitants of these regions have felt the effects of the regime of terror that has become embedded in their daily lives, as they have witnessed and become victims of innumerable forms of violence. In this context, fear is constantly brought to the present moment through rumors, threats, massacres, rapes and torture, and through orders to evacuate or the prohibition to circulate—actions taken by armed actors that intensify the climate of mistrust characterizing everyday life in an armed conflict zone.

The decision to take a shorter route (to the main municipality of the region) or a longer route (to Medellin) during displacement is associated with factors such as the presence of networks of relatives or persons from the same region in the place of arrival, perceptions of the security conditions in such places and opportunities for obtaining a basic economic means of survival. The final decision of whether or not to leave one's place of origin is based on an assessment of this balance of forces, resources and networks, and the mediation of fear as an emotional response to flee from danger. An additional factor characterizing mobility within the same country or region is that although short distances are covered in this type of displacement (from villages), the routes can be longer (in terms of time required) due to the many territorial borders to be crossed and restrictions on movements by the civilian population established by armed actors. Also, reaching a municipality or city does not guarantee protection since the armed conflict is also present in those places, generally with less intensity, but clearly there, and consequently new displacements are common, occasionally back to places of origin, or beginning a longer route to the capital city.

The continuity of fear hinders both the reconstruction of their lives as well as their local integration through conditioning individual and collective behaviour, the possibility or lack thereof of staying in the place of arrival and especially the decision of whether or not to return to the places from which they were expelled. In the case of intra-regional displacement we found differences in whether displaced persons felt protected according to: the attitudes towards internally displaced persons in the receiving society; the way in which local governments and government officials operate, and the presence of IDP's organizations. In the case of Eastern Antioquia, for example, efforts by the local population and some authorities to establish a basic system for supporting and expressing solidarity with displaced persons give the latter a stronger sense of protection as they confront the threats that provoked their exodus.

When we contrasted these experiences with those characterizing persons displaced within the city of Medellin—in the case of intra-urban displacement—we found that although the route taken was even shorter, fear persisted in tangible, identifiable manners that were associated, first of all, with the presence of armed groups in both sending and arriving places, but also with the lack of recognition for their situation as displaced persons by authorities and government officials. These factors further intensified the sensation of vulnerability and a lack of protection. In workshops, interviews and fieldwork with persons displaced within the city of Medellin, we learned that a significant number of these persons had previously experienced other intra-regional and intra-urban displacements. Here, one of the factors characterizing the phenomenology of fear was that not only were fears experienced and had their own history, but they were also reflected upon and analyzed, in terms of the ways they were used. For example, a group of men who participated in a memory workshop for persons experiencing intra-urban displacement noted that, as a result of their displacements and forced coexistence with conflict, they have accumulated lessons and skills in managing fear. To learn from and understand fear is vital in order to interact with armed groups and for one's neutrality to be acknowledged, as well as to know how to act toward these groups and maintain a less disadvantageous relationship with them, and even to avoid new re-displacements (Sánchez 2007). And thus, responses to fear and the mediation of factors such as previous displacement experiences became important in our work, in explaining variations in experience.

An analysis of local experiences, at both group and individual levels, allowed us to identify the continuities and variations in these experiences, to then outline some typologies that, as explained by Brettell (2000), constitute a way of theorizing similarities and differences, variations and contrasts, on the basis of which the phenomenon of the forced migration of Colombians in these localities can be characterized. From this perspective, the *routes taken and borders crossed* became increasingly important in the comparative analytical process, as primary factors in the construction of typologies that describe the relationships between sending and receiving contexts, the ways in which migration is organized, and the impact of the migration journey and local contexts on different groups of forced migrants. The route taken is structured as an analytical category that, as expressed by Díaz (2008), allows us to describe not only the paths, places and experiences of people in movement, but also the reconstruction of their identities, the marks they leave behind, the abandoned homes, accumulated knowledge, transformations of individuals, and narratives of the journey taken and their experiences of the past, present and future (Zierler 1992).

For Colombians who were displaced to Ecuador in their search for protection and shelter, for example, the binational border they must cross is a territorial border, but it is also a threshold between protection and risk, between safety and fear. Arriving at the border with Ecuador signified, in many cases, having managed to cross other borders within national territory, specifically those imposed by the different armed groups in order to control the circulation of the civilian population. As a result of this situation, crossing the border with Ecuador has a double meaning: on the one hand, displaced persons can feel safe from the threats experienced in Colombia, but on the other hand, they feel uncertainty and fear for what awaits them. We found in our field research that the Colombians who cross the border into Ecuador were generally unaware of the option of seeking refuge as a protection system. Those who were aware of this option avoided declaring at the border that they were fleeing from violence and needed protection, because they feared this acknowledgement could result in being denied entrance into Ecuador or being deported. In addition, we found that increased distance from the border did not necessarily make them feel safer or more protected.

In Quito—which of the three municipalities studied in Ecuador is the one located farthest from the border—fear was experienced within a more intense emotional system, since the increased presence of Colombians in the capital city has led to serious rumors of armed actors in the city, and in fact, some direct acts of aggression and threats have been documented. These fears became even more intense when combined with fear of the local police, and fear of discrimination and rejection by institutions. Colombians, especially those whose refugee claim was denied, but most of whom continue to live in Ecuador, expressed clearly and repeatedly their fear arising from police actions, especially the persecution aimed at confiscating the products they sell on the street, as well as their arbitrary detention or even deportation. This situation was even worse for women who frequently experienced sexual harassment. Added to this was a change in the attitudes of local residents toward Colombians who were viewed as direct threats, both in the labor arena and as a source of violence and criminality.

We found a significant contrast in San Lorenzo, a locality less than 20 km from the border that has received three massive displacements of Colombians from the Putumayo region (in southern Colombia). Colombians in that location expressed a greater sense of protection and security, and this was related to three factors. First was the welcoming attitude expressed toward Colombians by local residents and authorities, which can be explained to a significant degree by a history of continuous bonds based on cultural, commercial and migration exchanges between the two sides of the border. Secondly, as a border town, San Lorenzo also operates with a more ambiguous system in response to non-legalized trade, as well as arms and drug trafficking. Consequently, less persecution and fewer institutional barriers stand in the way of the most common activities for economic survival among refugees, specifically selling on the streets and informal trade. San Lorenzo had thus become a kind of 'informal' refuge for individuals whose requests for asylum have been denied. It was also the location of an organization of Colombians led by persons who identify themselves as 'denied' and who advocated for recognition of individuals in a refugee situation in Ecuador as persons deserving of rights and protection (independently of the State's formal recognition of refugees). They also advocated for the regularization of undocumented migrants, against deportation and in favor of political recognition of those who have been denied status as refugees and as Colombians (Nyers 2010).

This comparative analysis on different localities in Ecuador suggests that the *legal status* and *attitudes* of the receiving society shape and influence the variations in experiences of fear and forced migration. In this case *legal status* refers not only to legal and institutional processes and categories through which States recognize individuals with a need for protection, but also the practices and strategies through which the population struggles for this recognition, uses these categories, and identifies with or distances itself from such categories—in short, the way in which these categories are redefined on the basis of experience. The case of those who were denied refugee status illustrates how these modes of construction of 'legal status' and the organizational practices, and the resources used by individuals enter into play, to impact individuals' positioning and identification modes.

Our study of refugees' experiences in three localities in Canada concluded that the persistence of fear originating in painful events experienced in Colombia was transformed during the process of forced migration into fear that lives in one's body—that is not so tangible anymore but has remained in one's memory. This fear generates vulnerability in facing the challenges that refugees are forced to confront, specifically to assimilate the set of uncertainties arising from the arrival in a country that is culturally and linguistically different from their own. While fear accompanies migrants' journeys and their experiences of settlement independently of their status or category, there is an experience of embodied fear that is particularly intense for displaced persons and refugees, and especially for those who have been victims of violent actions (survivors of attacks, kidnappings, torture or rape, and witnesses of horrific acts). In some cases it could be characterized as an open wound from past experience, created as a result of a traumatic experience. In other cases, it could be described as a scar left on one's memory. It is important to explain this difference, since it directly affects refugees' processes of social incorporation. For some refugees in Vancouver and Sherbrooke who arrived in Canada directly from Colombia as government-assisted refugees, and who had suffered limit situations of armed violence, the fear embedded in their bodies was reactivated, for example, when there were rumors of the arrival of individuals potentially linked to one actor or another in Colombia's armed conflict. But fear was also reactivated by certain sounds or smells, or something they saw or heard, bringing the memory of the emotions they experienced during the traumatic event or the event itself to the present. This reactivation takes place in their bodies—as a sensory place where memories are stored (Creet and Kitzmann 2011). This difference in the experiences of fear among refugees who were recognized and assisted by the Canadian government indicates a differential impact or significance of fear that corresponds to the causes leading to their displacement. In this case, this difference highlights the impact from what we call the sending context—to indicate more than merely a place that is left behind, but a set of factors and causes of the forced migration—on the processes of reconstructing social worlds.

Those who arrive in Canada to seek refuge after having passed through or lived in the United States, as in the case of Colombians living in London, learned and confronted other fears during their migration journey. For some, passing through or living in the United States as undocumented migrants generated constant fear of authorities and other figures of power. These feelings, while living with the uncertainty of a non-regularized situation, together with the fear around living without a legal identity and of being deported at any moment, became a key factor in undertaking a new migration journey and confronting new risks. Initiating a new migration route and seeking refuge in Canada (for those who were living in the United States) corresponded to a strategy of protection and the search to regularize their situation—in other words, to obtain a legal status that will allow them to live without fear of being persecuted by the government due to their undocumented status. This goal of regularizing their legal status was given priority, even when it signified a decline in their standard of living (Díaz 2008).

The variation that stands out along the experiences related to the route taken by this group, which sought refuge at the border, and those who were resettled directly from Colombia, was the way in which the route taken became a factor that structured the experience, relationships and the acquisition of knowledge that allowed them to organize migration in such a way as to seek the most efficient manner to cross the border and to seek refugee status. Crossing the border symbolizes the threshold of risk and opportunity, and constitutes one of the central landmarks in the migration process for those who first went to the United States and then went to Canada. The routes taken by this group, furthermore, were not direct or unilinear, but rather encompassed many directions and re-locations in places of transit or residence. Passing through other countries, the intensity of experiences along the migration route, and their duration (which in some cases can be as long as ten years) modified the memory of events and violent situations that made it necessary to leave their own country. This contrasts—particularly in terms of the experience and memory of fear—with what happens for those whose migration journey is short, with a direct route, as in the case of refugees assisted by the government when they are still in Colombia.

In summary, our analysis of the forced migration experiences of displaced persons and refugees in multiple sites revealed a host of factors that shape and impact the journey of forced migration. Through analysis and discussion between our national teams, and during our seminars with the teams from the three countries, we were able to extrapolate these factors and identify their explanatory importance. This made it possible to describe variations, establish relationships according to the context and type of migration, and characterize the particular dynamics among the groups of displaced persons and refugees.

Therefore, the routes used by displaced persons and refugees became a key analytical category to describe the variations in the ways in which fear impacts and shapes the processes of social reconstruction and incorporation. In addition to this concept of the route taken, we understood that the economic, social and cultural resources that people have access to during the course of their migration process, the way in which they use these resources, and how these resources interact with other factors in the sending and receiving contexts also explained differences in experience and responses to fear on the part of the individuals who find themselves in this situation. The notion of the social organization of migration (Rivera and Lozano in this book) was helpful in identifying and naming this set of factors and in understanding the close relationship between sending dynamics and causes, individual profiles and resources, migration strategies and resources, and between the routes taken and the relationship with the receiving society. One factor that became important due to its capacity for explaining variations in experiences was *status*, understood as not only a person's legal situation but also the way in which individuals who experience displacement and seek refuge position themselves in relation to the institutional frameworks that may or may not recognize them, and in the actions they take to achieve such recognition.

## 4.4 Challenges and Reformulations

The comparative exercise presented a number of challenges to the research team. One of these challenges was related to modes of understanding the comparative method and the precise determination of cases for comparison. Our reflections on the limitations of studies on violence to describe the dynamics of mobility led us to consider whether a comparative analysis of displacement and refuge could contribute to bringing visibility to the impact of conflict beyond national-territorial borders, and its significance in the recent Colombian migration phenomenon. A review of the literature on forced migration indicated the potential of comparative studies for understanding the relationships between different forms of migration (for example, labor migration, forced migration, temporary work for migrants), the ways in which displaced persons/refugees construct their identities and their interactions with protection, assistance and reintegration policies (Lacroix 2004).

In the literature on this topic, authors such as Griffiths (2002) and Van Hear (2000, 2002) call attention to the importance of comparing the different forms of forced migration in order to develop more exhaustive theories on this phenomenon. However, only a few studies have carried out this exercise. We concluded from our review of this literature that a comparative approach involves considering the connections between forms of forced migration, but it also considers what an analysis of the human, subjective dimension of the experiences of forced migrants can tell us about the social forces that impact these experiences.

During the study, some of the tensions accompanying our definition of a qualitative study using a comparative methodology became evident. When we began the comparative exercise, we viewed displacement and refuge as discreet units of reference with cases that can be differentiated, whether by geopolitical borders of nation-states (distinguishing between exoduses that occur *within* or *outside* national territory) or by an international social-legal categorization (whose primary reference points would be the Convention on Refugees and the Guiding Principles on Internal Displacement). As we progressed in our studies by localities and documented the differences and similarities among groups of displaced persons and refugees (intra-group differences), we became aware of the heterogeneity and fluidity of the relations and processes that are grouped together in each one of these categories, and we questioned the way in which we were approaching the comparative exercise. We questioned the formulation of a comparative study *of two types* of forced migration, and we revisited the significance of formulating a strategy for observation and analysis identified as *relational*. This formulation assumed comparison to be a matter of construction, however we saw that using the contrast between two clearly defined types of forced migration—displacement and refuge—as a starting point risked obscuring the multiple relationships among the different forms of forced migration. In particular, it risked missing the various ways in which individuals position themselves during their migration and settlement journeys and the role of fear as an element that structures these experiences.

In response to these reflections, we reformulated the comparative exercise to connect it more vigorously to the relational perspective proposed. We changed our approach from an effort to define the types of forced migration in line with a set of intrinsic, clearly-defined characteristics, to focusing on understanding these types of forced migration as *social fields* of relations. The concept of *field* (Bourdieu and Wacquant 1995) describes nodes of relations that are configured in socially and historically constructed spaces. In other words, it describes the interactions established between different agents (displaced persons/refugees, armed actors, government officials), institutions, the set of policies and procedures that regulate the field, and in line with the differentiated positions of power they occupy (Bourdieu and Wacquant 1995). We began to understand displacement and refuge as structured social fields, or nodes of relations in which different social agents interact within hierarchized and differentiated systems of forces. In this sense, the relational comparative strategy captures the fluidity and complexity of social worlds of forced migrants and the ways in which they operate. This form of 'methodological relationism' prioritizes the observation and analysis of flows of relations, and avoids dichotomic approaches that tend to focus on the "ontological priority of structure or agent, system or actor, the collective or the individual" (Bourdieu and Wacquant 1995, p. 23).

A field places relations into play and structures them. It becomes a place of conflict, competition and action for maintaining or changing the order of these relations that interact under specific forces (Bourdieu and Wacquant 1995). In our research this field resulted from the inter-relations between *sending contexts* (dynamics of conflict, migration history, social networks, institutional presence); the *migration journeys* (social organization of migration, social and institutional resources used, social networks) and *receiving contexts* (individual and collective practices and responses of displaced persons/refugees, of local societies and institutions, and the sphere of public policies).

The experiences of fear and the responses by displaced persons and refugees and by government officials within the forced migration system and by the members of receiving societies were all shaped through this interplay of forces and relations, and depend on their position in this node of relations as well as in the forced migration system in general. As noted earlier, they also depend on one's set of personal resources, socio-demographic profile, history and social capital.

### 4.4.1 Ethics and Politics in Research Work

The topic of forced migration also presented methodological challenges associated with the post-structural epistemological framework of our research. From this perspective, we sought to construct knowledge that contributed to academic and political debates on this topic, that brought visibility to the humanitarian crisis and that impacted public policies on displacement and refuge. With this focus, ethics and epistemology came together in our research work (Lather 1991) as we also questioned how to construct knowledge on a highly sensitive topic. This was because the armed conflict continued; violence and trauma marked the experiences of participants, and the polarization in the three countries about displacement and refuge issues. We decided for this reason that a central element of the research was the analysis and interpretation of results in dialogue with research participants.

When we designed our methodological strategy, we recognized that the violence and fear that lead to forced migration, and the precariousness of the situation for individuals placed potential research participants in a vulnerable situation. We asked ourselves how we could study the effects of violence and forced displacement without dehumanizing and exploiting research participants. More specifically, we confronted questions regarding ways to build basic trust between researchers and participants amidst a generalized climate of fear and when the armed conflict was ongoing. This tension was present throughout the entire research process. Participation by Corporación Región, a social research and human rights non-governmental organization in Colombia, was crucial in identifying this tension, and in designing a methodological route that responded to these challenges in an ethical, responsible manner. From the beginning, we established consultation mechanisms with local organizations (non-governmental groups, displaced persons and refugees groups, and other groups involved in these issues) regarding the potential contribution and uses of our research, and regarding ways to invite and involve displaced persons and refugees.[9] The recognition of this tension was built upon the understanding that the type of relationship established with participants and the type of expectations emerging would influence what we learned and what we acknowledged as data and evidence. This also meant that as researchers, we had to sometimes 'position ourselves' in relation to the data. In other words, because highly sensitive information was involved, we had to make decisions regarding whether to use some of the information we gathered, how to approach the silences and disagreements that emerged among research

[9] In Canada, for example, agreements and cooperative arrangements were established with local organizations that provide services to refugees, such as MOSAIC in Vancouver, Cross Cultural Learner Centre in London, with the ColombiEstrie refugee organization in Sherbrooke, and with the Canadian Council for Refugees (CCR). In Ecuador we worked in collaboration with the Asociación Colombo Ecuatoriana, and in Colombia with the Human Rights team from Corporación Región in Medellín, with Opción Legal in Urabá, and with municipal Ombudsman's offices in Marinilla and Rionegro in the eastern part of the country.

participants, and the implications of risk or manipulation arising from the publication of certain stories or data.

In the recruitment process we sought to provide participants with information on the topic and purpose of our research and its potential impacts, and to assist individuals in making informed decisions regarding their participation. We also sought to facilitate understanding of their rights as research participants and the limitations of research in contributing to an agenda for change and long-term solutions. Basic agreements were negotiated with participants in the workshops and discussion groups to regulate interventions (including for facilitators and researchers), to foster an atmosphere of minimal trust in which stories and viewpoints could be shared, and as a point of reference for responding to conflicts or aggression.

Also, an important methodological and ethical strategy was the sharing of preliminary results with the participants and with governmental and non-governmental organizations working in this area. An important result of this strategy was that displaced persons and refugees drew differences and commonalities between their experiences and those of other research participants in other research sites. It was precisely when we shared research results from other countries that participants pointed to the similarity in experiences ('it's the same thing we've experienced'), or their differences ('they have it worse' or 'we're better of'). This information sharing also made it possible to present some of the preliminary findings to policy makers and service providers. And lastly, this information-sharing strategy facilitated maintaining a margin of reasonable doubt as to the pertinence and the academic and social usefulness of our analysis.

In conclusion, the alliances and coordination with community organizations and groups of displaced persons/refugees, the consultation mechanisms, the presentation of prior information on the research, and the negotiation of basic agreements with participants for research interaction and as a group contributed to the creation of an atmosphere of basic trust between researchers and participants. In all three countries this trust was progressively built through community consultations, through the field work carried out, when transcriptions were presented for verification, in the sessions organized in the nine localities for presenting and verifying initial research results, and in the final public forums on public policy issues organized in the three countries.

This article has described the primary reflections, questions and processes followed in our research on the forced migration of Colombians in Ecuador, Colombia and Canada. In the dialogue between research findings and the review of existing literature, new questions emerged and informed the ongoing dialogue between theory and data and particularly between participants and researchers. The perspective from which we approached reflections on the methodological validity and the analytical potential of our focus was based on its contribution to the fields of studies on armed conflicts and violence as well as migration studies. The fact that close to five million Colombians have been forced to abandon their homes, their lands and belongings, their plans for the future, has an impact on world order and mobility. It confirms the need for humanitarian systems designed to protect the population and assure that phenomena of this type do not continue to occur. But in order for these impacts to be acknowledged, we must construct new categories and approaches that capture this relationship and help us learn new ways of looking at and comparing the diverse modalities of human mobility.

## References

Ager, A. (Ed.), 1999: *Refugees: Perspectives on the Experience of Forced Migration* (London: Pinter).

Alto Comisionado de las Naciones Unidas para los Refugiados (ACNUR), 2006: *La situación de los refugiados en el mundo. Desplazamientos humanos en el nuevo milenio* (Barcelona: Icaria).

Alto Comisionado de las Naciones Unidas para los Refugiados (ACNUR), 2007: *Migración forzada y desarrollo. Foro Global sobre Migración y Desarrollo* (Brussels, 9–11 July); at: www.acnur.org/biblioteca/pdf/5152.pdf (September 2007).

Bilsborrow, R.; CEPAR, 2006: *The Living Conditions of Refugees, Asylum seekers and Other Colombians in Ecuador* (The Hague: Netherlands Interdisciplinary Demographic Institute).

Bourdieu, P.; Wacquant, L., 1995: *Respuestas por una antropología reflexiva* (Mexico City: Grijalbo).

Brettell, C., 2000: "Theorizing Migration in Anthropology. The Social Construction of Networks, Identities, Communities and Globalscapes", in: Brettell, C.; Hollifield, J. (Eds.): *Migration Theory. Talking Across Disciplines* (New York, N.Y.: Routledge): 97–136.

Castles, S., 2003: "Towards a Sociology of Forced Migration and Social Transformation", *Sociology,* 37,1: 13–34.

Colson, E., 2003: "Forced Migration and the Anthropological Response", *Journal of Refugee Studies,* 16,1: 1–18.

Conferencia Episcopal de Colombia, CODHES, 2006: *Desafíos para construir nación. El país ante el desplazamiento forzado y la crisis humanitaria (1995–2005):* (Bogota: Conferencia Episcopal de Colombia, CODHES).

Creet, J.; Kitzmann, A., 2011: *Memory and Migration: Multidisciplinary Approaches to Memory Studies* (Toronto: University Press).

Crosby, A., 2006: "The Boundaries of Belonging: Reflections on Migration Policies into the XXIst Century", at: http://www.interpares.ca/en/publications/pdf/boundaries_of_belonging.pdf (June 2008).

Daniel, V., 2002: "The Refugee. A Discourse on Displacement", in: J. MacClancy (Ed.), *Exotic no More. Anthropology on the Front Lines* (Chicago: The University of Chicago): 270–286.

Delgado y Márquez, 2010: "Una perspectiva del Sur sobre capital global, migración forzada y desarrollo alternativo", *Revista Migración y Desarrollo,* 16: 3–42.

Denzin, N.; Lincoln, Y. (Eds.), 2008: *The Landscape of Qualitative Research* (Urbana Champaign: University of Illinois Press).

Díaz, P., 2008: "Solicitantes de refugio en Canadá: trayectos, fronteras y redes", in: Riaño-Alcalá, P.; Villa, M. (Eds.): *Poniendo tierra de por medio. Migración forzada de colombianos en Colombia, Ecuador y Canadá* (Medellin: Corporación Región, University of British Columbia).

Gershon, W., 2008: "Qualitative Research, Intent and Expression", *Complicity: An International Journal of Complexity and Education.* Vol. 5,1: 121–124.

Griffiths, D. J. (Ed.) 2002: *Somali and Kurdish Refugees in London: New Identities in the Diaspora.* Burlington, VT: Ashgate Publishing Limited.

Gzesh, S., 2008: Una redefinición de la migración forzosa con base en los derechos humanos. *Revista Migración y Desarrollo,* 10, pp. 98–126.

Jaramillo, A., M. Villa & A. Sánchez, 2004: *Miedo y Desplazamiento*. Medellin: Corporación Región.

Jaramillo, A., R. Ceballos & M. Villa, 1998: *En la encrucijada. Conflicto y cultura política en el Medellín de los Noventa*. Medellin: Corporación Región.

Lacroix, M., 2004: Canadian Refugee Policy and the Social Construction of the Refugee Claimant Subjectivity: Understanding Refugeeness, *Journal of Refugee Studies*, 17,2: 147–166.

Lather, P., 1991: *Getting Smart. Feminist Research and Pedagogy within the Postmodern*. New York: Routledge.

Malkki, L. H., 1995: *Purity and exile: violence, memory, and national cosmology among Hutu refugees in Tanzania* (Chicago: University of Chicago Press).

Mármora, L., 1990: "Derechos humanos y políticas migratorias", in: *Revista de la OIM sobre Migraciones en América Latina* [Santiago: CIMAL-OIM], 8,2–3: 7–32 (August-December).

Maxwell, J. A., 2005: *Qualitative Research Design: An Interactive Approach* (Thousand Oaks: SAGE).

Nolin, C., 2006: *Transnational Ruptures: Gender and Forced Migration* (Aldershot: Ashgate Publishing).

Norwegian Refugee Council, 2008: *Internal Displacement. Global Overview of Trends and Developments in 2007* (Geneva: Internal Displacement Monitoring Centre).

Nyers, P., 2010: "No one is illegal between City and Nation", in: *Studies in Social Justice*, 12,4,2: 127–143.

Nyers, P., 2006: *Rethinking Refugees. Beyond States of Emergency* (New York, N.Y.: Routledge).

Penz, P., 2006: "Displacement by Development and Moral Responsibility: A Theoretical Treatment", in: F. Crepeau et al., (Ed.), *Forced Migration and Global Processes* (Lanham: Lexington Books): 63–91.

Riaño, P.; Colorado, M.; Díaz; P., Osorio, M.; 2007: *Migración forzada de colombianos. Canadá*. (Medellin: Corporación Región—Vancouver: University of British Columbia—Quito: FLACSO Ecuador).

Riaño, P.; Díaz, P., 2007: "Contextualización del refugio de colombianos en Canadá", in: Riaño-Alcalá, P.; Colorado, M.; Díaz. P.; Osorio, A. (Eds.): *Migración forzada de colombianos. Canadá*. (Medellín: Corporación Región—Vancouver: University of British Columbia—Quito: FLACSO Ecuador): 21–49.

Riaño, P., 2008: "Seeing the Past, Visions of the Future. Memory Workshops with Internally Displaced Persons in Colombia", in: Hamilton; Shopes, L. (Eds.): *Oral Histories and Public Memories* (Philadelphia: Temple University Press): 269–292.

Riaño, P., 2006: *Jóvenes, memoria y violencia en Medellín. Una Antropología del Recuerdo y el Olvido* (Bogotá: Instituto Colombiano de Antropología e Historia & Universidad de Antioquia, 2006).

Riaño, P., 2005: "El desplazamiento interno y los trabajos de la memoria. Los talleres de la memoria", in: M. N. Bello (Ed.): *Investigación y desplazamiento forzado. Reflexiones éticas y metodológicas* (Bogotá: Red Nacional de Investigadores, REDIF): 91–111.

Rivera, F.; Ortega, H.; Larreátegui, P.; Riaño, P., 2007: *Migración forzada de colombianos. Ecuador*. (Medellín: Corporación Región—Vancouver: University of British Columbia—Quito: FLACSO Ecuador).

Restrepo, B., 2008: "El desarraigo en su dimensión existencial. Opening presentation at seminar entitled", in: *Destierros y Migraciones. Experiencias, impactos y políticas migratorias internas y externas en Colombia*, Medellín, 17–19 September, Museo de Antioquia, Corporación Región, University of British Columbia.

Roniger, L., 2012: "Destierro y exilio en América Latina: Un campo de estudio transnacional e histórico en expansión", in: *Pacarina del Sur*; at http://www.pacarinadelsur.com/home/abordajes-y-contiendas/318-destierro-y-exilio-en-america-latina-un-campo-de-estudio-transnacional-e-historico-en-expansion#_edn1 (15 October 2012),

Salazar, Alonso; Jaramillo, Ana María, 1994: *Las culturas del narcotráfico* (Bogotá: Cinep).

Sánchez, A., 2007: "Medellín y el desplazamiento forzado", in: Villa, M., Jaramillo, A.; Sánchez, A., *Migración Forzada de Colombianos, Colombia* (Medellín: Corporación Región—Vancouver: University of British Columbia—Quito: FLACSO Ecuador): 41–81.
Schartz, M.; Walker, R., 1995: *Research as Social Change. New Opportunities for Qualitative Research* (London: Routledge).
Servicio Jesuita a Refugiados Ecuador, 2006: *Paradigmas del refugio colombiano en Quito* (Quito: Servicio Jesuita a Refugiados Ecuador).
Stepputat, F.; Sørensen, N. N., 2001: "The Rise and Fall of 'Internally Displaced People' in the Central Peruvian Andes", *Development and Change*, 32,4: 769–791.
UNHCR, 2008: *2007 Global Trends: Refugees, Asylum-seekers, Returnees, Internally Displaced and Stateless Persons* (Geneva: UNHCR).
UNHCR, 2010. Convention and Protocol Relating to the Status of Refugees, at: http://www.unhcr.org/3b66c2aa10.html (10 June 2013)
U.S. Committee for Refugees, 2005: *World Refugee Survey 2004. Warehousing Issue* (Washington: U.S. Committee for Refugees).
Van Hear, N., 2000: "Locating internally displaced people in the field of forced migration", *Norwegian Journal of Geography,* 54: 90–95.
Van Hear, N., 2002: *From 'Durable Solutions' to 'Transnational Relations': Home and Exile among Refugee Diasporas* (Copenhagen: Centre for Development Research): at: http://www.unhcr.org/cgi-bin/texis/vtx/home/opendoc.pdf?tbl=RESEARCH&id=3e71f8984 (March 2008).
Villa, M., Jaramillo, A. M. & A. Sánchez, 2007: Migración forzada de colombianos, Colombia. (Medellín: Corporación Región—Vancouver: University of BritishColumbia—Quito: FLACSO Ecuador).
Villa, M.; Sánchez, A.; Jaramillo, A. M., 2003: *Rostros del miedo. Una investigación sobre los miedos sociales urbanos* (Medellin: Corporación Región).
Zierler, W., 1992: "Footprints, traces, remnants: the operations of memory in Dan Pagis' 'Aqebot'" [poem discussing narrator's journey through past and return to present life], *Judaism: A Quarterly Journal of Jewish Life and Thought*, 41: 316–318.

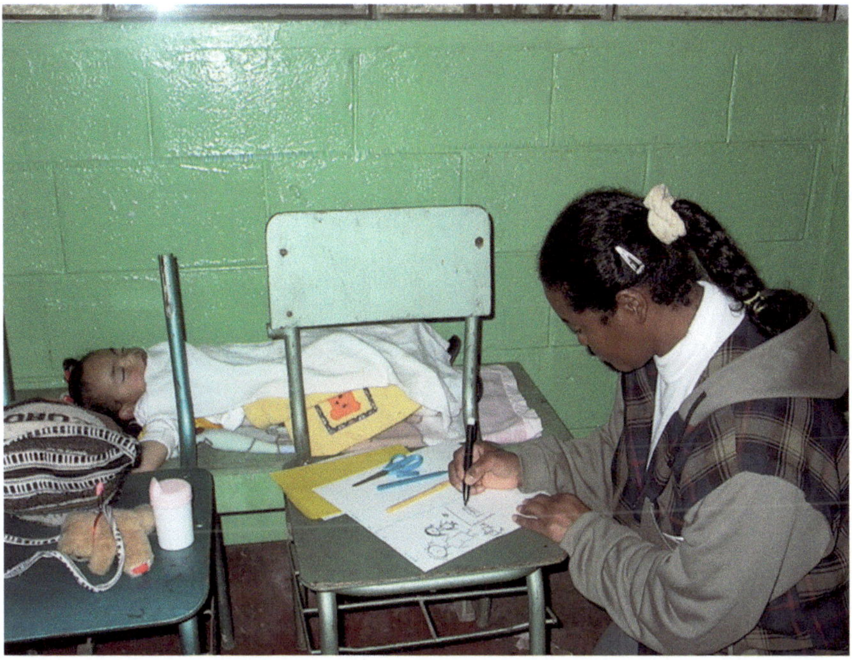

Project Presentation and Community Consultation in Apartado, Antioquia, Colombia, 2005. *Source* Photos by Pilar Riaño Alcalá and Marta I. Villa Martínez who granted permission

# Chapter 5
# Transnational Migration and the Reformulation of Analytical Categories: Unpacking Latin American Refugee Dynamics in Toronto

**Luin Goldring and Patricia Landolt**

**Abstract** This chapter contributes to comparative research on migration and incorporation. It offers a reconceptualization of analytical categories of research in Toronto into migrants from four Latin American countries whose migration is characterized as forced. The authors' initial research challenged assumptions about particular populations, similar contexts of departure, discreteness of contexts of arrival and the primacy of nationality. During fieldwork and subsequent analysis, the analytical categories were reformulated 'on the go'. The chapter documents the reformulation of *refugeeship*, unpacks the contexts of departure and reception, and identifies the socio-temporal interrelationships of arrival contexts. Drawing on dynamic approaches to culture, the centrality of national differences was reframed and *activist dialogues* were formulated as a category for interpreting variable patterns of incorporation and transnational engagements. The chapter contributes to comparative migration studies by offering a strategy for addressing some of the challenges of methodological nationalism, while also considering the specificity of history and culture.

**Keywords** Transnational · Refugees · Methodological nationalism · Canada · Latin Americans · Analytical categories

---

L. Goldring (✉)
York University, Toronto, Canada
e-mail: goldring@yorku.ca

P. Landolt
University of Toronto, Toronto, Canada

L. Rivera-Sánchez and F. Lozano-Ascencio (eds.), *The Practice of Research on Migration and Mobilities*, SpringerBriefs in Environment, Security, Development and Peace 14, DOI:10.1007/978-3-319-02693-0_5, The Author(s) 2014 

Comparative research offers the promise of enriching transnational migration studies.[1] Typical research designs build on the comparison of two or more *groups* in a given *destination* or one or more *groups* in more than one place of settlement and expand this to include their transnational social fields. Comparative research highlights the role of contexts of departure and destination in shaping distinct modes of incorporation and variation in the types, scope and sustainability of transnational engagements (Ostergaard-Nielsen 2001; Portes and Böröcz 1989; Portes et al. 2007). North American–based comparative research has theorized processes of immigrant integration, segmented assimilation and transnational engagements as multipath processes with potentially distinct group-level trajectories (Guarnizo et al. 2003; Itzigsohn and Saucedo 2002; Portes et al. 2005; Cheran 2007) and/or location-specific experiences (Landolt 2007). Recognizing the significance of these contributions does not preclude questioning the methodological limitations of the *experimental* paradigm on which much of this research is based or critiquing the application of methodological nationalism to immigrant experiences of incorporation and transnationalism (Wimmer and Glick Schiller 2003). In fact, we challenge researchers to *not* take for granted the role of nation-states as containers and fundamental organizers of social life, to interrogate the practice of using *given* populations, such as national or ethnic, as well as other categories associated with different 'groups' or study populations, and not take the constitution of contexts of departure and destination as self-evident.

Immigration scholarship has largely been anchored in a positivist epistemology, guided by a Cartesian concept of time–space and centered on experimental or quasi-experimental research methods (Bloemraad 2007; Smelser 2003), whether using quantitative, institutional, qualitative or mixed approaches to research design and data collection (Koopmans et al. 2001; Ostergaard-Nielsen 2001).[2] The bulk of migration research seeks to explain social processes over time. Linear, forward change over time is privileged (linear time leading to eventual integration, assimilation), and geographic spaces (for example, the home country, host society, immigrant neighborhood) are defined as discrete points on a two-dimensional social landscape (Harvey 1989; Kivisto 2003).

---

[1] This chapter is an updated version of a chapter published in a volume edited by Anna Amelina, Devrimsel Nergiz, Thomas Faist and Nina Glick Schiller (Goldring and Landolt 2012a). The original version of the chapter was published in Spanish in a collection edited by Liliana Rivera-Sánchez and Fernando Lozano-Ascencio (2009a). The two groups of editors and participants in the workshops leading to the original publication offered valuable comments. We are particularly grateful to Liliana Rivera-Sánchez, Marie Laure Cubés, Ninna Nyberg-Sørensen, Luis Guarnizo and Anna Amelina for their comments. We also acknowledge permission granted to reprint the updated version.

[2] This holds in spite of a vibrant body of scholarship offering other qualitative and interpretive frameworks, including various feminist and post-colonial or de-colonizing epistemologies and methodologies, and community-based research strategies (Guba and Lincoln 2005; Carroll 2004; Wilson et al. 2011). The reasons for this disjuncture are beyond the scope of this chapter, but may be related to the contested quality of immigration politics, and the role of research in policy debates.

Pan-ethnic latino consumption: "Latin American" foods in Kensington Market, Toronto, Canada. *Source* Photo by Luin Goldring who also granted permission

In comparative migration research, similar assumptions are reflected in how places and the people who inhabit them are conceptualized. Contexts of departure and reception are operationalized as geographic locations (home and host countries) and treated as independent analytical units within which the relevant contingencies remain the same over time and space (Portes and Rumbaut 1996). The analytical category of *contexts* is used to construct *de facto* units with which to compare two or more social groups from specified contexts of departure in a single context of reception, or one or more groups across multiple locations or contexts. The definition of *groups* is thus critical. Seen as containers of social life, national boundaries and nation-states are used to organize processes and define analytical categories in ways that are taken for granted. Data collection practices, such as a *national* census or the classification of immigrants and racialized minorities based on nationality, ethnicity, 'race' or culturalized region (for example, Latin American or South Asian) illustrate these processes (Cf. Hirschman 1987; Goldring and Landolt 2012b). The hegemony of state classification schemes can extend beyond large-scale data collection to shape how analysts and the public conceptualize 'groups'. In sum, the analysis of people and places begins with preconceived analytical categories whose composition and boundaries are taken to be self-evident rather than open to investigation (Ragin 2006).

Contemporary scholars of transnationalism and globalization focus on processes occurring in redrawn spaces and on multiple scales. They make explicit the assumptions about time–space and categories of analysis that are normalized in most immigration scholarship. Wimmer and Glick Schiller (2003) advanced the concept of methodological nationalism to critique how the social sciences work with container models of society; analytically, the bounded nation-state (or village, neighborhood and so on) approach to the *social* severs webs of social life that occur across borders or containers. Living lives across borders suggests a simultaneity of engagement with *here* and *there* that breaks assumptions of linear assimilation associated with mainstream theories of immigrant incorporation (Levitt and Glick Schiller 2004). Transnational social fields and related analytical categories—networks, practices and identities that span nation-state borders—are the conceptual starting point for studying social relations, formations and processes that are constituted without propinquity and not necessarily bound by place or national containers (Glick Schiller et al. 2006; Levitt and Jaworsky 2007; Pries 2008). While scholars of transnational engagements have alerted us to the pitfalls of national container models of social life, practical and theoretically informed 'solutions', particularly for *comparative* transnational migration studies, are being debated (Glick Schiller 2010; Pries 2008; Faist et al. 2013; Rivera-Sánchez Lozano 2009a). Glick Schiller and colleagues call on us to recognize non-national bases for collective action in locally situated spaces as well as transnational social fields, while paying attention to global hierarchies of power. Pries (2008) offers a model for specifying units of analysis in transnational studies. Both offer valuable pointers for addressing methodological nationalism from different epistemological orientations. Accordingly, we interrogate the constitution of analytical categories and add that this can be extended beyond those based on nationality and ethnicity.

The tensions between national and transnational ways of framing scholarship noted in this chapter emerged in our work as part of a larger collaborative and comparative project, *Social Cohesion and International Migration in a Globalizing Era: Transnational Solidarities and Newcomer's Incorporation in Canada.*[3] We designed a Latin American Research Group to examine transnational practices among four Latin American groups and their relationship to trajectories of incorporation. Given the dearth of research on Latin Americans in Canada at the time, we wanted to map out general patterns, paying particular attention to the relationship between Latin American organizations and Canadian civil society organizations, and to the relationship between incorporation and transnational engagements. Our interest in gathering data on immigrant organizations rested on the assumption that identities rooted in nationality would shape collective

[3] Michael Lanphier (York University) was the principal investigator of the Social Cohesion project, funded by the Social Sciences and Humanities Research Council of Canada (2003–2006). The project gathered 12 scholars from various disciplines to study 12 ethno-national groups in Canada (online at www.yorku.ca/cohesion). We formed the Latin American Research Group (*LARG*) together with Judith Bernhard to study four Latin American groups in Toronto. For more on LARG, see online at: www.yorku.ca/cohesion/LARG/html/largindex2.htm.

organizing and institution building in Toronto and in transnational social fields, including the countries of origin. A key objective was to compare patterns across the selected groups: Chileans, Salvadorans, Guatemalans and Colombians.

Our original formulation did not question mainstream methodological assumptions about how to construct the social and geographic spaces of contexts of departure and reception, or about place and time and their interrelationships. Guided by the tenets of comparative experimental methods, we planned to compare groups with ostensibly similar contexts of departure marked by forced movement in one settlement location, Toronto. Nationality organized our definition of *groups.* While their context of departure was considered similar, we distinguished three contexts of reception: Toronto in the 1970s when Chileans arrived, the 1980s when Central Americans appeared, and the 1990s and early 2000s when Colombians began showing up. Variation in patterns of incorporation would be attributable to the different contexts of reception encountered by broadly similar groups at different times, with Canadian civil society groups understood as an important social aspect of the context of reception. Explaining variable transnational engagements was left open because of the exploratory quality of the research, but we hypothesized they would relate to factors such as time in Canada, home country policies and patterns of incorporation in Canada, including interaction with Canadian organizations. We expected group-level variations without fully considering the implications of this assumption.

During the course of the research, we found it necessary to reformulate our analytical categories by unpacking contexts, interrogating given populations and related categories, and drawing on the sociology of culture. Our reformulations draw on comparative historical sociology, particularly McMichael's incorporated comparison approach, which "views all objects of inquiry as historical and historically connected" (McMichael 2000, p. 672). From this perspective, cases cannot be abstracted from their time–space location, and "[c]omparison is incorporated into the very process of defining the object of analysis" (2000, p. 672). McMichael developed this approach in the context of world systems theory, but it is relevant to other comparative projects, including studies of transnational migration (Comstock 2012). It has implications for our work, including our acknowledgment of the temporal and social interdependence of contexts of arrival—more specifically, how earlier migrants shape the contexts of reception for subsequent arrivals.

We reformulated conceptual categories and analytical strategies in response to three limitations we discovered in quasi-experimental comparative approaches. The first involved treating the four countries of origin as a single *type* of context of departure marked by forced migration, which together with Canadian policy, produced the category of *refugee.* This homogenizing framework erased relevant differences and contributed to methodological nationalism by making nationality a key marker of difference among migrants who shared a forced migration context of departure.

A second limitation was the use of cases and linear forward-directed notions of temporality to define *contexts of reception.* Typically, independent social and geographic categories are naturalized as discrete and thus rendered comparable. Comparative migration studies generally hold time constant by conducting synchronic studies (for example, Koopmans and Statham 2003; Ostergaard-Nielsen 2001). If time is considered, it is usually in terms of individuals' length of time in the country, or a group's peak period of arrival. Different periods of arrival become translated into potential differences in the context of reception. Alternatively, different cases are compared at various times, but time is not explicitly theorized (Itzigsohn 2000). Yet we discovered that a single context of reception is continually modified by *earlier arrivals* as they become part of and modify the local landscape for subsequent arrivals; thus, contexts as containers are generally not independent. In addition, there is often slippage between contexts as conceptual categories and units of analysis, with contexts taken as *de facto* comparable containers of units of analysis. Finally, local contexts are globally embedded and transnationally connected with consequent implications for understanding pathways of incorporation.

Third, using *Chilean, Salvadoran, Guatemalan*, or *Colombian* organizations as units of analysis assumed both the primacy of nationality and the ongoing importance of nationality over time. Our reformulation shifts from using "given populations" to considering how changing times transform elements of collective identities. This historically situated approach to populations and contexts of departure and reception draws on an understanding of political culture (and culture more generally) as a shared but not necessarily uniformly distributed tool-kit or repertoire of meanings and practices (Grimson 2011; Swidler 1986).

The next section situates the research and outlines our initial questions, data collection methods and analytical strategies. The third section identifies methodological problems and the subsequent adjustment of our research strategy and analysis. The closing section discusses implications of our conceptual reformulations.

## 5.1 Situating the Project

This section introduces the original research question of our project as well as the research context and methods, as well as the project's original ways to define populations.

### *5.1.1 Research Questions and Context*

Our research questions[4] concerning Latin American incorporation and transnational engagements were formulated in a specific context of knowledge production. At the start of the 2000s, Canada celebrated ethnic and cultural diversity but

[4] For information on the research questions and methods see Goldring and Landolt (2009) and Landolt and Goldring (various).

lacked breadth in immigration research. There was a dearth of studies comparing immigrant incorporation across groups, limited research on Latin Americans[5] and minimal scholarship on migrant transnationalism.[6] There was little research on forced migrants' transnational engagements; at the same time, work on refugee transnationalism (Al-Ali et al. 2001) was just emerging in Europe. With a few exceptions (Hamilton and Stolz Chinchilla 2001; Manz 1988; Menjívar 2000; Zolberg et al. 1989), US-based immigration research failed to theorize the specificity of Latin Americans as refugees, and the topic was absent from the literature on migrant transnationalism.

### *5.1.2 Data Collection, Methods, and Comparability*

In keeping with the larger project, our work was to be qualitative and institutional. To generate data comparable with those of other project researchers, we planned to do the following:

(1) Collect primary data through focus groups and interviews with key members of selected Latin American and Canadian organizations.
(2) Compile available secondary quantitative data (for example, government sources).
(3) Review existing literature.

### *5.1.3 Defining Study Populations*

Our mandate was to select Latin American refugee groups. As noted, we chose Chileans, Salvadorans, Guatemalans and Colombians to capture variation in the temporal context of arrival (1970, 1980, late 1990 and 2000s). We unreflectively defined our populations as *given* in two ways, assuming that each population of 'forced migrants' constituted a refugee-like movement and using national origin to define *groups*. The latter assumes the centrality of country of origin–based

[5] Unlike the US, where Latin Americans dominate the foreign-born population and research on immigration, in Canada, Latin Americans are less significant on both counts. When we began, research consisted largely of case studies and work on refugee adaptation and related issues (Basok 1986; Diaz 1999; Kendall 1992; Kowalchuk 1999a, b; Kulig 1998; Simmons 1993). Research on their economic incorporation was limited, partly because of limitations in data construction, disaggregation and access (Barragan 2001; Garay 2000; Mata 1985); work on their political incorporation was nonexistent. Researchers have since begun to address these gaps. On the political participation of Latin Americans, see Schugurensky and Giginiewicz (2006), Goldring et al. (2006), Veronis (2007) and Landolt and Goldring (2009, 2010).

[6] Exceptions include Kobayashi (2002) and Hiebert and Ley (2003). Collections edited by Satzewich and Wong (2006) and Goldring and Krishnamurti (2007) indicate the increasing research on migrant transnationalism in Canada.

identities and forms of organization and turns nationality into an analytical category informing the composition of the units to be compared.

### *5.1.4 Composing Categories for Comparison*

We initially conceptualized our *units of analysis* as Latin American country of origin–based organizations and related Canadian civil society organizations. Latin American migrant organizations and their activities were proxies for other analytical categories of comparison:

(1) Nationality-based patterns of organizing around transnational and settlement agendas (for example, Chilean versus Colombian organizing around homeland and Canadian-based agendas).
(2) Contexts of departure (for example, Chile under Pinochet or Colombia in the 1990s).
(3) Contexts of reception (for example, Toronto in the 1970 and 1990s).

Similarly, Canadian civil society organizations were conceptualized as part of the context of reception and as units of analysis. We posed questions to individual migrant and non-migrant 'activists' about the organizations in which they participated. We sought to map out patterns at the national group level rather than at the individual level because of the larger project's design.

We set out to conduct group interviews with Chileans, Salvadorans, Guatemalans and Colombians active in organizations framed around country of origin identifications. We assumed we would collect information on sports and cultural associations as well as locality or hometown and other types of organizations. As our previous research[7] had alerted us to the importance of both pan-ethnic umbrella groups (Latin American organizations) and gender (San Martin 1998), we planned to conduct group interviews with activists from the four national origin groups, women's groups and umbrella organizations. We soon recognized that these did not capture a broad enough spectrum, so we expanded the range of organizations.

The research topic was the relationship between Canadian civil society organizations and immigrant groups. The operationalization of the groups was left open but began with faith-based groups. In Canada, as in the US, religious congregations have a history of active participation in refugee resettlement and advocacy (Anderson 2003; Bibler Coutin 1993; Chute 2002). We conducted group interviews with faith-based, solidarity and refugee rights organizations.

[7] Goldring conducted exploratory research on the *civic engagement of Latin Americans in Toronto* with support from CERIS (CELAT project); Landolt studied Salvadorans in Los Angeles and Toronto.

### *5.1.5 Focus Groups*

Between October 2004 and June 2005, we conducted 18 group interviews with just over 100 Latin American and Canadian participants. While we asked participants for basic sociodemographic information about themselves, our focus was on them as participants in the collective life of their communities and organizations. As part of a 'mapping' exercise, we asked them to name organizations they had participated in or knew about; to provide information on the organizations' longevity, temporality, agendas, membership, organizational structure, interlocutors, and geographic and institutional orientation; and to address key internal debates and reasons for organizational change.

To summarize, we began with *given* populations and units of analysis rooted in the country of origin and refugeeness, or, for Canadians, in a particular political position and area of practice in civil society. As shown below, we re-conceptualized our analytical categories based on what we learned in the early part of the research. We reformulated our approach to contexts of departure and destination, with implications for addressing the practical challenges of methodological nationalism.

## 5.2 Reformulating Categories on the Go

This section presents three moments when we reformulated conceptual categories and analytical themes. It highlights the need to work through challenges rooted in methodological nationalism and illustrates solutions developed *on the go*.

### *5.2.1 Unpacking Contexts of Departure: Refugeeship, Violence, and Politics*

We initially framed the project as a study of four Latin American refugee groups, based on an assumption that their contexts of *departure* were similar and also distinct from others with less violence and forced movement. The term *refugee* is a state and supranational designation fraught with political, international relations, legal and budgetary considerations that does not necessarily respond to humanitarian crises (Hein 1993; Malkki 1995). Nonetheless, seeing commonality among the four groups made sense. People leaving Chile in the 1970s, El Salvador and Guatemala in the 1980s, and Colombia in the late 1990s and early part of this century were generally not 'economic' migrants but people fleeing polarized conflict and danger.

State policies in the national context of *reception* are also recognized as a crucial element shaping incorporation and transnational engagements (Hein 1993;

Koopmans et al. 2001; Ostergaard-Nielsen 2001; Portes and Boröcz 1989). Applying the term *refugee* to the selected groups seemed straightforward in formal terms, not only because of their contexts of departure, but also because the Canadian state has admitted Chileans, Salvadorans, Guatemalans and Colombians as refugees. While there are differences in how it has admitted people from the four countries, Canada has provided a relatively welcoming context of reception and refugee status. Thus, applying the refugee category to Chileans, Salvadorans, Guatemalans and Colombians should have been unproblematic.

### 5.2.2 Inhabiting the Refugee Category: Violence and Migration Narratives

Being a refugee does not have a constant meaning across groups or over time. There is variation in the experience of refugeeness and people's willingness to inhabit the category, regardless of formal or state-designated status. If one views community organizations as an expression of collective identities, Chilean, Salvadoran and Guatemalan groups have identified themselves more closely with categories of exile and refugee than Colombians. For the former, these categories convey the initial impossibility of return and the hope of returning in the long term when conflict is resolved. They are tied to a narrative that represents their departure from Chile, El Salvador or Guatemala in terms of their position in the political conflict. In contrast, for Colombians, the refugee category is ambivalent. It has negative connotations related to political affiliation or class, leading to an avoidance of the term or a reconstruction of refugee status as an 'accident' of conjunctural events (for example, kidnapping threats) and fortuitous policies (for example, Canadian policy recognizes Colombia as a refugee-producing country).

Thus, in addition to being a state-imposed category, refugeeness is a variably inhabited social category. It may be inhabited in ways that provide a basis for organizing and creating community, or it may be inhabited uncomfortably, a stigmatizing category to be avoided or hidden. While nationality becomes a shorthand for particular political experiences and processes of departure, it is not nationality or national culture *per se* that holds explanatory power as an analytical category. Thus, not all Chileans, by virtue of being from Chile or sharing 'Chilean culture', inhabit the refugee category in a particular way; rather, a social cohort of Chileans with a specific political experience identified with the refugee and exile categories.

The consequences of this finding go beyond recognizing the politics and power behind state and multinational institutions in designating refugees. It questions assumptions based on the experimental comparative approach—specifically, about the taken-for-granted dimension of defining *refugee* and the degree to which the meaning of the category is constant. It questions the assumptions that contexts of departure produce refugees in a relatively uniform manner and that the reception of groups formally recognized as refugees is similar and hence comparable in a quasi-experimental sense.

This finding also has implications for understanding variable forms of community organizing and transnational engagement. The actual experience of refugeeness is intimately tied to forms of violence and has a strong impact on migrant narratives that address 'who we are', 'why we came' and 'what we are doing here'. As we proceeded with the research and national group-level comparative analysis, we began to see connections between different forms and experiences of premigration violence, socially expected durations (*SEDs*),[8] sources of social capital[9] and nationally based differences in ways of doing politics in Canada—both transnational politics and locally oriented community organizing.[10]

Different approaches to refugeeness, narratives of departure and SEDs shape community organizing. Study participants from the selected countries formed organizations ostensibly based on national origin identities. However, we found that bases for organizing and identifications were complex and not static (see next section). For people from Chile, El Salvador and Guatemala, early forms of organizing centered on partisan affiliations and identities: political parties and social movements. Exile identity was central to Chilean organizations, and the initial assumption was that they would return. Salvadorans and Guatemalans did not articulate return as clearly (Nolin 2006), but they oriented much of their institutional activity around solidarity and support for movements and family in Central America. In the case of Colombia, transnational engagements look very different. Most organizations focus on settlement issues (family reunification, business and professional organizations), while a small network addresses the political situation in Colombia.

Our approach recognizes the state's power to designate and classify and the strategic use of personal narratives to negotiate borders and bureaucracies. Analyzing how organizations and social groups with specific experiences of violence, narratives of migration and SEDs relate to the refugee category highlights problems of population construction and specification that complement and go beyond current critiques of methodological nationalism. Potential variation in how groups inhabit the category means that the a priori assumption of uniform refugeeness as an invariant attribute of these populations is problematic, partly because of the arbitrariness of the state's application of the category and partly because differences in experiences of violence, political organization and so on, and the ways these are interpreted by Canadians, lead to variations in forms of organization both

[8] Socially expected durations (*SEDs*) are collectively patterned expectations about temporal durations embedded in social structures of various kinds (Merton 1984).

[9] Social capital is defined as the ability to secure resources by virtue of membership in social networks or larger social structures. Sources of social capital are distinguished by the presence/absence of overarching structures defining the character of the transaction and include both altruistic and instrumental sources (Portes 1998).

[10] A detailed discussion of these differences is not possible here, but see Goldring and Landolt (2009) and Landolt and Goldring (2010).

in Canada and transnationally, and to differences in people's use of the category. Again, it is not nationality *per se* that shapes variable identification with refugeeness. National history intersects with individual and collective political experience to produce patterns that appear to be 'national' but do not necessarily apply to everyone from a particular country, nor are they limited to a single nationality. Changes in the context(s) of destination also contribute to variation in how the refugee category is inhabited, thereby raising questions about the uncritical use of the "given population" of refugees. In spite of similarities, refugeeness and the definition of the refugee category need to be explained in the contexts of departure and reception.

### 5.2.3 Unpacking Contexts of Reception: Local Specificity, Transnational Connections and Path Dependence

When the context of immigrant reception is an important explanatory factor, conceptualizing place and the *local* becomes critical. Global hierarchies of power and transnational flows and circuits disrupt the assumption that locations—places of settlement or contexts of reception (and origin or departure)—can be analyzed as nationally framed and clearly bounded units suitable for comparison (Glick Schiller 2010; Rivera-Sánchez and Lozano-Ascencio 2009b). Multi-sited research that traces people as well as flows of ideas, goods and symbols offers a potential solution to this problem (Fitzgerald 2006; Marcus 1995). The challenge is capturing the *situated-specificity* of the local as it is embedded within global processes, transnational flows and social fields (Brettell 2003; Ley 2004). This has implications for constructing categories such as contexts of reception, trajectories of immigrant incorporation, and transnational engagement (Glick Schiller et al. 2006).

Three analytical challenges forced us to reconsider the spatial–temporal assumptions of the experimental comparative method. The first was our effort to come to terms with the non-independence and multivalence of territorial locations. Focus group participants mapped relevant organizations in time and space, creating a visual record of when organizations were established, how membership and agendas overlapped or competed and when they ended, as well as showing the networks between organizations and key interlocutors at various levels of geography and jurisdiction. Although conducted in one site, this mapping exercise responded to the methodological call to follow the webs of social life (Marcus 1995) rather than bounding social relations and formations according to preconceived notions about their spatial parameters.

The mapping exercise and corresponding discussions brought to light tensions between situated-specificity and transnational social fields. The organizational trajectories of the four 'groups' reflect the situated-specificity of the settlement city. An urban center's immigration history, political culture, traditions of civic participation, labor market structures, array of faith-based groups and ethno-racial composition and concentration constitute part of the context of reception and hence shape pathways of immigrant incorporation (Brettell 2003; Glick Schiller et al. 2006). A global immigrant gateway city, Toronto has received over 40 % of Canada's annual total of newcomers since the mid-1990s. Its labor markets reflect a decline in manufacturing and an increase in low-end service work characteristic of the new economy (Preston et al. 2003). There is a trend toward the deregulation of the labor process and an erosion of working conditions and workers' rights (Cranford et al. 2003). These features contour Latin American social and economic incorporation as a whole.

Our findings indicate that each study 'group' is embedded in a distinct transnational social field in which home country politics play a key role (Landolt and Goldring 2010). In the Chilean transnational social field, which includes Chilean and related solidarity organizations in Mexico, Venezuela, Cuba and multiple European locations, Toronto represents an important center in terms of decision making and fundraising for regime change. In contrast, Salvadoran and Guatemalan transnational politics revolve around Los Angeles and Chicago, respectively. Toronto Salvadorans or Guatemalans are minor political players to whom party orders are dictated; Toronto's social and political location as a city of minor import within the transnational social field affects their tenor and organizational dynamics (Landolt 2008).

Our second challenge was comparing multiple groups arriving at different times in a single location or *context of reception,* as this makes the requirement for independent cases difficult to uphold. We set out to compare place-making and modes of political incorporation (assimilative and transnational), with each population entering what we originally conceptualized as three discrete contexts of reception marked by different settlement landscapes and institutional opportunity structures. As noted above, Chileans arrived in Toronto at time one, Salvadorans and Guatemalans at time two and Columbians at time three. We found that the three contexts of reception were not discrete. Rather, the contexts changed over time in a path-dependent fashion so that the lessons and organizational outcomes of first-wave Latin American refugee migration (Chilean) informed subsequent interactions between Latin American refugees and previously arrived migrants as well as non-migrant populations and institutions. Political learning, demonstration effects and path dependencies constitute 'Latin American Toronto' as a single evolving context of reception. Within this single, fairly stable context, new groups encounter the organizations created by previous arrivals and migrant/non-migrant interactions as part of the emergent landscape. The context of reception can be understood as both an independent and a dependent variable, complicating causal ordering (McMichael 1990; Pero 2007).

The third challenge was the need to unpack the broad and homogenizing notion of a *welcoming context of reception* for refugees. In general terms, the four groups entered a *welcoming* context of reception; recognizing each country as refugee producing, the federal government established categories and programs to facilitate entry and settlement. In addition, the refugee rights lobby mobilized on behalf of each group. Nevertheless, certain institutional and discursive differences in the context of reception organized the four processes of incorporation and place-making. Our longitudinal analysis of Canadian refugee rights and solidarity advocates' engagement with Latin American refugee flows captures how contexts of reception constitute moments of discursive and organizational engagement. Broadly similar *welcoming* contexts of reception are rewritten as distinct political landscapes for refugee and migrant populations.

First, the settlement landscape varies over time. Chilean refugees faced a sparse settlement and social service landscape that was ill equipped to deal with the needs and customs of a militant and well-organized Spanish speaking population. In the 1980s, Central Americans accessed a variety of settlement and social services through ethno-specific Spanish-speaking agencies and frontline workers as well as faith-based organizations (Mennonites, Quakers) with growing expertise in the settlement of refugee populations. When Colombians arrived, settlement services had become highly bureaucratized. Today, local agencies are no longer as involved in setting settlement priorities, and the sector is underfunded.

Second, Canadian activist mobilization for the regulated entry of Chilean refugees and the political learning that occurred in the encounter between Chileans and Canadians helped to shape the subsequent production of the context of reception for Central Americans and Colombians. Each migrant/non-migrant encounter influences expectations about and the character of subsequent encounters. Similarly, Canadian state policy on Colombia and the mechanisms of policy delivery are influenced by the government's policy on Chilean and Central American refugees, which, in turn, is a product of the refugee rights lobby's ongoing work. Thus, our longitudinal analysis led us to unpack the notion of a 'welcoming' context of reception in terms of its dynamic organizational and discursive elements (Landolt and Goldring 2010).

### 5.2.4 Unbounding Nationality: From Nationality to Tool-Kits of Political Culture

In our original formulation, national origin was an analytical category informing our comparative analysis and the construction of organizations as units of analysis. Two moments in our research process prompted us to reformulate the significance and role of nationality:

- First, during the primary fieldwork, focus groups with country of origin–based activists revealed the importance of *non*-national origin organizations for the Latin American process of political incorporation in Toronto.
- Second, the comparative analysis of institutional relations between each of the study populations and Canadian civil society organizations showed important differences.

We were uncomfortable explaining these simply as a product of *national cultures*, with taken-for-granted containers of identity and organizers of political practice and institution building. We had already established the relationship between modalities of violence, migration narratives (SEDs, social capital), approaches to the refugee category and ways of doing politics. We drew on the sociology of culture to extend this argument.

#### 5.2.4.1 Organizational Polysemy

As we began to conduct group interviews using nationality as the starting point to identify organizations, we became aware of two patterns.[11] First, we discovered certain non-nationality-based identities and forms of organizing (artists, educational groups, church groups, mental health professionals) that we had not included in our original analytical categories or list of types of organizations (for example, Chilean refugees, Colombian refugees). Second, certain cleavages, divisions and forms of exclusionary and racialized classification threw into relief non-nationality-based identities (for example, indigenous Latin American identities) and affiliations (for example, political divisions). Figure 5.1 delineates our original conception of nationality as a container of immigrant organizing and organizations. It shows how pan-ethnic umbrella and women's intersectional pan-ethnic organizations overlap with certain nationality-based organizations.

Recognizing the limits of our original formulation, we conducted additional focus groups organized around emergent themes (religious congregations, mental health professionals, artists) to add relevant categories of collective identity and organizing. Figure 5.2 offers an alternative formulation of identity categories around which Latin Americans in Toronto have organized. It identifies the organizational forms that emerged among particular national origin groups, situates them outside or on the borders of the national circles and presents boundaries with broken lines to indicate porosity. Figure 5.2 summarizes but does not convey the temporal dynamics at play. Nationality is more important at first, but it clearly does not sufficiently capture the identities and forms of organization that we identified through the above-mentioned mapping exercise and group discussions. Elsewhere (Landolt and Goldring 2009), we trace the political trajectories of Latin American pan-ethnic sectoral and intersectional organizing (artists, women's organizations) to show that such organizations open up possibilities for cross-sectoral dialogue and alliance-building among Latin Americans while expanding the meanings of Latin American grassroots politics and generating forms of institutional mainstreaming and alliances with non–Latin American organizations and institutions. Despite having significant policy impacts, however, they have thus far failed to generate electoral gains or spark the interest of political parties.

[11] We draw on Morawska (2001), whose work on ethnicization emphasizes the multiplicity and polysemy of actors' practices and identities.

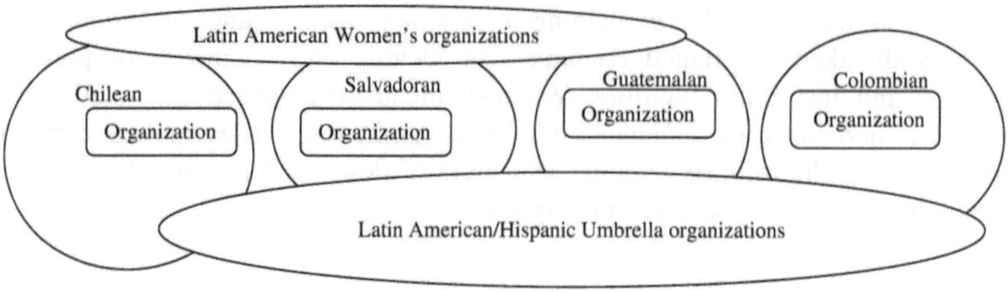


**Fig. 5.1** Nationality as container. *Source* The authors

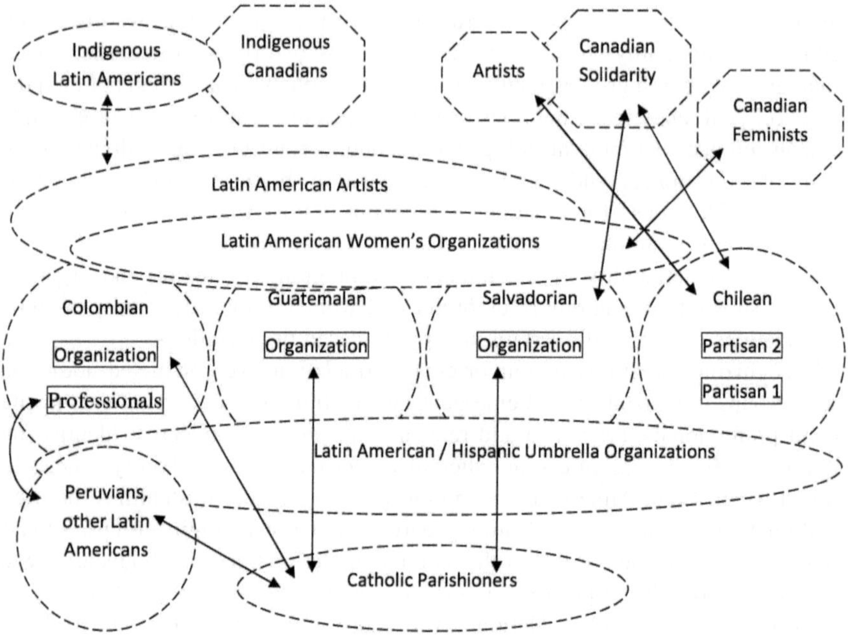


**Fig. 5.2** National, intersectional and pan-ethnic organizing. *Source* The authors

#### 5.2.4.2 From National Cultures to Cultural Tool-Kit

Levitt notes that immigration scholarship either ignores culture or takes it as an underlying set of shared, discrete and coherent unitary values (Portes et al. 2007) that explain human behavior (Levitt 2005, p. 52). As noted, we used nationality as an organizing category but were uncomfortable with the chauvinistic use of national cultures to explain difference. How then could we make sense of the Chilean case?

Chileans are an impressive presence in Latin American and Canadian organizations. Their leadership in a range of sectors (schools, unions), the mythologies generated about them and the genuine political camaraderie between progressive Canadians and Chileans all suggested there was something different about Chileans migrants. Time in Canada was not enough to explain this specificity, so we turned to Chilean exile politics and culture.

Some work in the sociology of culture has recast national culture as a cultural tool-kit, developing a notion of political culture that takes a dynamic approach to understanding ways of doing politics (Levitt 2005; Swidler 1986). Swidler notes that culture operates as a framework for explaining continuity, as in the case of immigrants following cultural traditions in a new setting, but argues that culture is also involved in developing "new strategies of action" (Swidler 1986, p. 278), particularly during periods of what she calls "unsettled lives," which occur both at the individual and macro levels in periods of heightened social transformation. She uses the metaphor of tool-kit to refer to elements of continuity and to the ability to integrate new strategies into an evolving repertoire of culturally informed action. Grimson's (2011) approach to culture and interculturality is similar; he argues against the extremes of either essentialist or constructivist approaches, insisting that cultural meanings and practices are not uniformly distributed among ethnic, national or cultural groups and that the boundaries around groups and their meaning-making practices are porous.

Drawing on these insights, we use *political culture* to refer to political repertoires that include values and actions manifested in particular strategies and repertoires of action (Landolt and Goldring 2010). This allows us to understand forms of organizing as building on political repertoires that migrants and refugees bring with them. To explain variations in ways of doing politics among people from Chile, El Salvador, Guatemala and Colombia, as well as the variable types of institutional alliances and relationships that develop between each group and Canadian social justice and solidarity organizations, we conceptualize community organizing and politics (including those of Canadian organizations) as informed by a tool-kit of political culture that people bring or have, but which is modified socially. Recognizing that cultural tool-kits and repertoires are rooted in but variably distributed among people from a particular ethnic or nationally constructed group (Grimson 2011) helps us interpret the variable group-level patterns of migrant activism, as well as the interaction between each group and 'Canadians.'

From this perspective, exile activists from Chile came with certain values, dispositions and strategies shaped by their previous socialization and history, political and otherwise. These strategies may be rooted in Chilean "national culture" in the sense that they are historically, socially, symbolically and politically situated. However, Chileans do not have a uniform political culture; some organize along partisan lines, others organize sports teams and still others stay home (do not organize). Post-coup migration consisted largely of opponents of the Pinochet regime who sustained various partisan affiliations and formed a variety of political and other organizations rooted in their political and cultural experiences in Chile. In the case of people leaving Colombia, we know from Riaño-Alcalá and

Villa Martinez's work (2009) and our own that Colombians in Canada (as elsewhere; see Guarnizo et al. 1999) mistrust other Colombians when it comes to stating political positions and organizing politically. Nevertheless, Colombians in Canada *have* organized in various ways, as for example, business and professional organizations, as well as groups advocating family reunification (Landolt et al. 2011; Riaño-Alcalá and Goldring 2006). The conflict in Colombia has generated ways of doing politics that produce variable political cultures of anti-politics as well as solidarity. This approach to political culture also informs our conceptualization of Canadian social justice activists' ways of doing politics (Landolt and Goldring 2010). More generally, it allows us to reformulate analytical categories, going from nationally framed categories (for example, Chilean or Colombian refugees, or Canadian solidarity) to categories (re)constructed on conceptual grounds and data pointing to dynamic configurations of strategies, identifications and alliances.

Our work thus shifts from cataloguing discrete individual or organizational practices (national organizing cultures) toward analyzing patterned interactions between migrants and non-migrant political actors. Chilean and Colombian activists sustain very different types of relations with Canadian activists. Chilean-Canadian activist dialogues reflect a convergence of political agendas and strategies of action grounded in a high degree of mutual intelligibility and an easy translatability of concerns. Meanwhile, Colombian-Canadian activist dialogues show a divergence of strategies of action that result in a deepening lack of respect, intelligibility and translatability. In temporal terms, the two types of dialogues are associated with long-term and sustained versus sporadic and *ad hoc* collaboration. Community activists from Colombia not only arrive with their own political culture tool-kit, they encounter arenas of political activity conditioned by preceding political dialogues between Chileans and Canadians and between Canadians and Central Americans. The 'dialogues' developed through earlier interactions have laid the basis for expectations for political practice that are sometimes at odds with Colombian activists' approaches. Thus, activists' political repertoires are shaped, albeit indirectly, by the political repertoire of earlier immigrant/refugee activists.

The character of activist dialogues helps us explain different pathways of political incorporation and transnational engagements (Landolt and Goldring 2010). The analytical category of activist dialogues replaces nationally framed culturalized approaches to organizing while recognizing porosity in ethno-culturalized boundaries and opening up the possibility of identifying and comparing patterns of interaction and social learning. In other words, the notion of exile political culture provides a basis for examining the interaction between selected Chilean activists and Canadian activists and the later interaction between Colombian activists and various Latin American and Canadian activists.

## 5.3 Implications for Comparative Studies of Migration and Transnational Engagement

Comparative studies of immigrant incorporation and transnational engagements enhance our understanding of both specific 'cases' and broader processes and patterns. What we derive from comparisons, however, depends on how we conduct them and whether we are willing to reformulate our categories and questions during analysis. Most comparative migration research is based on an experimental or quasi-experimental approach; it defines populations, categories, units and geographic contexts in ways shaped to varying degrees by methodological nationalism. Our questioning of this approach led to the reformulation of our categories and lines of inquiry in a bid to generate solutions and offer emergent methodological alternatives.

Briefly stated, we reframed three assumptions resting on the quasi-experimental approach to comparative research and implicitly informed by methodological nationalism. First, we initially treated the four contexts of departure as a single 'type' characterized by forced movement. This, together with our initial understanding of Canadian refugee policy, meant that we assumed the *refugee* category would be applicable across the four groups. The understanding was rooted in a methodological nationalism that privileged the state's power to classify and our analytical power to group 'contexts of departure'. We found that the comparability of the refugee-producing contexts and state category was problematic. This allowed us to question the classification of refugees based not only on the state's power to designate or recognize but also on the variable ways individuals and groups experience violence and movement and how they inhabit the category of *refugee*.

A second assumption involved the independence of the categories being compared and an approach to temporality that sees contexts of reception as discreet and independent. This aspect of the experimental comparative method gives the geographic container approach both temporal and territorial boundary-making power. We originally framed the temporal periods of arrival for each group as separate contexts and did not adequately theorize the effects of previous arrivals in shaping the context for later arrivals. We discovered, however, that the contexts were not independent, with consequent implications for understanding pathways and path dependency for incorporation and transnational engagements. In our reformulation, we understand the context of reception as continually modified by successive arrivals through a variety of mechanisms, including their interaction with Canadian civil society groups (Landolt and Goldring 2010) and their structuring of the policy and institutional landscape. Temporally, events in time one shape events in time two; thus, 'outcomes' in the former become part of the array of independent variables in the latter. At a macro level, this underscores the importance of viewing local processes as embedded in transnational spaces and contexts (McMichael 1990).

A third assumption led us to define *groups* on the basis of shared nationality. This form of methodological nationalism produces two tendencies. The first is to consider nationality as a valid 'container' and primary basis for defining and generating identities, practices and organizations. The second is to take for granted the durability of this primacy over time. Our reformulation rested on a mapping exercise that revealed a complex web of interactions; more specifically, intersectional and sectoral identities, practices and organizations changed over time and were conducted at variable geographic scales (Landolt and Goldring 2009). It should be noted that while we examine networks of action based on "ways of doing politics," other concepts may be equally useful.

Our process of reformulation has implications for comparative transnational studies. Rather than a quasi-experimental design, we argue for a strategy based on critical reflection on the composition of boundaries of social categories (cf. Lamont and Molnár 2002). This is not a call for a postmodern critique of epistemological foundations or a rejection of relevant categories but a call for critical and ongoing reflection on the relationship between conceptual categories—namely, the theoretical assumptions that guide their construction and boundaries—and the evidence gathered. Our methodology builds on McMichael's institutional and comparative-historical approach and contributes to recent innovations in migration scholarship. For example, Levitt (2005) calls for attention to culture in migration research; Bloemraad (2006) combines migration scholarship and social movement research. Others, including Glick Schiller and colleagues, address challenges of methodological nationalism.

Our reformulations allow us to *unpack* the contexts of departure and reception by paying close attention to units of analysis and measurement, identity, culture and temporality. First, as analysts of mixed migration now argue, forced migration contexts of exit are rarely uniform, nor are they necessarily distinguishable from those of 'voluntary' migrants. Together with a dynamic understanding of culture, this perspective on violence and migration establishes the importance of variable political cultures that make up the tool-kit that people bring with them as immigrants/refugees. The repertoire of culturally framed strategies has a national dimension, but national culture is neither the sole nor the primary determinant of political culture. In many contexts, experiences of violence, movement and political partisanship intersect with class, gender and racialization to generate variation in the political culture and dispositions that groups of people from a given country bring to a new context. National-level variation may have more to do with the specific experiences of a particular group defined by partisan affiliations or experiences of persecution in a particular temporal context than nationality *per se* and the experiences of particular social groups in the social and geographic context of reception. Receiving country state policies may classify refugees in terms of nationality, but in reality, they may select or facilitate the entry of more narrowly defined social groups.

Second, considering the temporal interdependence of contexts can shed light on key social processes. In Canada, successive arrivals from Latin America encountered civil society organizations with whom they set up patterns of interlocution based on political culture. These 'dialogues' varied due to differences in political culture and the way earlier dialogues conditioned expectations and subsequent dialogues. The context of reception is dynamic; it changes with policy shifts and with migrant and civil society agency. The contours of this agency are shaped, in part, by the political culture tool-kits that Latin American and Canadian activists bring to bear on their dialogues, but the process and quality of the dialogues modifies subsequent engagements and dialogues. However, it is not enough to add *types of violence* or *types of dialogues* to the analysis. We must consider a broader set of questions, including how populations and units of analysis are defined; whether certain bases of organization and identification are privileged while others are obscured; the changing importance of intersectional, sectoral and pan-ethnic identities and organizations; the ways in which contexts may be temporally and socially interdependent, and so forth (Landolt and Goldring 2009, 2010; Landoltet al. 2011; Goldring and Landolt 2012b).

Research on migrant political engagements needs to consider a wider range of identities and bases for organizing. There is a disconnect between scholarship that recognizes the importance of faith-based groups, community-based organizations and other non-national grassroots activism and work that emphasizes nationality as a basis for organizing. We question whether nationality is as important in organizing identities and community organizations as is generally assumed. We call for a nuanced, reflective approach to understanding 'given' populations, categories and units, including *refugee, nationality* and *context.* We also ask colleagues to consider the role of narratives in constructing powerful metaphors and identities that help to structure practice and to examine the role of interactions with other collectivities, including non-migrant associational forms and institutions. When the latter are considered in more fluid forms, we will develop a better understanding of social organization and social change in and across transnational social fields.

## References

Al-Ali, N.; Black, R.; Koser, K., 2001: "Refugees and transnationalism: The experience of Bosnians and Eritreans in Europe", in: *Journal of Ethnic and Migration Studies*, 27: 615–634.

Anderson, K., 2003: *Weaving Relationships: Canada Guatemala Solidarity* (Waterloo, ON: Wilfrid Laurier University Press).

Barragan, J., 2001: *Hispanic Immigrant Women in Toronto's Labour Market* (Toronto: University of Toronto).

Basok, T., 1986: "Central American refugees: Resettlement needs and solutions", in: *Refuge* (Canada's Periodical on Refugees), 5,4: 7–9.

Bibler Coutin, S., 1993: *The Culture of Protest: Religious Activism and the U.S Sanctuary Movement* (San Francisco: Westview Press).

Bloemraad, I., 2006: "Becoming a citizen in the United States and Canada: Structured mobilization and immigrant political incorporation", in: *Social Forces*, 85: 667–695.

Bloemraad, I., 2007: "Of puzzles and serendipity: Doing research with cross-national comparisons and mixed methods", in: DeSipio, L.; Kossoudji, S.; Garcia y Griego, M.

(Eds.): *Researching Migration: Stories from the Field* (New York: Social Science Research Council).

Brettell, C.B. (2003) "Bringing the city back in: Cities as context for immigrant incorporation", in: Foner, N. (Ed.) *American Arrivals: Anthropology Engages the New Immigration* (Santa Fe, NM: School of American Research).

Carroll, William K. (Ed.). 2004: *Critical Strategies for Social Research* (Toronto: CSP).

Cheran, R., 2007: "Transnationalism, Development and Social Capital: Tamil Community Networks in Canada", in: Luin Goldring; Sailaja Krishnamurti. (Eds.): *Organizing the Transnational: Labour, Politics and Social Change* (Vancouver: University of British Columbia Press): 129–144.

Chute, T., 2002: "New El Salvador directors know about taking risks", in: *Canadian Mennonite*, 6: 32.

Comstock, S., 2012: "Incorporating Comparisons in the Rift: Making Use of Cross-Place Events and Histories in Moments of World Historical Change", in: Amelina, A.; Nergiz D.D.; Faist, T.; Glick Schiller, N. (Eds.): *Beyond Methodological Nationalism: Research Methodologies for Trans-national Studies* (London: Routledge): 176–197.

Cranford, C.; Vosko, L.F.; Zukewich, N., 2003: "Precarious employment in the Canadian labour market: A statistical portrait", in: *Just Labour: A Canadian Journal of Work and Society*, 3: 6–23.

Diaz, H., 1999: *Chileans* (Toronto: University of Toronto Press).

Faist, T.; Fauser, M.; Reisenauer, E., 2013: *Transnational Migration* (Cambridge, UK – Malden, USA: Polity).

Fitzgerald, D., 2006: "Towards a theoretical ethnography of migration", in: *Qualitative Sociology*, 29: 1–24.

Garay, E., 2000: *Integrated Settlement Planning Project: Social, Economic and Demographic Profile Hispanic Community* (Toronto: Hispanic Development Council).

Glick Schiller, N., 2010: "A global perspective on transnational migration: Theorising migration without methodological nationalism", in: Baubock, R.; Faist, T. (Eds.): *Diaspora and Transnationalism: Concepts, Theories and Methods* (Amsterdam: Amsterdam University Press): 109–129.

Glick Schiller, N.; Çağlar, A.; Guldbrandsen, T.C., 2006: "Beyond the ethnic lens: Locality, globality, and born-again incorporation", in: *American Ethnologist*, 33: 612–633.

Goldring, L.; Krishnamurti, S.V. (Eds.), 2007: *Organizing the Transnational: The Experience of Asian and Latin American Migrants in Canada* (Vancouver: University of British Columbia Press).

Goldring, L.; Landolt, P., 2009: "Reformulación de las unidades, identidades, temporalidad, cultura y contextos: Reflexiones sobre la investigación de los movimientos migratorios", in: Rivera Sánchez, L.; Lozano-Ascencio, F. (Eds.) *Encuentros disciplinarios y debates metodológicos: La práctica de la investigación sobre migraciones y movilidades* (Mexico City: Miguel Angel Porrúa—Cuernavaca, Mor.: CRIM-UNAM): 125–161.

Goldring, L.; Landolt, P.; Bernhard, J.; Barriga, M., 2006: "Toronto Hispano, Toronto Latino: Latin American institutional community development in the greater Toronto area (1973–2005)", in: Schugurensky, D.; Giginiewicz, J. (Eds.): *Ruptures, Continuities and Re-Learning: The Political Participation of Latin Americans in Canada* (Toronto: OISE, Transformative Learning Centre): 58–71.

Goldring, L.; Landolt, P., 2012a: "Transnational Migration and the Reformulation of Analytical Categories: Unpacking Latin American Refugee Dynamics in Toronto"; in: Amelina, A.; Nergiz D.D.; Faist, T.; Glick Schiller, N. (Eds.): *Beyond Methodological Nationalism: Research Methodologies for Transnational Studies* (London-New York: Routledge): 41–64.

Goldring, L.; Landolt, P., 2012b: *The Impact of Precarious Legal Status on Immigrants' Economic Outcomes*, IRPP Study 35 (Montreal: Institute for Research on Public Policy, October).

Grimson, A., 2011: *Los límites de la cultura: Crítica de las teorías de la identidad* (Buenos Aires: Siglo Veintiuno).

Guarnizo, L.E.; Portes, A.; Haller, W., 2003: "Assimilation and transnationalism: Determinants of transnational political action among contemporary migrants", in: *American Journal of Sociology*, 108: 1211–1248.

Guarnizo, L.E.; Sanchez, A.I.; Roach, E., 1999: "Mistrust, fragmented solidarity, and transnational migration: Colombians in New York City and Los Angeles", in: *Ethnic and Racial Studies*, 22: 367–396.

Guba, E.; Lincoln, Y., 2005: "Paradigms, controversies contradictions and emerging confluences," in: Denzin, Norman, K.; Lincoln, Yvonna S. (Eds.): *Handbook of Qualitative Research* (Thousand Oaks: Sage): 191–215.

Hamilton, N.; Stolz Chinchilla, N., 2001: *Seeking Community in a Global City: Guatemalans and Salvadorans in Los Angeles* (Philadelphia: Temple University Press).

Harvey, D., 1989: *The Condition of Postmodernity: An Enquiry into the Origins of Cultural Change* (Cambridge: Blackwell).

Hein, J., 1993: "Refugees, immigrants, and the state", in: *Annual Review of Sociology*, 19: 43–59.

Hiebert, D.; Ley, D., 2003: *Characteristics of immigrant transnationalism in Vancouver*, Working Paper 03-15 (Vancouver: Vancouver Center of Excellence, Research on Immigration and Integration in the Metropolis).

Hirschman, C., 1987: "The Meaning and Measurement of Ethnicity in Malaysia: An Analysis of Census Classifications", in: *The Journal of Asian Studies,* 46,3: 555–582.

Itzigsohn, J., 2000: "Immigration and the boundaries of citizenship: The institutions of immigrants' political transnationalism", in: *International Migration Review*, 34: 1126–1154.

Itzigsohn, J.; Saucedo, S.G., 2002: "Immigrant incorporation and sociocultural transnationalism", in: *International Migration Review*, 36,3: 766–798.

Kendall, P.R.W., 1992: *The Spanish-speaking community in Toronto. Ethnocultural and health profiles of communities in Toronto*, Vol. 7 (Toronto: Department of Public Health, Health Promotion and Advocacy Section).

Kivisto, P., 2003: "Social spaces, transnational immigrant communities, and the politics of incorporation", in: *Ethnicities*, 3: 5–28.

Kobayashi, A., 2002: *Transnationalism, Citizenship and Social Cohesion: Changing Concepts of Citizenship among Recent Immigrants from Hong Kong* (Kingston, ON: Queen's University).

Koopmans, R.; Statham, P., 2003: *How National Citizenship Shapes Transnationalism: Migrant and Minority Claims-Making in Germany, Great Britain and the Netherlands* (New York: Palgrave Macmillan).

Koopmans, R.; Statham, P.; Costa-Lascoux, J.; Hily, M.-A., 2001: "How national citizenship shapes transnationalism. A comparative analysis of migrant claims-making in Germany, Great Britain and the Netherlands", in: *Débats contemporains* [Current debates], 17: 63–100.

Kowalchuk, L., 1999a: "Guatemalans", in R.P. Magocsi (Ed.): *Encyclopaedia of Canada's Peoples*, (Toronto: University of Toronto Press 9. 626–630.

Kowalchuk, L., 1999b: "Salvadorans", in: Magocsi, R.P. (Ed.) *Encyclopaedia of Canada's Peoples* (Toronto: University of Toronto Press): 1109–1115.

Kulig, J.C., 1998: "Family life among Salvadorans, Guatemalans, and Nicaraguans: A comparative study", in: *Journal of Comparative Family Studies*, 29,3: 469–479.

Lamont, M.; Molnár, V., 2002: "The study of boundaries in the Social Sciences", in: *Annual Review of Sociology*, 28: 167–195.

Landolt, P., 2007, "The institutional landscapes of Salvadoran refugee migration: Transnational and local views from Los Angeles and Toronto", in: Goldring. L.; Krishnamurti, S. (Eds.): *Organizing the Transnational: Labour, Politics and Social Change* (Vancouver: UBC Press): 191–205.

Landolt, P., 2008: "The transnational geographies of immigrant politics: Insights from a comparative study of migrant grassroots organizing", in: *The Sociological Quarterly*, 49: 53–77.

Landolt, P.; Goldring, L., 2009: "Immigrant political socialization as bridging and boundary work: Mapping the multi-layered incorporation of Latin American immigrants in Toronto", *Ethnic and Racial Studies*, 37: 1226–1247.
Landolt, P.; Goldring, L., 2010: "Political cultures, activist dialogues and the constitution of transnational social fields: Chilean, Colombian and Canadian organizing in Toronto", in: *Global Networks*, 10: 443–466.
Landolt, P.; Goldring, L.; Bernhard, J., 2011: "Latin American immigrant political incorporation in Toronto: A dynamic and multi-layered social field", in: *American Behavioral Scientist*, 55,9: 1235–1266.
Levitt, P.; Glick Schiller, N., 2004: "Conceptualizing Simultaneity: A Transnational Social Field Perspective on Society", in: *International Migration Review,* 38,3: 1002–1039.
Levitt, P., 2005: "Building bridges: What migration scholarship and cultural sociology have to say to each other", in: *Poetics*, 33: 49–62.
Levitt, P.; Jaworsky, N.B., 2007: "Transnational migration studies: Past developments and future trends", in: *Annual Review of Sociology*, 33: 129–156.
Ley, D., 2004: "Transnational spaces and everyday lives", in: *Transactions of the Institute of British Geographers*, 29: 151–164.
San Martin, R.M., 1998: *Picking up the Thread: An Oral History of the Latin American Women's Collective in Toronto 1983–1990* (Toronto: University of Toronto).
Malkki, L.H., 1995: "Refugees and exile: From 'refugee studies' to the national order of things", in: *Annual Review of Anthropology*, 24: 495–523.
Manz, B., 1988: *Refugees of a Hidden War: The Aftermath of Counter Insurgency in Guatemala*, (Albany: State University of New York Press).
Marcus, G.E., 1995: "Ethnography in/of the world system: The emergence of multi-sited ethnography", in: *Annual Review of Anthropology*, 24: 95–117.
Mata, F., 1985: "Latin American immigration to Canada: Some reflections on the immigration statistics", in: *Canadian Journal of Latin American and Caribbean Studies*, 10: 35–40.
McMichael, P., 1990: "Incorporating Comparison within a World-Historical Perspective: An Alternative Comparative Method", in: *American Sociological Review*, 55, 3: 385–397.
McMichael, P., 2000: "World-Systems Analysis, Globalization, and Incorporated Comparison", in: *Journal of World-Systems Research*, 6,3: 668–690.
Menjívar, C., 2000: *Fragmented Ties: Salvadoran Immigrant Networks in America* (Berkeley: University of California Press).
Merton, R.K., 1984: "Socially expected durations: A case study of concept formation in sociology", in: Powell, W.W.; Robbins, R. (Eds.): *Conflict and Consensus: A Festschrift for Lewis A. Coser* (New York: The Free Press).
Morawska, E., 2001: "Immigrants, transnationalism, and ethnicization: A comparison of this great wave and the last", in: Gerstle, G.; Mollenkopf, J. (Eds.): *E Pluribus Unum? Contemporary and Historical Perspectives on Immigrant Political Incorporation* (New York: Russell Sage Foundation): 175–212.
Nolin, C., 2006: *Transnational Ruptures: Gender and Forced Migration* (Aldershot, UK-Burlington, VT: Ashgate).
Ostergaard-Nielsen, E., 2001: "Transnational political practices and the receiving state: Turks and Kurds in Germany and the Netherlands", in: *Global Networks*, 1: 261–282.
Pero, D., 2007: *Anthropological perspectives on migrants' political engagements*, Working Paper *No.* 20 (Oxford: Center on Migration Policy and Society [COMPAS]).
Portes, A., 1998: "Social capital: Its origins and applications in modern sociology", in: *Annual Review of Sociology*, 24: 1–24.
Portes, A.; Böröcz, J., 1989: "Contemporary immigration: Theoretical perspectives on its determinants and modes of incorporation", in: *International Migration Review*, 23: 606–630.
Portes, A.; Escobar, C.: Walton Radford, A., 2007: "Immigrant transnational organizations and development: A comparative study", in: *International Migration Review*, 41: 242–281.
Portes, A.; Fernandez-Kelly, P.; Haller, W.. 2005: "Segmented assimilation on the ground: The second generation in early adulthood", in: *Ethnic and Racial Studies*, 28,6: 1000–1040.

Portes, A.; Rumbaut, R.G., 1996: *Immigrant America: A Portrait* (Berkeley: University of California Press).
Preston, V.; Lo, L., Wang, S.; 2003. "Immigrants' economic status in Toronto: Stories of triumph and disappointment", in. Anisef, P.; Lanphier, M. (Eds.): *The World in a City* (Toronto: University of Toronto Press): 192–262.
Pries, L., 2008: "Transnational societal spaces: Which units of analysis, reference, and measurement?", in: Pries, L. (Ed.): *Rethinking Transnationalism: The Meso-Link of Organisations*, (Oxon, UK-New York: Routledge): 1–20.
Ragin, C.C., 2006: "How to lure analytic social science out of the doldrums", in: *International Sociology*, 21: 633–646.
Riaño-Alcalá, P.; Goldring, L., 2006: "A Colombian diaspora? Characteristics, tensions and challenges in transnational engagements", in: International Centre for Knowledge for Peace: *Expert Forum on Capacity Building for Peace and Development: Roles of Diaspora* (Toronto: University for Peace).
Riaño-Alcalá, P.; Villa Martínez, M.I., 2009: "Migración forzada de colombianos: Una mirada relacional", in: Rivera-Sánchez, L.; Lozano-Ascencio, F. (Eds.): *Encuentros disciplinarios y debates metodológicos: La práctica de la investigación sobre migraciones y movilidades* (Mexico City: Miguel Angel Porrúa—Cuernavaca, Mor.: CRIM-UNAM).
Rivera-Sánchez, L.; Lozano-Ascencio, F. (Eds.), 2009a: *Encuentros disciplinarios y debates metodológicos: La práctica de la investigación sobre migraciones y movilidades* (Mexico City: Miguel Angel Porrúa—Cuernavaca, Mor.: CRIM-UNAM).
Rivera-Sánchez, L.; 2009b: "Entre los contextos de salida y las modalidades de la organización social de la migración: Una radiografía del proceso de investigación", in: Rivera-Sánchez, L.; Lozano-Ascencio, F. (Eds.): *Encuentros disciplinarios y debates metodológicos: La práctica de la investigación sobre migraciones y movilidades* (Mexico City: Miguel Angel Porrúa—Cuernavaca, Mor.: CRIM-UNAM): 189–232.
Satzewich, V.; Wong, L. (Eds.), 2006: *Transnational Identities and Practices in Canada* (Vancouver: University of British Columbia Press).
Schugurensky, D.; Giginiewicz, J., 2006: *Ruptures, Continuities And Re-Learning: The Political Participation of Latin Americans in Canada* (Toronto: OISE, Transformative Learning Centre).
Simmons, A., 1993: "Latin American migration to Canada: New linkages in the hemispheric migration and refugee flow system", in: *International Journal*, 48: 282–309.
Smelser, N.J., 2003: "On comparative analysis, interdisciplinarity and internationalization in sociology", in: *International Sociology*, 18: 643–657.
Swidler, A., 1986: "Culture in action: Symbols and strategies", in: *American Sociological Review*, 51: 273–286.
Veronis, L., 2007: "Strategic spatial essentialism: Latin Americans' real and imagined geographies of belonging in Toronto", in: *Social and Cultural Geography*, 8: 455–473.
Wilson, R.M.; Landolt, P.; Shakya, Y.B.; Galabuzi, G.; Zahoorunissa, Z.; Pham, D.; Cabrera, F.; Dahy, S.; Joly, M-P, 2011: *Working Rough, Living Poor: Employment and Income Insecurities Faced by Racialized Groups in the Black Creek Area and their Impacts on Health* (Toronto: Access Alliance Multicultural Health and Community Services).
Wimmer, A.; Glick Schiller, N., 2003: "Methodological nationalism, the social sciences, and the study of migration: An essay in historical epistemology", in: *International Migration Review*, 37: 576–610.
Zolberg, A.R.; Suhrke, A.; Aguayo, S., 1989: *Escape from Violence: Conflict and the Refugee Crisis in the Developing World* (New York: Oxford University Press).

Ramírez, [illegible]

[illegible]

Sayad, A. [illegible]

[illegible]

Schiller, N. G. [illegible]

Schiller, N. G., Basch, L., & Szanton Blanc, C. [illegible] *Immigrant Organizations* [illegible]

Schmitz, [illegible]

# Chapter 6
# Between Contexts of Departure and Modalities of Social Organization of Migration: A Radiography of the Research Process

**Liliana Rivera-Sánchez and Fernando Lozano-Ascencio**

**Abstract** This chapter offers a methodological reflection on the research process into migration and social transformation in the Mexican state of Morelos, an emergent area of migration to the United States. It presents an overview of the research process that discusses how the research was conducted and how the main findings were obtained. It includes the theoretical and methodological arguments prompting the research, how these arguments were subsequently modified over time, the process by which analytical categories were constructed, and the data construction process. The analysis is based on the concept that both the original research proposal as well as its subsequent enrichment are closely linked not only to the type of academic formation and field of study of the participating researchers, but also to the questions each of them has posed and the debates they have engaged in during their particular trajectories.

**Keywords** Research process · Context of departure · Social organization of migration · Morelos · Mexico

## 6.1 Introduction

The objective of this chapter is to analyze and describe the research process in the project entitled *Migration and Social Transformation: Morelos in the context of contemporary migrations*, carried out at CRIM-UNAM during 2005 and 2007. We will discuss how the study's analytical and methodological strategies, and its conceptual and analytical instruments, were enriched and modified over time, and

L. Rivera-Sánchez (✉) · F. Lozano-Ascencio
Centro Regional de Investigaciones Multidisciplinarias (Regional Center for Multidisciplinary Studies), Universidad Nacional Autónoma de México (National Autonomous University of Mexico), Mexico, Mexico
e-mail: rivesanl@correo.crim.unam.mx

L. Rivera-Sánchez and F. Lozano-Ascencio (eds.), *The Practice of Research on Migration and Mobilities*, SpringerBriefs in Environment, Security, Development and Peace 14, DOI:10.1007/978-3-319-02693-0_6, The Author(s) 2014

we will present the most important reconsiderations and key theoretical and methodological reformulations. This document is therefore not a report on research results, but rather a reflection on how our research was conducted and how our main findings were obtained.

The strategy used in developing this chapter was to present the study's starting point and final point, including the theoretical and methodological arguments prompting the research, how these arguments were subsequently modified over time, the process in which analytical categories were transformed, and then the data construction process. Thus, the final point—which also constitutes the starting point for new stages of the project, or new and different lines of study—expresses the dialectic nature of the research process. Our analysis is based on the notion that both the original research proposal as well as its subsequent enrichment are closely linked not only to the type of academic formation and field of study of the participating researchers, but also to the questions each of them have posed and the debates they have engaged in during their particular trajectories.

The chapter is organized into three main parts. In the first part we present our reflections on how the research problem was proposed and the analytical areas of focus were constructed, as well as the interaction among these elements in the research process and their subsequent re-formulation. With these aims in mind, we discuss the original objective of our research, and some theoretical assumptions supporting the initial proposal, related to the conformation of certain migration patterns and trajectories in line with migrants' places of origin. Also presented in this section are the categories we define as the *context of departure* and *social organization of migration*, which are the analytical of focus that guided our research. Finally, we present our principal assumptions, with the aim of demonstrating how we reformulated our research questions and constructed our units of analysis, with the objective of discussing the symbiotic interaction characterizing contexts of departure and modalities of social organization of migration.

The second part of this chapter is divided into two sections. In the first section we analyze in detail the methodological strategy used for understanding the analytical relationships between contexts of departure and the social organization of migration. To achieve this objective, we develop some specific analytical categories and present some problematic points encountered throughout the different research stages. In particular there is a process of constructing variables and analytical categories, and two different ways of constructing data are illustrated, for the purpose of demonstrating different ways of approaching knowledge production. In other words, we present two epistemological modalities involved in the strategy for researching the migration process in Morelos and its forms of social organization. Thus, through the analytical category of *oriundez*, we illustrate the complexity of the research process, and specifically we discuss how *data* is understood in this study, how data is constructed, and how an analytical category can also be operationalized as a variable. In particular our intention is to demonstrate how different types of data are generated and how in the end this exercise resulted in a constructivist proposal that constantly prompted the reformulation of analytical categories. On the basis of these elements, we propose some ideas around the dialectic process accompanying data construction and the research process itself.

The chapter concludes with a presentation of the study's methodological design and some reflections on how units of observation were identified, as well as the methodological implications for conducting case studies when working with an analytical category such as the context of departure. Finally, we present the methodological instruments we used in our field work, specifically ethnographic observation and in-depth interviews and a questionnaire.

In the third and final part of the chapter, we present some reflections on the levels of analysis in our research and their methodological implications. We end with some thoughts on the dialectic nature of social science research.

## 6.2 Reflections on Analytical Strategy

### *6.2.1 Research Problem, Initial Study Objective and Hypothesis*

This research was based on certain problematic objectives and questions proposed by the researchers in the project's initial design (questions that were also present in the individual agendas of each of the two researchers). Originally, the design was focused on giving an account of how contemporary international migrants develop diverse migration strategies and trajectories, in line with whether they are originally from urban or rural localities, using a comparative analytical strategy.

Strictly speaking, the idea of comparing the characteristics of migration dynamics and international migrants originating from rural and urban localities is associated with the particular history of Mexican migration to the United States. During the first half of the twentieth century and continuing up to the late 1970s, Mexican migrants traveling to the United States were predominantly from rural areas. They migrated for certain periods of time, and were male adults, most of whom were married, with economic dependents remaining in Mexico. They worked primarily in agricultural activities and remained in the United States for less than a year (Cross and Sandos 1981). This particular international labor market was structured on the basis of the demand for labor in seasonal agricultural activities in the United States. The most eloquent expression of this international labor market was the bilateral program established by the Mexican and US governments between 1942 and 1964, known as the Bracero Program. The flow of seasonal migrants originating from rural areas in Mexico and employed in US agricultural activities was the dominant type of migration up until the mid-1960s.

Towards the late 1970s, and more clearly during the 1980s, the predominance of emigration from rural areas began to diminish. The major surveys conducted in Mexico pointed to a gradual transition from a rural migrant profile to one more clearly urban and characterized by increasing participation by younger Mexicans with higher levels of education who traveled to the United States to explore the labor market, and were more likely to enter the neighboring country with a tourist visa. Many of them migrated a single time, were not likely to enter into a pattern of migration circularity, remained for a longer period of time in the United States, and at the same time, were less likely to return to Mexico and experienced less support from family networks and friends during their migration (Cornelius 1992; Lozano 1999; Roberts and Hamilton 2005; Durand and Massey 1992). There are diverse explanations for this breakdown (see Lozano 2002).

There is broad consensus, however, that the increasing participation of the urban population in the migration flow to the United States is due, on the one hand, to the accelerated, disorderly urbanization experienced in Mexico from the 1950s on. This involves, among other things, massive emigration from rural areas to cities and metropolitan areas—a process that unleashed what some authors describe as a 'rural exodus' (Arizpe 1981)—and also a profound transformation and crisis in agricultural activities. In terms of changes on the US side of the border, activities other than agricultural activities began to require significant contingents of non-native (cheap and flexible) labor, especially for activities linked to industries and services—a process that demonstrates the consolidation of this labor market in US cities (Roberts et al. 1999).

The objective with which this research began consisted of studying the differences and similarities in the contingents of emigrants to the United States originating in Mexican urban and rural localities, specifically in one state considered to be characterized by emerging international migration: the state of Morelos (Durand and Massey 2003). The study was focused on studying the selectivity of migrants departing from rural and urban localities, with the aim of explaining differences not only on the basis of the particular attributes of individuals (human capital), but by analyzing the effects of rural and urban environments on this migration selectivity.

The main hypothesis of our research was that the profile of international migrants of rural origin was different from the profile of those of urban origin–further expressed in migration dynamics that were also different. We attempted to demonstrate that there is a close relationship between the urban or rural characteristics of migrants' places of origin and migration dynamics—the latter consisting of the way in which migrants organized themselves to reach and cross the border, the type of social networks they used to this end, the type of jobs they obtained in the country of destination, the duration of their stay, and other characteristics.

Our central research question was: How does the rural or urban nature of localities of origin impact the selectivity of international migrants and the dynamics of migration to the United States, or in other words, the conformation of differentiated migration patterns? We decided to study, from a comparative perspective, the selectivity of migrants originating from both types of localities and to establish whether rural or urban environments influenced the selectivity of migrants and the dynamics of migration to the United States.

#### 6.2.1.1 Changes in Research Strategy and the Design of New Analytical Axes

The initial objective and research question presented some conceptual problems that hindered progress in our work. We considered the localities we had defined for our comparative analysis, one rural and one urban, as international migrants' *places of origin*. Let's take a closer look at this. The study of the selectivity of migrants in their places of origin supposes that the places from which international migrants depart when they begin their migration process are, at the same time, their places of birth. This is common in rural localities, although not necessarily all of the inhabitants in a rural locality were born in that place. This assumption is less likely to be true in urban areas, not only due to the presence of migration associated with the formation of cities, but also due to the link between displacements of the population within a country and between countries (i.e. the relationship between internal migration and international migration). This means that the "origin" of urban migrants is not necessarily the urban locality where they were residing and from which they left for some international destination such as the United States. Their true origin is their place of birth (probably in the rural sector), while the urban locality from which they begin their journey to the United States may be an intermediate point or a link in their migration route.

Thus, if our objective was to investigate the way in which urban life (or the urban environment) influenced or impacted on international migration (or the conformation of a specific migration pattern), we were not taking into consideration that urban localities were not necessarily the origin of many international migrants. Instead, what we gradually began to find is that a significant portion of 'urban' migration dynamics could be explained by the rural origin of international migrants and not exclusively by their urban experience and/or contact. This type of approach pointed to the need to situate the rural and urban migration flow in time and space, which necessarily led us to review the concepts of *place of origin* and *place of destination*. The most important lesson from all of this, in methodological terms, was the importance of not limiting the study of migration to a probable place of origin—which would obstruct observation of the global movement of migration flows, in different directions, in different localizations and at different moments.

In the context of the state of Morelos, Mexico, selected for this research study, it is even more difficult to study the origin of international migration, especially if we take into consideration that this state has attracted especially the population from Mexico City and neighboring states like Guerrero, the state of Mexico and Puebla, and to a lesser degree, Veracruz and Oaxaca.[1] Many of these internal immigrants who have settled in the state of Morelos have joined the ranks of the

[1] According to the population surveyed in Mexico's 2000 Population Census, 71 % of the population residing in Morelos is native to the state, 10 % is from Guerrero, 6 % from Mexico City and 4 % from Puebla.

contingent migrating to the United States, and this means that the 'origins' of a significant number of international migrants leaving Morelos are actually neighboring Mexico City and the states of Guerrero, Mexico and Puebla.[2]

The two researchers responsible for this work have suggested various hypotheses in terms of the link between internal and international migration throughout their academic work. Fernando Lozano-Ascencio studied the internal migration antecedents of Mexican international migrants, and also discussed how international migration can be an internal migration strategy (Lozano 1999; Lozano et al. 1999). Liliana Rivera-Sánchez, in her research on the transnational migration circuit associated with the Mixtec region of Puebla, clearly identified different internal and international trajectories in the same migration circuit (Rivera-Sánchez 2004, 2007, 2008). Strictly speaking, Liliana Rivera's incorporation into this project, and in particular, the initiation of documentary research work, ethnographic work and the initial interviews conducted, led to a substantial re-formulation of the research study.

The authors of this chapter strongly questioned the hypothesis of a causal relationship between rural or urban characteristics of migrants' localities of origin, on the one hand, and migration selectivity and migration dynamics, on the other—in other words, the existence of a rural or urban migration pattern dependent on whether migrants originated in rural or urban localities in Mexico. Our intention was no longer to study the dynamics of international migration from the urban and/or rural localities of an emerging state, but rather to discuss the relevance of understanding places of departure "…as *contexts*, or in other words, as complex spaces inserted in regional dynamics that extend beyond boundary lines between states, municipalities and localities, spaces that link together the logical basis for internal migration, local–regional social dynamics alluding to the conformation of societies and their relationship with territories, with the ups and downs of national and international economies, as well as the particular restructuring of US labor markets and immigration policies" (Rivera and Lozano 2006, p. 51).

So, the first significant change in our research methodological strategy took place. By replacing the locality of origin (rural or urban) category with the *context of departure (ruralized or urbanized)*, we moved beyond the notion that 'rural' and 'urban' are characteristics or attributes that are determined, pre-existing and defined by a particular population size or specific type of predominant economic activity. To the contrary, we conceive of contexts of departure as

[2] For example, of the total population of *migrants returning from the United States*, registered in the 2000 Population Census—in other words, of the total population reporting having lived in the United States in 1995, and at the time of the census were residing in Morelos—52 % were natives of Morelos, 20 % were from Guerrero, 12 % from Mexico City, 3 % from the state of Mexico and 3 % from Puebla. This data, together with the figures from the previous footnote, point to the significant presence (selectivity) of non-native individuals in the contingent of international migrants departing Morelos.

> spatial, historic and societal products of the relationship between regions and peoples… expressed in the link between the historic formation of territory and the conformation of local societies. In other words, the experiences of those inhabiting these places have paved the way for the conformation of territories and regions, but at the same time, the social places, landscapes and spaces established within these territorial dynamics provide elements for outlining the contexts…defined more by the scope of the social relationships established by those who live there than by the official boundaries between states and municipalities (Rivera and Lozano 2006, p. 53).

The *context of departure (urbanized or ruralized)* category was therefore converted into the first analytical focus in our study.

A second significant change in our study's analytical strategy was replacing the migration dynamic category with the social organization of migration. As the reader will recall, the initial research question revolved around the existing relationship between the type of locality of origin of international migrants (rural or urban), and the selectivity of migrants and characteristics of migration dynamics, with the latter understood as the emergence of various *migration patterns* resulting from displacements from rural or urban localities. In other words we were interested in finding opposing, differentiated rural and urban migration patterns. We intended to develop a characterization of those patterns, and on the basis of a comparative analytical strategy, work to understand their differences and similarities. Our initial hypothesis was oriented much more toward finding differences than similarities in the migration patterns derived from rural or urban localities.

The methodological design of the rural and/or urban migration pattern category was based on the logic of the definition of the *place of origin* (rural or urban), presented earlier here. We expected a certain degree of correspondence between the type of place of origin and the conformation of rural and urban migration patterns. In fact this argument constituted the study's initial hypothesis. Nevertheless, by replacing the *place of origin* category with the *context of departure* category, we were obliged to analyze the relationship between the latter and migration dynamics in a different way. Along the way we established that these migration dynamics were deeply influenced by the particular processes of contexts of departure, such as the localization and (economic and social) integration of the places selected for the study, the place of birth and place of origin of international migrants—in other words the relationship between internal and international migration, the forms of local-community organization, the depth of the history of migration to the United States from the places selected, and the role of social networks in the migration process.

This complex range of variables characterizing the context of departure had an influence, in turn, on migration dynamics, that is, on the strategies used by migrants when crossing the border and on the places of destination selected in the United States, on the modalities of these displacements to the *north* (for example, whether *coyotes* or *polleros* were involved in the trips to the United States), on the forms of networking used by migrants with their families living in the place they left, and on the modalities of concentration or dispersion of migrants at certain points in the United States. We identify this new set of processes as the social organization of migration—a category that replaces the migration dynamics category, and becomes the second analytic focus in our research.

At the same time that we established the contexts of departure and social organization of migration as the study's new analytical areas of focus, we verified that the urban locality we had selected was not a strictly urban environment, and the locality we had identified as rural was not a strictly rural environment. The notions of the *countryside* associated with primary activities (basically crop-growing and livestock production), and the *city* as the exclusive environment for industry and manufacturing were no longer accurate, to a significant degree because agriculture was no longer the axis around which rural economies revolved, and manufacturing activities were being relocated to non-urban spaces. de Grammont (2004) points out that

> the countryside-city relationship is now much more complex than the old dichotomic relationship, characterized by unequal exchange and the migration of the rural poor to cities to become part of the industrial reserve army. The conceptualization of *rural* as a space occupied by social groups associated with agricultural production, in contrast with *urban* as a space occupied by social groups associated with industry and services no longer has explanatory value in the context of globalization (de Grammont 2004, p. 279).

In general we can say there is consensus on analyzing regional environments on the basis of considering the *interaction* between rural and urban, and the *linking* of these regional environments with national and global processes, as part of the our current complex reality.

All of this, together with the discussion on analytical areas of focus, led us to reformulate our hypothesis, arguing that there is a close relationship between contexts of departure (urbanized or ruralized) and the development of certain types of migration trajectories and networking modalities between migrants and their families–in other words, a strong relationship between the context of departure and the social organization of migration. In reality, the meaning of the hypothesis was not modified. What was changed radically was the way in which the research problem was stated and the analytical categories and axes used.

#### 6.2.1.2 Reformulation of the Research Question and Unit of Analysis

The identification and definition of the study's analytical axes, together with the modifications in the study's objective, led us necessarily to reformulate the research question. This was a fundamental step, since the research question constitutes not only the connecting thread for the study, but derived from the research question is also, first of all, the analytical strategy, and secondly, the methodological strategy and the research design in which different instruments are used, or in other words, the specific type of research techniques and sources to be used, whether qualitative, quantitative or a combination of the two (Oxford 2007).

In the previous section we indicated that our research question at the beginning of the study was: How the rural or urban nature of localities of origin influence the selectivity of international migrants and the dynamics of migration to the United

States, or in other words, the conformation of specific migration patterns? The elaboration and inclusion of the two new analytical axes (contexts of departure and social organization of migration) led us to reformulate the research question into three basic questions: (a) how does the context of departure influence on the social organization of migration, and vice versa? and more specifically, (b) what type of migration trajectories do individuals departing from rural and urban contexts develop? and (c) what type of links and practices are developed among international migrants and their families residing in the places of departure (rural or urban)?

Of the variables defining the social organization of migration to the United States, we decided to focus specifically on a comparative analysis of *migration trajectories* originating in *ruralized* and *urbanized* contexts of departure. The latter are understood not only as travel routes or itineraries, but as displacements of population characterized by a particular historicity. They are closely linked to the social, economic and political processes of migrants' places of birth, defined by the specific use of social networks or other types of local and non-local actors or agents (such as *coyotes* or *polleros*) for traveling to the *north* and crossing the border, and in general, with specific forms of social organization, such as family, extended family or *paisanaje* (village ties) that define a concentration or dispersion of migrants in the places of destination in the United States.

With this broad vision of migration trajectories, it was necessary to precisely define the *unit of analysis* for our research, and on the basis of that definition, to precisely select and design specific research methods and techniques for the type of questions proposed. To conclude the first section of this chapter, we will present the discussion that led to the definition of our basic unit of analysis, leaving discussion on the elaboration of our methodological strategy and the design of instruments for our field research to the next section.

One aspect that we needed to take into consideration in defining our study's unit of analysis consisted of migration histories, both of individuals residing in the selected localities, and also non-residents who had emigrated to another region of Mexico (a different municipality or state) or to the United States. It was necessary to identify the place of birth for these individuals, their place of residence at the time of our field research, the intermediate points of residence between their place of birth and their most recent place of residence, as well as their family relationship to the head of the family household in the locality of departure. In other words we were interested in reconstructing the migration histories of individuals residing in the localities selected in Morelos, as well as of individuals having some type of family connection and residing in other regions of Mexico and the United States. And this is how we came to establish our basic unit of analysis as the *family nucleus* "...composed of all the household members residing in the locality, plus the sons and daughters not residing in the locality, and living in the United States or in some (Mexican) state other than Morelos" (Rivera-Lozano 2006, p. 49).

It is worth clarifying that the individuals making up the family nucleus, as defined here, may be members of different households. For example, if a son emigrated to the United States during the 1990s, and in 2005 was living with his wife and children in Chicago, Illinois, this individual has his own household in the United States. However, for our purposes, he is also a member of the family nucleus, the head of which resides in one of the Morelos localities selected for our study. Strictly speaking, we are interested in establishing the connections between the migration histories of the members of the family nucleus, the family arrangements characterizing internal and international migration processes, and also the links and relationships among the members of the family nucleus who emigrate and those who do not.

A risk we assumed in attempting to reconstruct the migration histories of all the members of the family nucleus was in not obtaining precise information regarding those household members residing in the United States or in other parts of Mexico. In reality this is a risk taken when asking individuals interviewed or surveyed for information regarding third persons, whether parents, sons or daughters, or brothers and sisters. Nevertheless, we decided to maintain this strategy, since it was our only possibility for reconstructing the migration history of the family nucleus.

## 6.3 Notes on the Methodological Strategy

### *6.3.1 Between the Theoretical Frameworks and Methodological Instruments*

Our methodological strategy went through some important adjustments and reformulations throughout the various stages of our research work. These changes had an impact not only on the re-elaboration of the analytical strategy, as expressed in the previous sections of this chapter, but also particularly on the integration of the methodological strategy, designed for carrying out the field research work, and for responding—through the use and design of specific variables and indicators—to the study's central questions, or in other words, for presenting the relationship between the contexts of departure, both urban and/or rural, and the modalities of social organization of migration in Morelos.

Thus, throughout the various stages of the research process, some dilemmas presented themselves, both theoretical and methodological in nature. This led us initially to construct some alternative analytical categories and to design or refine instruments for the successful use of the methodological strategy. Then, we also refined the analytical strategy for the analysis and presentation of results, for presenting the relevant findings from the work carried out.

In relation to elaborating the methodological strategy, the most significant changes occurred after our field work was initiated, and after the subsequent discussion among an interdisciplinary research team with regard to the initial findings. For this reason, our intention in this part of the chapter is to demonstrate the particular circumstances, empirical evidence, and also the problems in analysis that led to certain key changes that in turn resulted in the analytical and methodological redefinition of our research. Obviously, not all of these key changes had the same intensity in the exchange among the interdisciplinary team. And not all the changes carried out during the process were necessarily immediate or had a substantial impact on strategy. Some required more time and in fact some are still to be resolved.

In some cases these changes were taken note of as pending matters, and in other cases new lines of work were opened up for initiating new research projects in the coming years. The detection of explanatory gaps, new findings and certain changes in problematic lines of research led us, on the one hand, to strengthen the idea of working as a team, to complement the ways in which we conduct research and to reinforce our academic vision of interdisciplinary work, thus making the best use possible of the differences from our professional preparation. And within this framework, the *CRIM-UNAM Migration and Transformation Team* was created, leaving each researcher to independently conduct his or her individual projects but offering a great opportunity for proposing other larger-scale collective research projects.

On the other hand, the studies conducted simultaneously by the participants in this project—in their respective fields of specialization—as well as those carried out during previous time periods, significantly enhanced the discussion and enriched the project's initial proposals. Primarily, however, they contributed toward the initial findings from the state of Morelos entering into play with those from other Mexican states. In the following sections of this chapter, we will present some of these key changes and problematic aspects that became interwoven throughout the entire process, allowing for the design of the research strategy. In order to facilitate describing how and during what stages certain problematic areas arose, we will identify the various stages of the research work conducted in Table 6.1.

#### 6.3.1.1 Initial Empirical Evidence and its Effect on the Methodological Strategy

One of the first decisions that impacted our methodological strategy responded to the need for understanding local dynamics in a regional context, not only in the state of Morelos, but also in interaction with Mexico City and the neighboring states of Guerrero, Puebla and the state of Mexico. In particular we observed that dynamics in the localities where we conducted our study were directly associated and intrinsically instilled in longer-term regional processes, in relation to both time and space.[3] For example the evidence established in the initial in-depth interviews conducted in the Alta Palmira neighborhood—particularly those with individuals living in households in which some family member was in the United States or had

[3] Research work was conducted in two localities in the state of Morelos: the first was a complex urban neighborhood that still has some *ejidal* lands, located in the Cuernavaca metropolitan area and known as Alta Palmira; and the second was a locality in the Mazatepec municipality, in an agricultural area of the state, and known as Cuauchichinola.

**Table 6.1** Research stages

| First stage | Second stage | Third stage |
|---|---|---|
| • Ethnographic observation | • Application of questionnaire | • Comparison of both phases and instruments |
| • In-depth interviews: conducted in two phases: (a) key informants; (b) other informants (see section on *In-depth interviews*) | • Processing of preliminary results | • Processing of results<br>• Re-elaboration based on findings, certain concepts and categories used |

*Source* The authors

emigrated there at one time, revealed interesting clues as to the presence of some former *braceros*, who were participants in the guest worker program during the second stage of that program between 1951 and 1964. This initial evidence led us to think of the historicity of international migration in this particular region and to ask ourselves about the pertinence of basing our research on the supposition that migration is an emerging process in the state of Morelos.

In addition our interviews with former *braceros* contributed evidence that allowed us to suppose a connection between *bracero* migration and subsequent undocumented migration after the program ended. The empirical evidence suggests that all the former *braceros* interviewed in both Alta Palmira and Cuauchichinola have sons or daughters who are currently international migrants. Therefore, migration by *braceros* may have effectively contributed toward tracing out certain routes and motivating contemporary migration, as some authors have supposed (see, for example, García y Griego 1996), or may have socialized and encouraged the experience of undocumented migration to the *north*.

An important piece of evidence that made it possible to open up another area of analysis in our research was the fact that the experience of participating in the guest worker program took place in relation to the *braceros*' places of *origin*, specifically localities in the states of Guerrero or Mexico in the case of Alta Palmira residents, and particularly from the state of Mexico in the case of Cuauchichinola residents.[4] This evidence reinforces the idea that the population of Morelos has clearly experienced inter-regional displacements during diverse time periods. For example, some of the Bracero Program participants had settled in Alta Palmira since the 1960s, and others two decades later. We can therefore suppose a significant relationship between the processes of internal migration and contemporary international migration, and even more so, between certain processes of inter-regional displacement and the conformation of specific regions in central Mexico. Furthermore, such translocal interconnections and regions may be, at the present time, defining or influencing the conformation of migration circuits with inter-linking internal and international routes (see Rivera 2004, 2007; Rivera and Lozano 2006).

[4] In Alta Palmira we found a greater number of former *braceros*, while in Cuauchichinola we only conducted four interviews with former braceros.

These initial findings had two consequences for our methodological strategy. First was a change in relation to the scale of analysis used in our case studies, one urban and one rural, for visualizing regional processes. Secondly, we began to consider the points at which we were conducting field research work not as *places of origin*, in the case of the trajectories of international migrants, but rather as points of departure. These reflections led us to design a complex analytical category that we have identified as *contexts of departure*,[5] with the idea of understanding regional processes of internal displacement, together with contemporary processes of international migration. The analytical implications from these two considerations, in relation to the scale of analysis and places of departure, point to reconsiderations of a methodological nature, in relation to both time and space in the study of population movements, but also involve reconstructing analytical categories and reflecting upon the theoretical concepts that might contribute to empirically explain and theoretically substantiate our research proposals and initial findings.

This initial evidence in the first phase of our research process opened the way for beginning to seek and then construct explanatory, comprehensive variables of regional processes—*contexts of departure* was coined with this aim in mind—and this variable led us to correlate it analytically with a second variable, which would express the *social organization of migration* in line with *urbanized* or *ruralized* contexts of departure.

Therefore, in both contexts studied—and it is worth emphasizing that the contexts studied in this second phase no longer refer to only geographic spaces defined by localities, but rather their *social spaces*, understood as spaces intersected by logical explanations and relationships beyond what we would typically define as the space of a locality—we observed a significant relationship between the places of family origin (interegional migration) for those who are currently emigrating from the state of Morelos to international destinations, on the one hand, and on the other, the patterns of migration (Adams and Hoelscher 2001). The latter refers specifically to the time period of migration, the place of destination and the point where the border is crossed, as well as the strategy for crossing the border—and even more importantly, whether local *coyotes* or *polleros* are involved and the forms of settlement in international destinations (what we refer to as concentration/dispersion).

To explain the relationship between these two analytical categories (contexts of departure and social organization of migration) generated from the first phase of research, we identified a series of complex variables for analyzing in detail the contents of the categories defined, and for developing—from the perspective of these categories and variables—the problematic areas of focus for the research underway. In the end these two categories and their respective variables (Table 6.2) constituted the analytical focus for our research.

On the basis of these complex variables we attempted to reformulate our initial hypotheses, to establish the close relationship between the categories that guided

[5] For an extensive discussion on this category, see Rivera and Lozano (2006, pp. 50–53).

**Table 6.2** Complex variables identified in research

| |
|---|
| 1. Localization and integration |
| 2. Relationship between internal and international migration |
| 3. Historic formation of territory: differentiation/fragmentation |
| 4. History (particularly: the beginning) of emigration to the United States |
| 5. The role of social networks in the migration process |
| 6. Modalities of settlement in the United States: concentration/dispersion |

*Source* The authors

our research and then defined our methodological strategy. In other words, the construction of these variables was initially influenced particularly by the findings from the first phase of our research, in which we carried out our ethnographic field work and in-depth interviews. The evidence revealed in this phase of our work led us to organize the set of questions on the questionnaire and introduce these analytical axes into the survey design, so as to study the same research questions using more than one instrument.

We were then led to construct some variables that could also be observed and operationalized through the questionnaires, in which we attempted once again to document the relationship between internal and international migration (variable no. 2 in Table 6.2). This required particular indicators for establishing the direct relationship between internal migrations or certain inter-regional displacements and international migration, on the one hand, however we also found a significant relationship between internal and international migration when we observed the processes of territory formation (variable no. 3) and the modalities of settlement in destination points for contemporary international migrants (variable no. 6).

Once the complex variables entered into play, making it possible to study the correlation between contexts and social organization of migrations, we designed another analytical category. This allowed us to fully establish such relationships and thus identify the key points of interaction among the various categories and their respective variables. We named this new category *oriundez*, although we recognize that this term does not fully reflect the conceptual implications we attribute to this category—as will become clear in the following paragraphs. We then proceeded to operationalize this category with a particular focus on *oriundez* corresponding to the state of Guerrero. The latter appeared repeatedly as an explanatory factor of various inter-regional processes, particularly when our analytical *lens* was focused on the processes of interconnection from the perspective of contexts of departure.

The *oriundez* category became, in turn, a complex variable as soon as results from the questionnaire conducted were integrated (see CRIM-UNAM Morelos Migration Survey questionnaire, 2005). To this end we recovered information from the initial *basic form* filled out from the questionnaire, in which the place of birth of the head of household and his partner were recorded. Then on the basis of these references to places of origin, we proceeded to extend the characteristic to members of the family nucleus, in which we recorded the head of household and/or partner as originating from Guerrero. This characteristic was attributed to all members of this family nucleus, and thus *oriundez* was used as an explanatory variable. *Oriundez* is considered to be not only an attribute or characteristic of family nucleuses (an aggregate characteristic) but also useful in the analysis of the individual trajectories of persons. We will see in the next section how the *oriundez* variable was constructed and how it was integrated into the study design throughout this research, that is, as both an *analytical category* and a *variable*.[6]

#### 6.3.1.2 The *Oriundez* Variable as an Analytical Category

According to the *Diccionario de la Lengua Española*, *oriundez* refers to the quality of being *oriundo*, or in other words, a native who was born in the place specified, or who originates from that place. In this case, originating from a place does not necessarily imply having been born in that place, but being rooted in terms of family ties to that place, or in other words, having a father and/or mother who was born in that place. Now then, *oriundez* is an attribute that is extended to family members of the same group, who acknowledge originating from a determined place. For our purposes here, *oriundez* in relation to the state of Guerrero signifies having been born in that state, or originating from some localities in that state—which means belonging to a family nucleus in which the head of household and/or his partner was/were born in that state.

*Oriundez* is an attribute acknowledged beyond a place of origin, in relation to others who are native to a place or who originate from that place. Thus, *oriundez* is necessarily a relational variable, and at this level should be used analytically to explain *originating from*, in relation to 'another,' in order for it to have meaning. The use of this variable is only relevant in contexts in which it is possible to find persons with different *oriundez* in the same social space.

Thus, *oriundez*, to the extent that it refers to *originating from*, it also refers to mobility, or in other words, it necessarily means that someone who originates from a place is not native to the place in which he/she is residing at the time his/her origins are being defined. And here we find a certain richness from using a variable like *oriundez*, because it does not only refer to one's place of origin, but also to the place from which one was displaced to now be in the place where information regarding one's origins is being gathered.

---

[6] An *analytical category* is a theoretical-empirical construct that makes it possible to establish relationships between diverse variables in an analytical process. Throughout this chapter, we have considered analytical categories to be instruments for the analysis and interpretation of findings. A *variable*, for its part, is the translation of an analytical category into an element that can be measured. Nonetheless, we have also acknowledged that some variables become analytical categories due to their importance in analysis and acquire a different status, depending on the research stage, which depends to a significant degree on the process of developing instruments for analysis.

This variable—which is relatively simple to operationalize, through an analysis of places of birth and migration sequences (based on information gathered through the questionnaires)—is associated with various analytical categories in this research. On the one hand *oriundez* in relation to Guerrero helps us to understand, in a regional context, the importance of the shared border between Morelos and Guerrero, and the contemporary relationship between internal and international migrations in the case of migrants who leave Morelos for international destinations. It also helps to establish the dynamics of certain inter-regional displacements, both contemporary and long-standing in nature,[7] and to understand the conformation of certain Morelos territories penetrated by the arrival of persons originating from other states. As well, *oriundez* allows us to establish the complexity of local–regional spaces immersed, on the one hand, in logical explanations of a greater regional scale, and on the other hand, in particular socio-historic dynamics resulting from long-standing social interactions between these territories. Therefore, even though the variable is simple in terms of its operationalization, it has significant heuristic value in this research, since it makes it possible—when inter-related with other variables–to discern certain processes in local and regional dynamics.

To offer evidence of what we have just stated, we can note that the social dynamic of fragmentation in the Alta Palmira neighborhood is characterized by certain processes of social differentiation. These processes are also associated with the convergence of inhabitants originating from different places. For example, inhabitants residing in the lower part of the neighborhood, with access to public services, are those who arrived when this urban housing division was established. Alta Palmira is located in the Temixco municipality, and while currently referred to as a neighborhood, it was originally constituted as a collective *ejido*. The first inhabitants identify themselves as originating from Morelos, although various families among those who founded the neighborhood were originally from Palpan de Baranda, which at one time belonged to the state of Mexico, but is currently part of the Miacatlán municipality in Morelos.

Those who arrived later to inhabit this neighborhood settled in the *higher* part of the neighborhood (in terms of elevation). Since their arrival they have suffered from inadequate infrastructure and public services, and this has served to accentuate the division between 'those up above' and 'those down below', defined primarily by *oriundez*.

Those originating from Guerrero are considered by the family members of the neighborhood's founders as not only the recent arrivals to the neighborhood, but also as being from another state, as 'upstarts' who furthermore 'have other customs'. Thus, within the social dynamics of the neighborhood, *oriundez* and particularly *originating from Guerrero*, refers not only to the state from which one originates, but this social classification is based on criteria including skin color,

---

7 Displacements of recent internal migrants and even those who left their places of origin to participate in the Bracero Program, and who have been residing in the state of Morelos for more than 40 years.

customs related to food and hygiene, musical preferences, forms of celebrating, modalities in conflict processing, among other factors. This social border that divides some from others, and that imprints particular relationship-based dynamics among inhabitants, also currently impacts the configuration of differentiated international trajectories.

Consequently, while *oriundez* does not refer to a particular identity, but rather to the state from which one originates, it is experienced in these local spaces as an important element of classification. For the purposes of our research, we use *oriundez* in relation to Guerrero as a variable that allows for understanding certain logical explanations of social differentiation and, thus, of social mobility and exchange. In fact the *context of departure* analytical category was coined in light of the consideration that *oriundez* prefigures certain characteristics of the context, and that such characteristics might place an important role in the modalities of social organization characterizing international migration from the state of Morelos.

*Oriundez* became an explanatory variable for certain processes that establish the relationship between contexts of departure and the social organization of Morelos migration. In other words, the *oriundez* of international migrants departing from Morelos is a key element in understanding contexts of departure and their relationship with the dynamics of international migration, including factors such as concentration in certain places of destination, or to the contrary, dispersion, as well as the definition/selection of certain points for crossing the border, the migration strategies of family nucleuses in Morelos and the conformation of certain international migration sequences and trajectories—which also involve internal migration routes and sites of origin.

To illustrate the above, we can say—based on on the analysis of our survey and also of course from previous evidence from interviews—that there is a significant relationship between *oriundez* and places of destination in the United States. Specifically, there is a high correlation between leaving Alta Palmira to the United States, originating from Guerrero, and arriving in Chicago as one's international place of destination. Historically, a well-defined migration circuit has been established between Alta Palmira and Chicago, to the extent that 65 % of all those who leave Alta Palmira to emigrate to Chicago originate from Guerrero. In contrast, migrants from Alta Palmira who originate from Morelos emigrate to varying places of destination and use different points to cross the border. In summary, originating from Guerrero is an organizing element for certain migration sequences and trajectories in the case of international migrants from Alta Palmira.

These considerations regarding the significance of originating from Guerrero for those living in the Alta Palmira neighborhood do not necessarily refer to particular expressions of identity, since *oriundos* from Guerrero who inhabit the Alta Palmira neighborhood are also *from* Alta Palmira, and thus also *from* Morelos. In other words, their forms of action and interaction are also mediated or impacted by their socialization in this particular space (the neighborhood). What we would like to emphasize through the above considerations is that while family networks and *oriundez* do not necessarily determine their strategies for action in everyday life, they do influence them, and lend them certain meaning and orient some courses of action in the social space they inhabit. Therefore, migrants from Alta Palmira express different levels of belonging and different identity practices in their action strategies. In summary while *oriundez* orients the course of certain exchanges and displacements, and in this case particularly migration sequences, the social organization of migration is a more complex process that requires an analysis of the interaction among various variables, which intervene in migration trajectories and the various mobility strategies.

## 6.4 The Data Construction Process

### *6.4.1 What is Data?*

We conceive of two different ways of understanding and constructing *data*. First, a piece of data can be considered, as typically the case in basic sciences, as a number, a piece of certain information, an initial experimental piece of evidence, or an empirical finding (in the case of social sciences), that has a referent in reality and that may come from direct field work, from documentary sources, or from other previously conducted studies. In this case we use the term *first order data*, acknowledging that it is also a construction, but it is constituted in the early phase of a research study.

Secondly, a piece of data is also a theoretical-empirical construction, or in other words, a product of the exercise of *filtering* initial evidence obtained in exploratory field work, or the initial stage of research, through the analysis strategy developed with conceptual and methodological structure. This new data, then, is constructed in this way, and can specifically be a result of research. This is what we refer to, throughout this text, as *complex data* or *second order data*.[8]

Thus, data construction is necessarily a complex process that requires different approaches, and does not necessarily follow linear, inflexible formulas. This does not indicate a lack of scientific rigor, and to the contrary, represents the possibility of approaching knowledge production from different paths (cf. for example Corona Berkin and Kaltmeier 2012).

Below, we will present two processes through which data was constructed in our research. The two schemes illustrate the epistemological modalities in the production of knowledge related to the migration process and forms of social organization in Morelos. The first demonstrates the design and transformation of the *oriundez* category, as the analytical strategy was being developed and re-formulated. The second demonstrates how this category is constituted as *complex data*, as a consequence of the research and the subsequent exercise of

[8] The reference to first or second order does not have a value-related connotation, but instead refers exclusively to different moments in time during the research process, or different forms of data construction.

contrasting between different types and levels of findings. We present these two processes separately with the aim of facilitating an understanding of the logic used in the design of the analytical strategy and its lights and shades.

#### 6.4.1.1 Process of Construction and Transformation of the Oriundez Analytical Category: From First Order Data to Indicator and/or New Data (Second Order Data)

The *oriundez* category, considered one of the analytical categories that organized and facilitated the interpretation of our initial findings, had different connotations, depending on the various stages of the research process (see Table 6.3). From *first order data* constructed during the initial stage of gathering information in the field—through ethnographic work and interviews—it became a *complex variable* in the second stage of our research, coinciding with the application of questionnaires and the processing of the initial survey results. During the third stage, this complex variable adopted two analytical modalities: on the one hand, as an *indicator*, a product of the process in which the research strategy was developed and operationalized, and on the other hand, as *oriundez*—in this case Guerrero *oriundez*. It also adopted the modality of a research *finding*, which in turn can be considered as *new data* (or *second order data*).

This process, which begins with first order data and culminates with second order data, makes it possible to illustrate the dialectic nature and complexity of the construction of analytical categories, data, variables and indicators—in other words the research process itself, particularly in social sciences. This new data, while *second order* at this moment during the research, can become *first order*, if it constitutes the starting point for a different phase of research, or is picked up by other researchers for beginning new research. Table 6.3 summarizes the process just described.

#### 6.4.1.2 Data Construction Process: From Indicators to Complex Data

Presented below is the data construction process throughout the three stages of analytical strategy design. In the first stage we carried out field research work, using ethnographic observation and in-depth interviews. During this stage we

**Table 6.3** Process of constructing and transforming the *oriundez* category, in line with research stages

| First stage: (Ethnographic work and interviews Initial findings) | Second stage: (Questionnaire application and initial results from survey) | Third stage: (Contrasting the two phases and instruments) |
|---|---|---|
| Oriundez *as first order data* | Oriundez *as complex variable* | Oriundez *as indicator, new data or second order data* |

*Source* The authors

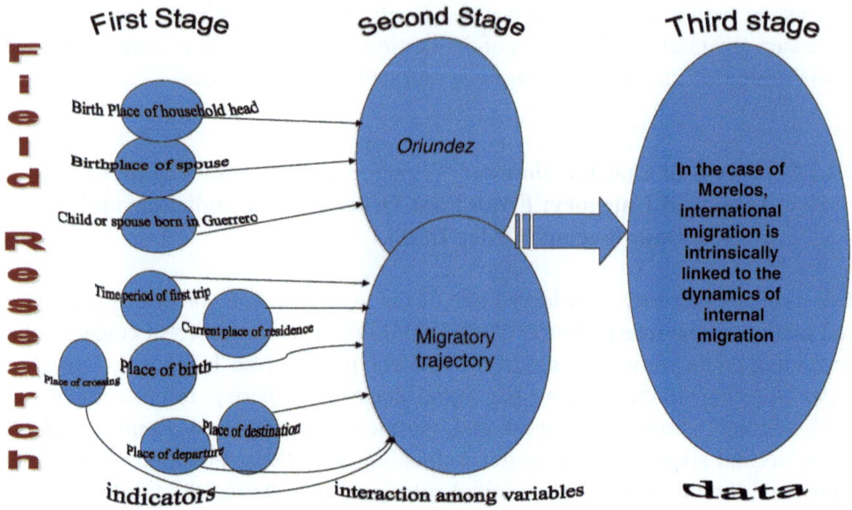


**Fig. 6.1** Data construction process. *Source* The authors

identified the primary indicators for analysis. In the second stage we constructed variables by contrasting and placing into perspective the findings and indicators from the previous stage. It was then possible to design a questionnaire that clearly incorporated the indicators generated in the first stage. The main analytical exercise in the second stage consisted of interaction among the variables created, to establish associations among them and identify their level of meaning. A third stage was represented by the moment in which certain second order data presented as research results were constructed and generated. Presented in the scheme below is the construction process for two variables: *oriundez* and migration trajectory, with their respective indicators. This scheme illustrates the second modality used in data construction (Fig. 6.1):

We can observe in this scheme that indicators were defined in the first stage, through field research work, to be used later in constructing variables. In the second stage, when the *oriundez* variable interacted with another variable, such as *migration trajectory*, new data was generated, making it possible to gradually define some results associated with our initial hypotheses. We can affirm from this, for example, that Morelos international migration is much more complex than the dichotomy between rural-origin and urban-origin migration. We can also maintain that

> the *oriundez* of international migrants departing from Morelos constitutes a key element in understanding contexts of departure and their relationship with the dynamics of international migration, such as *concentration* in certain places of destination, or *dispersion*, as well as the definition of places for crossing the border, the migration strategies of family nucleuses in contexts of departure, and the conformation of some international migration sequences and trajectories (Rivera and Lozano 2006, p. 75).

Consequently, if more variables interact in our analysis, we can increase the complexity of our data and reach the point of sustaining the findings previously proposed. Furthermore, this process allows us to illustrate how the *oriundez* and migration trajectory variables—when they intersect (in the third stage of the process)—generate complex data that indicates a research result: “In the case of the state of Morelos, international migration is intrinsically linked to the dynamics of internal migration” (Rivera and Lozano 2006, p. 75). This seemingly simple result is a product of the interaction among diverse variables and is sustained in the correlation between these variables, in an exercise that allows for *de-constructing* variables into indicators, to then organize the variables and their level of explanatory meaning once again, and understand their inter-connection with other variables.

In summary the methodological strategy of this study adopted a *constructivist notion of data* throughout the research process, that is, the need to gradually construct and generate new data in each phase, based on the findings at different levels and complexities. Therefore, the methodological strategy was built upon two different modalities for constructing data. In the first modality we can observe the process of the conversion of an analytical category, in which first order data are transformed into variables and then into indicators, or can become new data. We can also observe that, according to the scheme illustrating the second process, certain indicators are generated on the basis of the initial field work and a prior review of the literature on a certain topic. These indicators, in turn, become variables, and in the interaction among these variables, new data or second order data are generated.

These two processes make it possible to demonstrate that the initial research hypotheses do not necessarily have to be proven in order for new data or research results to be generated. Instead, the hypotheses serve as guidelines for clarifying and generating analytical categories—which orient both the strategy and development of the methodological design through various instruments, and also generate different types of data, some more complex and others less so. The data are gradually defined on the basis of the categories, or as products of the data construction process itself in the course of the research.

In fact, another characteristic of the methodological strategy consisted of complementing and verifying information and hypotheses that emerged from the first stage, particularly in the first phase involving ethnographic work and interviews. The strategy was gradually enriched with information gathered through the questionnaires, resulting in the construction of new variables and complex data, based on the findings emerging from the various methodological instruments and research stages.

### *6.4.2 Methodological Design and Field Work: Devices for Understanding the Relationship Between Contexts and Social Organization*

The methodological design was formulated using three instruments (ethnographic observation, in-depth interviews and questionnaires applied to family nucleuses), to propose three central questions, which actually constitute the research questions that guided the study: (a) What type of trajectories are developed by migrants who depart from urban contexts and from rural contexts in the state of Morelos? (b) How does the context of departure impact the social organization of Morelos migration and vice versa? and (c) What type of links and practices are developed among Morelos migrants and members of their families residing in the places of departure?

#### 6.4.2.1 Units of Observation and Case Studies: How They Influenced the Comparative Strategy

Our field research work was conducted over a period of 8 months, between November 2004 and June 2005, in two spaces, specifically an urban neighborhood known as Alta Palmira and a rural locality in the Mazatepec municipality known as Cuauchichinola. The selection of the urban neighborhood and rural locality responded basically to the project's initial objectives, contemplating the comparison between migrants who depart from a rural space and those who depart from an urban space, with a focus on observing the subsequent development of international migration trajectories and sequences. In relation to the latter, the intention was to understand family and community strategies that are involved in the migration process, and that reveal the construction of networks and, fundamentally, modalities of networking between migrants and their families residing in the localities from which they began their journey to the *north*.

The idea of conducting two case studies was included in the initial research design, with the aim of comparing two processes that we assumed were differentiated—unlike the more common strategy in contemporary migration studies of using in-depth case studies to document local endogenous processes. The urban neighborhood and rural locality were experimental points of reference for testing some initial suppositions regarding the behavior of urban and rural migrants. These prior assumptions had been elaborated after a review of the literature, and made the distinction between urban and rural migration patterns. The two localities selected, defined by the official boundaries between states and municipalities, were the *units of observation* for defining our field work and also defining the initial scope of our research.

The selection of locations for conducting our field research was not oriented by indexes of international migration intensity or a notion that international migration was an extensive phenomenon in the region—since neither of the two localities selected are located in municipalities with particularly high migration intensity, according to the migration intensity indexes elaborated by the National Population Council (*Consejo Nacional de Población*—CONAPO 2000). We did, however, have some prior evidence leading us to assume that international migration was an experience within the everyday dynamics characterizing both places. Consequently, what we had particularly identified were certain key informants in each locality. And, we had basic sociodemographic information regarding the characteristics of the two localities, however less information regarding the contexts in which the two localities were inserted.

The characteristics of the two locations selected led us to suppose that we would necessarily have highly-differentiated research results. And this could lead us to return once again to our initial suppositions, which anticipated differentiated migration patterns, one rural and one urban. Nevertheless, the initial empirical evidence indicated that the two locations were not necessarily characterized by major differences, and in fact some processes were actually similar and others were only slightly different. We therefore began to look at the contexts of regional dynamics in which the two spaces were inserted.

It is important to highlight that the cases studies proposed in this research have the potential for constructing data from both documentary information as well as information from on-site research—in other words, from both direct field research and documentary sources. Fundamentally, however, these cases were proposed for generating information that contributes toward understanding the relationship between the contexts from which Morelos migrants depart for international destinations and the particular forms of social organization in the localities from which we are observing the displacements.

In this sense the heuristic value of comparison also enhances the analysis of scenarios and dynamics through case studies (Ragin and Becker 1992). Thus, our research proposed the need for *comparatively* studying these migration patterns on the basis of certain contexts of departure, considering the places as *test sites*, or units of observation, from which comparisons can be made of migration trajectories, individual vital sequences, and also the dynamics among the family nucleuses involved in the migration experience. Nonetheless, such comparison remains focused on the fact that what are comparable are the processes carried out on the basis of these contexts of departure, not the places in and of themselves. In other words, these processes should be analyzed as rooted in regional contexts, however without forgetting that contexts are not only the frameworks in which differentiated courses of action are produced. They are also in continuous interaction with processes, through the experience of multiple mobilities, and then mutually impacting each other.

This is the reason for which the comparative strategy was not proposed in the redesigning of our research as a central objective, since because discreet units are not recovered for subsequent comparison—as is usually the case in conventional comparative studies—but instead the processes and trajectories generated from certain contexts of departure are observed, comparison points to a redefinition of objectives, and even more so, to the construction of a methodological strategy for simultaneously documenting processes, finding their particularities as well as similarities with those generated from other contexts of departure. In the end the ongoing comparison made it possible to establish a dialectic inter-relationship between the context of departure and social organization.

## *6.4.3 Methodological Instruments*

### 6.4.3.1 Ethnographic Observation

A set of guidelines for observation was designed for the *ethnographic work* to be carried out, to facilitate specific observations of the social context of the locality in question as the unit of observation.[9] These guidelines facilitated organizing visits and recording observations, ordered on the basis of identifying the various places of social centrality mentioned by inhabitants and selected by those carrying out the field work after a number of trips had been made through the localities. The important spaces in which families residing in the localities meet and interact were located and marked in the logbook, to create a type of map (including primarily sports fields and areas, parks, certain street corners, stores, small restaurants, government offices, churches, and the locations of some local celebrations), and a search was made to reveal the everyday dynamics of relationships among inhabitants in the locations, with the aim of learning about the prevailing forms of social organization. This work was complemented in an important way with information from some historic documents containing elements revealing dynamics (including references of certain local families), the urban landscape, distributed lands and *ejidal* lands, conurbation processes and the introduction of some public services, as well as various moments in time during the formation of social spaces.[10]

There were significant, decisive moments during the field work that influenced the ways in which these places were viewed. One of these was the first visit made to Cuauchichinola, where we found that there were eight religious establishments in a relatively small locality, giving us an idea of the local religious diversity, and later helping us to understand the mobility between religions and also religious conversions. Another moment was the first interview with the municipal agent that gave us an idea of the political plurality in the locality. We learned that during the last four terms of municipal government, the locality had been governed by four different political parties.

---

[9] See Grills (1998) regarding the importance of conducting ethnographic field work using guidelines designed for ethnographic observation, as an instrument for filtering interpretative aspects (what people say) and interactive aspects (how people act in their social environments).

[10] In reference to the ethnographic observation in the field of migration studies in Mexico cf. Hirai and Shinji (2012). Additionally see classical articles on ethnographic research linked to migration studies, such as Marcus, 1995 (English version) and 2001 (Spanish version) and also, Gupta and Ferguson (2008).

Meanwhile, one element that emerged repeatedly in Alta Palmira, from the initial field visits and trips, was the persistent division characterizing the neighborhood, manifested in many ways in the inhabitants' discourses and practices. The constant references to 'upper' and 'lower,' and between 'them' and 'us,' revealed the presence of a significant population from the state of Guerrero, as opposed to the population from Morelos, with the latter having founded the neighborhood and settled in the lower part. These characteristics of local dynamics helped to refine the perspective for preparing interviews and attempting to understand the relationship between these contexts of departure, social dynamics and migration as a complex social process.

#### 6.4.3.2 In-Depth Interviews

The second instrument consisted of *in-depth interviews* designed to tell life stories, outlining migration trajectories by reconstructing the vital history of migrants and their families. We conducted 32 in-depth interviews in the two communities, at two different times. The interviews were initially directed at local authorities, representatives of churches, and individuals previously identified as international migrants, including not only young, recent migrants but also individuals who had participated in the Bracero Program (1942–1964). Some of the latter had prolonged their stay or diversified their routes in the United States, or had facilitated the migration of the next generation—their sons and daughters—to the United States, sometimes with immigration documents.

Later, in-depth interviews were conducted with members of the migrants' families, basically migrants' wives, mothers and/or parents whose husbands or sons were working in the United States at that time (in this group, 65 % of those interviewed were women). One of the central topics during this phase of the interviews was associated with the forms of networking used by families residing in the localities and the members of their families who were immigrants in the United States, the frequency and modalities of their contact, and the vital experience generated by distance.

The interviews helped us in reconstructing the translocal and transnational topographies of displacements, and identifying the places of destination, of transit and of border crossings, as well as the strategies used by migrants for moving from one place to another (cf. Velasco and Gianturco 2012), their jobs, the intensity and modalities of networking, the contact between migrants and members of their families remaining in the localities, the frequency of movements and number of trips, the sending of remittances, gifts or other goods, as well as some of the characteristics of the context of departure that may or may not affect the way in which migrants construct social networks or establish themselves in common or differentiated destinations.

In the end these elements made it possible for us to refine and design the analytical categories for reformulating the analytical areas of focus, on the one hand, and then, to introduce new elements to also explore through the use of a questionnaire.

### 6.4.3.3 Comprehensive Questionnaire

Our ethnographic work and interviews were notably enriched with the *2005 CRIM-UNAM Morelos Migration Survey*—our third methodological instrument—with the application of a comprehensive questionnaire[11] to family nucleuses in both localities. The sample of family nucleuses was selected by mapping the blocks and housing units per locality and constructing stratified random samples in the two localities being studied, taking into account the total housing units, not only those with migrants. A total of 374 questionnaires were applied, 180 in Alta Palmira and 194 in Cuauchichinola, during the month of June 2005.

The questionnaire's basic unit of analysis is the family nucleus, defined as all the members of the household residing in the locality, plus the sons and daughters who do not live there, and reside in the United States or in a different Mexican state. Using this concept of the family nucleus makes it possible for us to gather information regarding sons and daughters, how they are related to the rest of the family nucleus and the arrangements made in families within internal and international migration processes. It also makes it possible for us to identify the links and relationships maintained by family members who do not emigrate, with those who do, and this is precisely the information that can potentially respond to the concerns proposed in the initial research design. The questionnaire's unit of analysis was also, of course, constructed with the intention of responding to the particular research objectives, although some of the instruments we reviewed when designing our own did not use this unit of analysis in their survey.

The questionnaire has three basic sets of questions including an initial section in which the general information on household members is recorded (name, age, sex, schooling, family relationship, place of residence), a second section in which the migration trajectory of each member of the family nucleus is recorded, independently of where they reside, as well as their economic participation in the household through remittances, for example. If a member of the family nucleus has international migration experience, an additional form is filled out, specifying experiences in crossing the border, strategies used in their trip, use and cost of *coyotes* and *polleros*, the place where they were hired, and their particular trajectories as international migrants.

One of the characteristics of this questionnaire is that it contains closed and semi-closed questions that typically appear in similar questionnaires for gathering

[11] The comprehensive questionnaire follows the design and logic of open interviews in some sections, and uses some aspects of the design from the *Mexican Migration Project* ethno-survey, however with significant *ad hoc* additions to the characteristics of family nucleuses in the localities where the instrument was applied and to the particular objectives of this study. Prior to designing and applying the questionnaire, we had conducted ethnographic work and in-depth interviews, and consequently were familiar with both localities. We consider this instrument to be a comprehensive questionnaire, because it reveals information that can be both quantified and *qualified*, specifically allowing for interpretations that can be generalized as well as interpretations of the particular characteristics of families and individuals.

information on migration processes, but also very notable are open questions that allow for recording qualitative information on the regional dynamics of migration in Morelos, particularly in relation to two topics: forms of social networking and practices of exchange between migrants and their families.

## 6.5 Some Reflections on the Dialectic Nature of Research

This research proposal falls within what Faist (1997) identifies as research at the *meso* level of analysis, aimed at looking at the intermediate structures between the micro and macro levels (Faist 1997, p. 255). Consequently, the last objective of our study was not to understand exactly the structural conditions that make migration possible, or the modalities in the decision-making by individual migrants, but was focused particularly on analyzing the ways in which the structures and social connections between actors, including both individuals and groups, influence migrants' social strategies, and in the concrete case of this study, how certain migration trajectories evolve and how diverse modalities of networking between migrants and non-migrants are established in accordance with contexts of departure. Throughout this text the latter has been noted as the relationship between contexts of departure and the social organization of migration, which became the analytical axes that gave structure to the research strategy used and that set the tone for thinking postfactum about the way in which the research process was conducted—beginning with the original proposal, including the diverse processes of data construction, and concluding with the presentation of findings.

It is important to establish the level of analysis adopted because we can then identify the perspective from which the researchers developed both their conceptual framework and their strategy for analysis. Also, this consideration leads to reflection on the explanatory scope of such a strategy by looking through this particular analytical lens, confined in spatial terms to units of observation from which researchers attempted to reveal contexts of departure and their interrelationship with the social organization of migration. Therefore even when the instruments for gathering information were methodologically designed to capture diverse strategies of mobility, through the connections established beyond the places where the questionnaires, interviews and ethnographic observation took place, they were limited methodologically by the experiences of those who were our informants in the Alta Palmira neighborhood and in Cuauchichinola. And they were also limited to the experiences registered in the places of departure.

In other words even though the analytical lens of this research was focused on taking a 'panoramic' approach to the social relationships established from these contexts of departure, we find that the social organization of migration is a complex process that makes it necessary to also consider the contexts of arrival and the way direct research evolves in these places constructed/influenced by the other contexts involved in migration dynamics (contexts of arrival and transit). It was not possible to fully develop the latter in our study, even though we could identify certain effects of migration strategies and trajectories in the places of destination. Thus, the lens used and its consequent theoretical-methodological strategy did allow for a certain degree of analytical depth, by observing the processes from the contexts of departure, however it also imposed certain methodological limitations that should be considered in order to fully understand the relationship between contexts of departure and the social organization of migration.

Despite the methodological limitation indicated, the research became increasingly profound analytically, and for example, allowed for analysis of both structural processes as well as subjective processes involved in the dialectic relationship between contexts of departure and the social organization of migration. A notable example of this is the analytical category of *oriundez*. Another is the consideration that the social space constructed as a result of the social organization of migration depends on the interaction of variables both structural in nature—such as the characteristics of the economic activities carried out in the neighborhood and the locality—and also subjective in nature—such as those that refer to the particular forms in which modalities of social differentiation are generated and expressed in these places (religious groups, political preferences, amount of time residing in a single place, musical preferences, daily habits, skin color, social origins, and others) (cf. Rivera Sánchez 2012). These topics that refer to both structural as well as subjective processes are included in the various devices prepared for field work (questionnaires, interview guides, ethnographic observation and recording). Also, the information regarding both processes was studied through both the closed questions included in the questionnaires, as well as in the open questions developed for both the guidelines for the in-depth interviews and in some modules of the questionnaire—and for this reason we refer to this latter instrument as a comprehensive questionnaire.

In addition ethnographic observation was focalized on these same topics, and allowed for specifying the characteristics of, for example, complementary family income strategies, or the combination between formal and informal employment, as well as other topics associated with involvement by *coyotes*, who are significant local actors for understanding the social organization of migration, or other elements conditioning social dynamics, such as the role of religious diversification in these particular contexts, or the role of the alliances and networks derived from *paisanaje* and *padrinazgo*, to mention only a few examples.

The need to identify both structural and subjective processes undoubtedly comes from the original hypotheses and research proposal. Thus, the re-formulation of the analytical axes, research questions and categories of analysis required a strategy with a lens focused on these two spheres. However, it is also true that the multi-method design made it feasible to maintain a perspective of meso level of analysis, prioritizing the inter-relationship between the macro and the micro, structural and subjective processes, and lastly, the meso level of social relationships, as a dimension of sociological analysis. In this way the methodological design became an important factor for constructing and redesigning both the methodological and analytical strategies (cf. for example Pedreño 2010; Lara 2010). Despite the methodological limitations noted earlier, the strategy demonstrated great analytical potential for successfully carrying out the research proposed.

Finally, the process of reconstructing both the methodological strategy and the theoretical-analytical framework of the various phases of our research made it possible to illustrate what has been mentioned throughout this chapter as a constructivist strategy. This is not only in relation to data construction specifically, as demonstrated in the second part of this chapter, but to the research process itself, of complexity. This process of *give and take*, of constructing and deconstructing from its initial conception to the presentation of results—since this process has involved going back and forth in the definition of categories, variables, indicators and data with different levels analytical categories and other variables, and of generating different data is what has been referred to—at different moments throughout the exchange of viewpoints during the methodological seminars that gave rise to this book—as the dialectics of social research.

## References


Adams, Paul C.; Hoelscher, Steven; Till, Karen E., 2001: "Place in Context. Rethinking Humanist Geographies", in: Adams, Paul C.; Hoelscher, Steven; Till, Karen E. (Eds.): *Textures of Place. Exploring human geographies* (Minneapolis: University of Minnesota Press): xiii–xxxiii.

Arizpe, Lourdes, 1981: "The Rural Exodus in Mexico and Mexican Migration to the United States", in: *International Migration Review*, 15,4 (Winter): 626–649.

Carton de Grammont, Hubert, 2004: "La nueva ruralidad en América Latina", in: *Revista Mexicana de Sociología*, 66, special edition 2004: 279–300.

Cornelius, Wayne, 1992: "From Sojourners to Settlers: the Changing Profile of Mexican Immigration to the United States", in: Bustamante, Jorge; Reynolds, Clark; Hinojosa, Raúl Eds.): *US-Mexico Relations: Labor Market Interdependence* (Stanford, CA: Stanford University Press).

Cross, Harry E.; Sandos, James A., 1981: *Across the Border: Rural Development in Mexico and Recent Migration to the United States* (Berkeley, CA: University of California, Institute of Governmental Studies).

Corona Berkin, Sarah; Olaf Kaltmeier, 2012: *En diálogo. Metodologías horizontales en ciencias sociales y culturales* (Barcelona: Gedisa).

Durand, Jorge; D. Massey, 2003: *Clandestinos, migración México-Estados Unidos en los albores del siglo XXI* (Mexico: Miguel Angel Porrúa–Zacatecas: Universidad Autónoma de Zacatecas).

Durand, Jorge; Massey, Douglas S., 1992: "Mexican Migration to the United States: A Critical Review", in: *Latin American Research Review*, 27, 2.

Faist, Thomas, 1997: *The crucial meso-level analysis*, working paper.

García y Griego, Manuel, 1996: "The importation of Mexican Contract Laborers to the United States, 1942–1964", in: Gutierrez, David G. (Ed.): *Between Two Worlds: Mexican Immigrants in the United States* (Wilmington, Delaware: Scholarly Resources Inc.): 45–85.

Grills, Scott, 1998: *Doing Ethnographic Research. Fieldwork Settings* (Los Angeles, CA: Sage).

Gupta, Akhil; Ferguson, James, 2008: "Discipline and Practice: 'The field' as Site, Method, and Location in Anthropology", in: Khagram, Sanjeev; Levitt, Peggy (Eds.): *The Trasnational Studies Reader* (New York: Routledge): 87–103.

Hirai, Shinji, 2012: "¡Sigue los símbolos del terruño!: Etnografía multilocal y migración transnacional", in: Ariza, Marina; Velasco, Laura (Eds.): *Métodos cualitativos y su aplicación empírica. Por los caminos de la investigación sobre migración internacional* (Mexico, D.F.: Universidad Nacional Autónoma de México; Tijuana, B.C.: El Colegio de la Frontera Norte): 81–111.

Lara Flores, Sara, 2010: "Movilidad y migración de familias jornaleras. Una mirada a través de genealogías", in: *Empiria: Revista de Metodología de las Ciencias Sociales*, 19: 184–203.

Lozano Ascencio, Fernando, 1999: *Immigrants from Cities: New Trends in Urban-Origin Mexican Migration to the United States* (Doctoral dissertation, City, University of Texas at Austin, August).

Lozano Ascencio, Fernando, 2002: "Migrantes de las ciudades: Nuevos modelos de la migración mexicana a los Estados Unidos", in: García, Brígida (Ed.): *Población y Sociedad al Inicio del Siglo XXI* (Mexico, D.F.: El Colegio de México): 241–325.

Lozano-Ascencio, Fernando; Roberts, Bryan R.; Bean, Frank D., 1999: "The Interconnectedness of Internal and International Migration: The Case of the United States and México", in: Pries. Ludger (Ed.): *Migration and Transnational Social Spaces*, Research in Ethnic Relations Series (Ashgate, Aldershot): 138–161.

Marcus, George, 1995 (English version): "Etnografía en/del Sistema mundo: el surgimiento de la etnografía multilocal", in: *Alteridades,* 11,22: 111–127.

Oxford, Connie G., 2007: "Changing the Research Question: Lessons from Qualitative Research", in: DeSipio, Louis; García y Griego, Manuel; Kossoudji, Sherri (Eds.): *Research Migration. Stories from the Field* (New York: Social Sciences Research Council); at: http://www.ssrc.org/pubs/researching_migration.pdf. pp. 116–129.

Pedreño Cánovas, Andrés, 2010: "Familias inmigrantes: el trabajo de los padres y las estrategias de trabajo de los hijos en las áreas mediterráneas de agricultura intensiva", in: Lara Flores, Sara María (Ed.): *Migraciones de trabajo y movilidad territorial* (Mexico: Miguel Angel Porrúa): 333–365.

Ragin, Charles; Becker, Howard, 1992: *What is a case? Exploring the foundations of social inquiry*. (London: Cambridge University Press).

Rivera Sánchez, Liliana, 2007: "La formación y dinámica del circuito migratorio Mixteca-Nueva York-Mixteca. Los trayectos internos e internacionales", in: *Norteamérica,* a journal co-published by the Centro de Investigaciones sobre América del Norte (CISAN-UNAM), and the Center for North American Studies at the American University, Mexico, 2,1 (January–June): 171–203.

Rivera Sánchez, Liliana, 2008: "El eslabón urbano del circuito migratorio Mixteca -Nueva York -Mixteca: Los migrantes de Nezahualcóyotl, Estado de México", in: Levine, Elaine (Ed.): *La migración y los latinos en Estados Unidos: Visiones y conexiones* (Mexico, D.F.: Centro de Investigaciones sobre América del Norte (CISAN-UNAM): 53–73.

Rivera Sánchez, Liliana, 2012: "Las trayectorias en los estudios de migración: Una herramienta para el análisis longitudinal cualitativo", in: Ariza, Marina; Velasco, Laura: *Métodos cualitativos y su aplicación empírica. Por los caminos de la investigación sobre migración internacional* (Mexico, D.F.: Universidad Nacional Autónoma de México–Tijuana, B.C.: El Colegio de la Frontera Norte): 455–494.

Rivera-Sánchez, Liliana, 2004: *Belongings and Identities. Migrants between the Mixteca and New York* (doctoral dissertation, New York: New School for Social Research, June).

Rivera-Sánchez, Liliana; Lozano, Fernando, 2006. "Los contextos de salida urbanos y rurales y la organización social de la migración", in: *Migración y Desarrollo*, No. 6, first semester (Mexico, D.F.: Red Internacional de Migración y Desarrollo): 45–78.

Roberts, Bryan R.; Frank, Reanne; Lozano-Ascencio, Fernando, 1999: "Transnational Migrant Communities and Mexican Migration to the United States", in: *Ethnic and Racial Studies*, 22, 2 (March): 238–266.

Roberts, Bryan; Hamilton, Erin, 2005: *The New Geography of Emigration: Emerging Zones of Attraction and Expulsion, Continuity and Change*, Working Paper Series (Princeton, N.J.: Princeton University, Center for Migration and Development).

Velasco, Laura; Gianturco, Giovanna, 2012: "Migración internacional y biografías multiespaciales: una reflexión metodológica", in: Ariza, Marina; Velasco, Laura (Eds.): *Métodos cualitativos y su aplicación empírica. Por los caminos de la investigación sobre migración internacional* (Mexico, DF: Universidad Nacional Autónoma de México – City; El Colegio de la Frontera Norte): 115–150.

Women from Socarte, Ecuador. Photo by Gioconda Herrera who granted permission

# Chapter 7
# Investigating at the 'Source': Rethinking the Transnational Social Space from the Contexts of Departure

**Alicia Torres and Gioconda Herrera**

**Abstract** This chapter presents a research project that analyses the dynamic of a social space in Ecuador with a long migratory tradition. It examines the process through which conceptual tools, as well as questions and the methodological strategy described at the beginning of the study, were progressively changed as a result of experience in the field. Its specific subject is how the initial plan to study networks and transnational ties turned into a study of the social and cultural construction of the migratory experience. This meant, in methodological terms, moving from a research strategy addressing both the source and receiving countries to concentrating on the 'source' as the research space. With this reformulation, the chapter attempts to problematize the importance assigned, in studies on transnational migration, to the departure contexts. It addresses the relatively simplistic readings of the places of origin of migrants that tend to homogenize them to the same extent that they homogenize the labour markets into which migrants are inserted on arriving at their destinations.

**Keywords** Ecuador · Migration · Methodology · Place · Transnationalism

## 7.1 Introduction

This chapter presents a reflection on a research project in progress that analyzes the dynamic of a social space with a long migratory tradition in Ecuador. The purpose of the project is to examine the way in which the migratory experience has affected the reconfiguration of relations of inequality and exclusion in the area, the

A. Torres (✉) · G. Herrera
Facultad Latinoamericana deCiencias Sociales, Quito, Ecuador
e-mail: atorres@flacso.edu.ec

G. Herrera
e-mail: gherrera@flacso.org.ec

L. Rivera-Sánchez and F. Lozano-Ascencio (eds.), *The Practice of Research on Migration and Mobilities*, SpringerBriefs in Environment, Security, Development and Peace 14,
DOI:10.1007/978-3-319-02693-0_7, The Author(s) 2014

kind of articulation among the global, national, and local that comes into play in this reconfiguration of social space, and the way hierarchies of class, gender, and ethnicity are being changed in the process. This study is part of an interpretative concern regarding how the relation between globalization and social inequality are translated in their local manifestations.

The chapter examines the process through which both conceptual tools, as well as questions and the methodological strategy stated at the beginning of the study, were progressively changed in the course of the investigation, as a result of confrontations on the ground; it seeks to demonstrate how the study's early findings resulted in the elimination of some conceptual tools, the strengthening of others, and the refining of still others, determining, at the same time, changes in methodological options. The objective of the article is to make explicit the way the study was redefined and to bring into relief the constant movement, back and forth, between concepts and findings in the field in the construction of our interpretations.

The specific subject that we illustrate is how the initial plan to do a study about networks and transnational ties created by families and migrant communities between Ecuador and Spain turned into a study on the social and cultural construction of the migratory experience and, more precisely, of the feelings of family and community belonging in this experience. This meant, in methodological terms, moving from a research strategy in the source and receiving countries to concentrating on the "source" as the research space. With this reformulation, we attempt to problematize the importance assigned, in studies on transnational migration, to the departure contexts. We seek to complexity the relatively simplistic readings of the places of origin of migrants that tend to homogenize them to the same extent that they homogenize the labor markets in which migrants are inserted on arriving at their destinations. In so doing, there arises the challenge of how to understand this complexity in a productive fashion, without getting lost in a forest of interrelations that cause further confusion.

Responding to this challenge generated the need to look for a way to think about the presence of the transnational beyond that which a bi-directional focus of migration calls 'source'. We opted for an exploration of the spatialization of the transnational in the source contexts from two dynamics closely related to forms of inequality: how gender and family relations have been reconfigured and what has happened with the process of ethnic identification.

On the other hand, as a result of this reflection, we also explore the use of comparison in this research experience as a tool to control levels of complexity. In effect, while at first we considered comparison among different receiving countries as a way to understand the diversity of 'departure' and arrival situations, now we argue that comparison makes sense if the relation with receiving states and the times of migration is abandoned, and it becomes instead a way to better understand the differences in the social fabric in the source societies.

The study takes place in the province of Cañar, in southern Andean Ecuador, specifically, in Cañar County which, since the beginning of the twentieth century, has experienced migrations. At first, residents migrated to coastal areas specializing in sugar cane production and, beginning in 1950, to the United States. In the last decade, Spain has become an important destination, especially for the indigenous population, which had also been a major source of labor for sugar cane plantations for various decades. This is an eminently agricultural area, whose residents have combined subsistence farming with internal and external migrant labor. That is, it has been inserted in both the internal and international markets principally through its labor force.

Currently, male and female indigenous and mestizo migrants from Cañar feed the agricultural labor force in the agro-exporting area of Murcia (Spain) and also the construction, textile manufacturing, and service (gardeners, kitchen help, waiters, domestic labor, and caretakers) sectors in New York City. With more than 30 years of international migration and 9 % of its population living abroad, Cañar's landscape has gradually changed, revealing the presence of remittances in new urban and consumer forms though, it seems, with little impact on poverty rates that, according to official figures, remain among the highest in the country. At the same time, mobility has transformed the demographic characteristics and the family structures of the area. The presence of international migration is felt in the more rapid drop in fertility rates than on the national level, the reduction of the younger cohorts (20–44 years of age), and in family composition which, contrary to the tendency in Latin America and nationally, demonstrates a predominance of extended families. Today, these represent 41 % of all homes in the county and 62 % of homes with a migrant family member (ODNA 2008).

Below, we present the path that led to the reformulation mentioned earlier. In the first part, we present the conceptual starting points, then we contrast the setting constructed at the beginning of the study with the setting found in the study's exploration phase. A third section presents the reformulations in terms of the conceptual tools and methodological strategy that this implied. A fourth part is dedicated to the lessons and challenges that remain in this study.

## 7.2 Our Interpretive Points of Departure

In our initial proposal, the reconstruction of transnational ties was theoretically conceived from two entry points: on the one hand, from a feminist political economy perspective in order to visualize the different forms of gender and class inequality and exclusion present in transnationalized social reproduction. At the same time, we intended to work with ethnicity as a process of political construction that takes into account, historically, the different forms and practices related to identity and how this is politicized, in what contexts, and in light of what social dynamics.

As for the first, inequality is understood, according to feminist political economy, as a structural dimension of globalization with concrete expressions at the regional, local family, and subjective scales, and these can be examined through social reproduction practices. According to Bakker and Gil (2003), the political global economy generally is explained as the product of the interrelation between states and the market, leaving aside all those aspects related to social reproduction, understood as the transformation of social processes and the mechanisms, institutions, and practices necessary for the sustenance of communities. This implies, fundamentally but not exclusively, the social organization of care-giving, in addition to the more general process of life sustenance. Feminists thus propose recovering in analyses of globalization aspects related to social reproduction and the sustainability of life at its various scales, that is, both at the places of arrival and in the reorganization of the departure contexts.

Analyses from the feminist political economy point of view proved useful to the extent that they allowed us to examine the logic of recent female migration: how have care-giving activities been distributed and redistributed in the international system in which the immigrant work force provide care in rich countries, through domestic labor, for example, in many cases, in detriment to the care and social protection provided to populations in the countries of origin (Hondagneu-Sotelo and Ávila 2003; Hondagneu-Sotelo 2001; Salazar 2001; Ehrenreich and Hochschild 2003). The reconstruction of the global care chains permits an analysis of the different links in globalized social reproduction, centering on the critical nodes precisely where care is most vulnerable: the source societies. In this sense, care-giving had to be examined not only within the framework of gender relations but in overlapping class, ethnic, regional, and geopolitical relations.

Understanding the dynamics of female migration, transnational motherhood, and care arrangements in connection with transnational dynamics, that is, to the extent that links in the global care chains, seemed to be an interesting path for research into gender relations and migration at the local, regional, and global scale. This framework served to interpret the female Ecuadorian migratory experience, of urban origin; it was thus valid to think that a study of a rural, indigenous environment, such as Cañar, could provide new clues regarding how to understand these links in social transnational reproduction.

In addition, we took up the work of other researchers in the gender and migration field, whose authors emphasized the need to take into account how transnational relations were marked by power relations between the genders. Examples of this were the deployment of mechanisms to control remittances, by transnational husbands vis-à-vis their wives, or the control, through networks of relatives, of women's sexuality (D'Aubeterre 2001; Hondagneu-Sotelo and Avila 2003; Herrera 2006). That is, from the gender relations point of view, these networks are spaces for the reproduction of relations of power and inequality among men, women, father/mothers and children. Thus, for example, the work of D'Aubeterre (2001) demonstrates that transnational families do not necessarily break with hegemonic family patterns, in spite of upsetting many daily practices.[1]

In the same sense, with respect to ethnic inequalities and the process of politicization of the ethnic, the starting point was the discussion regarding

---

[1] This criticism has already been presented by feminist anthropology, demonstrating that on treating the family like a unified and uniform whole, unequal power relations existing within, cultural and ideological values that permeate role assignment, the construction of identities, and the reproductive conditions of persons were rendered invisible (Moore 1988).

community as a uniform classification, in both territorial and identification terms. That is, the starting point was a preliminary classification, first to delimit a space, the community, and, second, to identify the difference between the indigenous and the non-indigenous, a discussion that will lead us to the problem of identity or, better, to the processes of identity construction. However, before dealing with the identity issue, we have to point out that on speaking of community, it is assumed that this is a place that is "particular, differentiated, and opposed to other places" (Gupta and Ferguson 1997, p. 13), politically constructed through the practices incorporated, where the communal and the communitarian are not "simply the recognition of a cultural similarity or of a social contiguity, but a classificatory system founded on various forms of exclusion and of the construction of *otherness*" that defines personal and collective identifications (Gupta and Ferguson 1997, p. 13). At the same time, we proposed looking at the process of identity construction as "a relation of difference almost always unstable and mobile" (Gupta and Ferguson 1997, p. 13), not as an essence, not as a primordial element; "identity is not a problem of recognition of a communality already present, nor is it the invention of an identity originating in a void, but, rather, it is the effect of structural relations of power and inequality. Rather than being a product of the same culture, of the same community, or of the same place, identity is a domain forever in dispute" (Gupta and Ferguson 1997, p. 14).

With respect to the production of identity, we return to Brubaker (2000, p. 4), who asks what identity is, and proposes that some key terms in the interpretative social sciences are, at the same time, categories of social and political practice[2] and a category of socio political analysis, and situates the term identity with this double function. As a category of practice, it is used by common actors to make sense of themselves, their activities, and to situate the difference from others, and it is used by those "political entrepreneurs to persuade the people to understand themselves, their interests…to persuade people that they are 'identical' to one another and, at the same time, different from others, and to justify and organize collective action…" (Brubaker 2000, p. 5). But, for Brubaker, this "reality" does not justify using the term as a category of analysis because one runs the risk of doing that which the category does in practice: essentialize and reify. Thus, the analytical category should take into account that reification process.

If identity is taken as a historical process of the construction of difference, this assumes the presence of actors and, to take that into account, Brubaker proposes the category of identification, "which invites the analyst to specify those agents making the identification" (Brubaker 2000, p. 14). These identification processes are generated in diverse contexts: the actor (self-identification in relation to the "other"); relational identifications (family, boss-client, etc.); categorical identifications (in reference to class, race, gender, nationality, citizenship, etc.). This

---

[2] A category of practice defines them as those of daily social experience, developed and deployed by common social actors (Brubaker 2000, p. 4).

process also assumes taking into account who produces said identifications and categorizations and from what place (Brubaker 2000, p. 15).

However, identifications do not necessarily need a specific actor, but, rather, the process can take place through discourses and narratives that permeate ways of thinking and talking about, and making sense of, the social world (Brubaker 2000, p. 16).

Approaching the subject of community and identify means debating with tradition in studies of communities, especially in the Ecuadorian case, of associating a form of social and economic organization of indigenous groups with a form of territorial occupation. That is, long and torturous definitions and discussions have always had as their starting point the amalgam of these two aspects: the community is equal to social organization plus territory. To this is added the role of the indigenous movement in politicizing ethnicity as part of their gestation process and their political identity, and of promoting the reinvention and putting into practice traditions, beliefs, and forms of social and family organization. One of these reconstituted forms, in which that political ethnicity is condensed, is precisely the indigenous community. Thanks to the organizing process and the political nature that identity acquires, the community is converted, supposedly, into the center and the place where that ethnic identification is recreated, endowed with ancestral elements, with practices of equality and complementarity that serve to reaffirm the difference from the 'other'. International migration proposes, in fact, the questioning of said identification, and that we ask ourselves how to conceive a community without communal property, without a territory prior to the 'creation' of that space, as a space for the construction of identity and of social and economic relations.

Our third point of departure will be the concept of transnationalism that emphasized the need to transcend the space of the national state in the analysis of migration, and to underline the importance of the double frame of reference to understand the dynamics of migrants, both men and women, as well as the dynamics of local space. Methodologically, we constructed the social transnational field by going back and forth, beginning with the experience from the context of the departure, moving to the destination countries, and then taking into account the return. In other words, we maintained a perspective of reconstruction of the *social organization of migration*, of its networks, its internal inequalities, both here and there, in the most synchronic fashion possible, in order to capture the simultaneity of migratory dynamics and the double frames of reference in which the strategies of migrant families and political organizations unfolded.

## 7.3 The Strategy that We Constructed and the Setting We Found

Studies on international migration in Ecuador are recent, in spite of the fact that in some areas of the country, it has been an extensive practice since the 1940s; both for certain urban sectors of Quito and Guayaquil in the 1970s and 1980s and for indigenous groups, the Otavalo Kichwa, for example, and peasants from the south of the country who combined in their trajectories internal migration with movements to the United States.[3] More recently, academic interest in this phenomenon arose, primarily, beginning with the exodus that took place at the end of the 1990s, in which a more urban and impoverished middle class profile predominates.[4]

Choosing Cañar as the research setting had to do with making complex the look at recent migration to Europe, centering the analysis in an area with a longer migratory trajectory, with a variety of destinations, and in which interethnic relations are relevant given the significant presence of the indigenous population and their high levels of politicization.

In effect, in the Cañar region two, or even three, moments in Ecuadorian migration converge: internal migration, urban and rural (parish) to the United States, and indigenous migration to Spain. It is also an area of strong politicization of ethnic identity. In effect, beginning in 1990, as in many other areas of the Sierra and the Amazon in the country, indigenous organization in Cañar began to acquire a leading role in the local political dynamic, managing to destabilize the traditional domination of mestizo groups and achieving a degree of negotiating power with the state. In that sense, this was an appropriate area for exploring the encounters and des-encounters between international migration and the politicizing of ethnic identity. The study proposes to look at the whether the migratory process was changing interethnic relations in the area and, at the same time, how the migratory experience of the indigenous people could be questioning forms of ethnic politicization.

At the same time, this contrast between previous and recent migration took on meaning for the purpose of understanding continuities and transformations in family arrangements and gender relations given that traditional male migration seemed to be giving way to the migration of women, either in family reunification processes or in the form of independent migrants.[5]

Cañar thus appears to be an ideal setting for comparing two migratory flows, recent and past, to two different countries, with potentially different family arrangements due to female migration and as a space for analyzing the ways in which ethnic identity is constructed. That is, we began with a perspective that conceived the times of migration, the destinations, and the actors as stable and permanent elements that responded more to the construction of a typology.

Thus, two studies of transnational homes and transnational cultural/political organizations were proposed in the source and receiving countries. The idea was to do a follow-up of the trajectory of migrant homes with children in the country of

[3] Peasant migration to the United States has been studied by Kyle (2000), Pribilsky (2007), Miles (2004).

[4] Migration to Europe has been analyzed in the following works: Herrera et al. (2005), Ramírez and Ramírez (2006), Pedone (2006), Lagomarsino (2006), Camacho (2005), Herrera (2006, 2007), among others.

[5] According to ODNA (2008), the number of women leaving increased more than that of men between 2000 and 2007, both to Spain and to the United States.

origin, and of organizations to understand from that point of view the characteristics of transnational ties.

The setting or context that we found marked a change in our approach to the area and also implied change in our analytical frameworks and methodological strategies. One of the first matters confirmed was that the migratory dynamic took place in broader spatial and temporal frameworks. To begin with, the times of migrations previously identified–internal, to the United States, and, more recently, to Spain–had become much more complex. In effect, we found that migration to the United States was also recent, and also much more significant than migration from the area to Spain, and that the former took place in conditions of high risk and greater vulnerability, compared with earlier experiences. In addition, there were more migratory destinations and the presence of a migrant population from countries bordering Ecuador. That is to say, the levels of mobility of the population were far greater than those we had imagined and, above all, seemed to have different rhythms. It was not so much a matter of an increase in mobility in recent times but, rather, of a permanent movement with different rhythms of intensity. It was thus necessary to explore what factors had provoked this mobility and how to begin to characterize the social dynamics of the region from on that basis of movement and not only on the basis of transformations caused by the movement of some persons.

In the second place, the politicizing of ethnic identity did not appear as clear cut as imagined, based on the history of organizations in the region. In effect, the emigration of community members and the formation, at the destination point, of associations of indigenous migrants from Cañar who seek to be involved in the application of public policies in countries of both origin and destination, has presented challenges to the traditional ways of organizing and of the politicization of the ethnic, raising question about power relations within the organizations, about traditional forms of representation, about participation, and, definitely about the very conception of the community as an expression of identity.

In the third place, an initial approach to gender relations and the upsetting of care arrangements caused by migration in the area demonstrated that the setting was not solely one of the feminization of migrations; men, and especially young people, continued to migrate, and transnational family dynamics did not necessarily correspond to the different times or destinations of migration but, rather, different dynamics coexisted. On the one hand, there are those derived from male migration that cause a series of negotiations and tensions for women who stay behind, from processes of empowerment to dynamics of social and sexual control by the family group and social networks. On the other hand, what seems to have been accentuated are those homes with two migrant parents, which assumes more complex restructurings of social reproduction strategies and in the social organization of care, an element often exposed to greater vulnerability. Finally, we also found among female emigrants mothers without a partner whose leaving has different implications, both in terms of care practices and in relation to gender ideologies present in the local context.

This led us to believe that transnational family relations were going to be marked by these diverse gender configurations, given that each would illustrate different power games both within family networks and in relation to the community.

But in addition, this first look at homes and migrant families based on the impact on care practices and gender ideologies left out other dimensions of the family that became relevant in exploratory visits. In effect, what was striking was the proliferation of discourses on family disintegration that we heard locally, expressed by both actors directly related (family members) and indirectly involved (teachers, public servants, non-migrant families) with migration. These discourses seemed to have been activated especially when women departed, that is, in relatively recently, and often resulted in negative representations of female migration. This was in contrast to the meticulousness and the resources invested in family events, such as baptisms, 15th birthday parties, marriages, in which the "good health" of migrant families seemed to be put to the test, as though the vulnerability to which family ties were subjected with international migration were being symbolically counteracted with these collective practices demonstrating the importance of family ties for transnational homes.[6]

Finally, separation and physical distance contrasted with the presence of absent family members through transnational ties: 81 % of children from homes with migrant parents receive remittances, 91 % have telephone contact with their father or mother at least once a month, 56 % receive other gifts, and 78 % have received photos or videos (ODNA 2008).

That is, following that proposed by Pribilsky (2007), analysis of the migrant family had to go beyond economic and social reproduction strategies and investigate the meanings—the tensions and contradictions—that arise from these practices for members of both transnational homes and communities.

In other words, the setting of the initial comparative research proposal between migratory destination and migratory times—past and recent—did not hold up. There was a need to rethink how to approach that reality in order to restate questions that would get at the complexity of the departure contexts, the logics of underlying power, and the meanings assigned by social agents to the transformations of institutions such as the family and the community.

The dialogue between the initial proposal, both analytical and methodological, and the information that we received from the 'field' led us to abandon our initial premise, that is, of viewing the study area as susceptible to type-casting. We needed to break with the initial construction of the research setting and find a set of conceptual tools that allowed us to formulate new questions, that recovered perspective on the process, in which times, destinations, and actors were seen in an overlapping fashion.

[6] Jason Pribilsky, in his study of another community in the province of Cañar, points out that these festive events serve to counteract the dominant discourses of family disintegration, coming especially from urban mestizo sectors, and suggests looking at the family, at its reconstruction in the country of origin, as a symbolic refuge in the face of the difficulties inherent in the migratory experience (2007, pp. 21, 22).

## 7.4 New Questions and Reformulation of Tools of Analysis

Neither global care chains nor deterritorialized communities, though dressed in constructivist notions that aimed at dismantling power relations, were tools that allowed us to come face to face with the complexity of the departure contexts we found. The view of the transnational that we had constructed methodologically tended to homogenize and des-historicize the departure space, to analyze it in a fixed fashion, and, thus, to make invisible the social dynamics and the transformations that occurred there. It was at this point that we understood that we were not interested in getting to the bottom of the social organization of migration or the last link in a chain of global inequalities but, rather, in understanding the transformation that would be occurring in the local space, both in relation to the senses of belonging to a specific idea of community and with respect to the senses associated with the idea of family and family ties. It was a matter of understanding how the local is constantly reconstructed in its relationship with the global, in this case, with practices derived from the migratory experience and how this reconstruction of the local, of that related to family and community implied—or not—a new relation among the families, in the construction of communities and also with the local political space (Ward 2003, pp. 84–86).

This implied, in turn, an emphasis on the importance of reconstructing migratory dynamics from a historical perspective that would allow for seeing the construction of transnational social spaces as an irregular process, with moments of greater and lesser intensity, and underlining social agency in a local transnationalized dynamic. That is, it was a matter of getting away from the initial typecasting to bring out the process and the way in which, in this process, the social senses of belonging, local as well as community and family, had been constructed.

The first element requiring redefinition was that of space, of territory, of place, the elements constituting the community (Low/Lawrence-Zúñiga 2003, pp. 13–15). It was a matter now of exploring how the relation between ethnicity and community was constantly recreated in a dynamic play between territoriality and deterritoriality (Torres 2009). In this context, the initial questions had to be complexified with new elements: In what form do the indigenous Kañaris recreate community–now deterritorialized and defined by new elements–as a space for the construction of ethnic identity, as a space of social cohesion and social, political, and economic relations? How did the Kañaris reinvent their identity and what are the new anchors of that ethnicity? The research interest, then, no longer centered so much on finding out if transnational ties existed or not among local indigenous organizations and those in the destination countries, but in the imaginaries that migration provoked in the senses of ethnic and community belonging as an expressed form of that identity.

And, so, it was necessary to return to notions of territory and of place and the concept of identification seemed to be a useful analytical category to explain the process of identity and of the construction of the senses of belonging within relations of inequality and power (Guerrero 2010, pp. 161–238). These preliminary definitions of territory, of the community, and of identity-identification permitted us to question static and essentialist visions of community; we proposed thinking about the community historically, starting with the fact that it was formed in connection with other hierarchically organized spaces.

Looking at territory and space, culture and identity as a constant process of the construction of difference makes it possible to propose, finally, looking at how local territories, or places, are constructed in a process of differentiation and identification (Glick Schiller and Çağlar 2009, pp. 178–179).

By that same token, the idea of identifications, both individual (self-identification) as well as relational, makes it possible to interpret the forms in which individuals, men and women, and families recreate and transform themselves on the basis of their transnational ties, without leaving aside concerns for inequality and gender and generational hierarchies that are reproduced in daily life in the departure context. The practices of migrant families, both the daily and the festive, would be constructed thus in very dynamic processes of identification and of differentiation that arise in response both to local surroundings (for example, discourses on family disintegration or the search for status) and to respect for the migrants' surroundings, marked by precariousness and exclusion, in the destination societies. In this fashion, we were able to go beyond the somewhat linear vision of the "chains" that looked at origin as a link of inequality but did not allow for understanding the contradiction that arise from the local dynamics made tense by the migratory experience. In this sense, gender becomes a crucial dimension in the inequalities present in the transnational migration experience, not only due to real and ideological tensions that the migration of women entails but because it is a component part of representations that are constructed in the local space about migration and the family, about motherhood and also about fatherhood.

In this sense, congruent with this position, as a result of the constant debate between analytical categories and empirical information, we opted for the perspective of recovering the history of place, conceiving it as a transnational space "that includes individuals who without crossing borders are connected through social relations with persons in distant and diverse localities" (Glick Schiller 2004, p. 457); individuals and relations that form part of the construction of the everyday in their place of origin, as well as in that of destination; relations that assume the exchange of information, of resources, of goods, of services, of ideas. What we sought is to analyze the spatialization of these transnational forms in terms of processes of ethnic identification and transnational ties among families. Here it becomes again pertinent to return to the difference that Glick Schiller proposes between transnational ways of belonging and transnational ways of being. The transnational ways of being would include "those daily acts through which people live across distance…"; acts that include the raising of children, the supporting of families, facing family tensions and rivalries within transnational networks; maintaining, constructing, and breaking couple relationships, friendships; getting involved in business and investment activities and the sending of goods and information.

Transnational ways of belonging, on the other hand, lead us to the production of a cultural representation, to identity, to the field of ideology, elements that allow for approaching migrants through memory, nostalgia, and the imagination. "Transnational belonging is an emotional connection with persons wherever they may be, whether that be a locality or a region, or a religious group, or a social movement, but persons who are united by a sense of history and shared destiny" (Glick Schiller 2004, p. 59). A transnational way of belonging that, as a social construction, can change in time because transnational subjects adopt different forms of cultural representation that do not refer to fixed categories but, instead, to processes.

The transnational ways of being might reflect the everydayness of care and the transnational ties that families maintain through remittances, gifts, and communication; this would include gender and generational negotiations around decisions about what to do with remittances and kinds of consumption, and also the education of children, health and care of elders, control of women's sexuality, etc. The transnational ways of belonging could be an allusion, in the case of transnational families, to special recreational events and the cohesion of family ties through family parties and religious events sponsored by certain families in which the goal is the reproduction of certain ways of belonging and of social status.[7]

On the other hand, from the point of view of the social organization of care, this double perspective of looking at ways of being and belonging, the practices and process of identification, contributes to toning down one of the limitations of the concept of global care chains, which is its structural determinism. While it is a very effective category for spatially and geopolitically locating strategic instances of the reproduction of gender, class, and ethnic inequalities at the global level, it is not very effective for taking into account the complex power games that this global belonging implies from local spaces. In this sense, a category is needed that allows for understanding, in terms of social agency, the tactics and strategies that actors deploy to interweave these transnational ways of being and belonging within the framework of local domination. Brubaker's concept of identification is a tool that, given its dynamic character, makes it possible to capture changes and resistances in the game in processes on a smaller scale, such as those deployed in families.

But it was also necessary to reflect on a concept of family that contemplated both feminist criticism and this new sense of cohesion/tension that we found. We opted for Bryceson and Vuorela's concept of the transnational family, which allowed us to capture both the ties and the tensions present in the migratory experience: "like any other family, transnational families have to mediate forms of inequality among their members: differences in access to mobility, to resources, to various kinds of capital and life styles" (Bryceson and Vuorela 2001, p. 5). What is important for these authors is that transnational families act as supports and are sources of identity but, at the same time, their very structure produces constant risks and instabilities. Thus, transnational families, more than any other type of family, find it necessary to work on their family ties, to forge them constantly in a variety of ways in order to mitigate the risks that distance creates to guarantee their

[7] For a recent analysis of mobilities, Glick Schiller and Salazar (2013).

reproduction. This perspective proposes, precisely, the analysis of multiple mechanisms of materializing family distance, of strengthening family ties, and also of looking at symbolic constructions of the family. In this sense, in the absence of physical proximity, the family needs to be rationalized.

On the basis of these reflections, a set of new questions arises that will guide the study: In what way is the family rationalized in the rural context of Cañar? What are the tensions that arise in these processes of rationalization? On what ethnic and gender hierarchies are these conceptions created? What are the cultural and social presuppositions that sustain the practices and ties of transnational families? Are there conceptions of the family that are in dispute? What has the role of female migration been in unleashing these disputes regarding the meaning of families? How does this affect care arrangement practices?

## 7.5 Changes in the Proposed Methodology

At the beginning, in light of our research trajectories, we were inclined toward different interests, molded by our disciplinary formations. According to sociology, the dynamic of institutions, whether the state or families, is key to understanding processes of social change and the role of social actors in those changes. According to anthropology, the social construction of identities is the fundamental dimension for examining the social and political agency of actors. The turn toward the relevance of a historical perspective as the point of entry to understanding the complexity of existing social dynamics is an element both researchers share and an important option in the study's methodological strategy; according to Joan Scott (2008, 1991), a way of understanding the role of differences in the configuration of domination and inequality is precisely by looking at the process of said role's constitution. In this sense, beyond looking for an interdisciplinary perspective, the option has been to combine our disciplinary views, that is, make them complementary on the basis of their specificity, a strategy that was feasible through problematizing the construction of belonging of communities and families in a migratory territory.

At the beginning, we visualized a study in the countries of origin and destination through which we could be able to reconstruct the networks and ties among families and among communities. After reformulating the aspects of the study mentioned above, a redefinition of the methodology was produced in which destination was gradually accorded less weight in the methodological strategy in favor of a denser look at the departure contexts. If, as Fitzgerald (2006, p. 3) states, we consider that the 'field' of ethnography is not simply a geographic place but a conceptual space "whose limits are constantly negotiated and constructed by the ethnographer and the members (of this field)," in this process the field of ethnography in Cañar was in a state of flux. We moved from emphasizing a leave-taking and an arrival to concentrating on the density of the ethnographic field of the leaving-taking, or of the place of origin, depending on what one wants to call it. Now it was a matter of paying special attention to the complexity of the society of origin as a place in which the transnational was spatialized. While we are interested in looking at how these spaces are being informed by practices in the distinct destination societies and states, the relevance of these factors comes to be conferred by the degree to which they overlap with local dynamics.

The choice of emphasizing the complex heterogeneity of the area of origin of migration also has to do with the need, in migration studies, to carry out "dense" studies in the place of origin, that can be contrasted with those undertaken in places of destination and that refer to the place of origin with lesser intensity. This strategy has special relevance for the Cañar case due to its population's long migratory history, a fact has been made invisible for decades.

And this confirmation led us to the second methodological option, that of undertaking a historical ethnography that combines the gathering of studies on the area, investigating the information and explanations contained in these with information from local and regional archives as a way to reconstruct what has formed "the culture of emigration" (Fitzgerald 2006, p. 12).

This historical ethnography is an attempt to come to know the place of origin of migratory trajectories, understanding place as that geographic space which, through practices of historical social subjects, is beginning to be constructed as a cultural place. It is an attempt, in this sense, to look at the territory of departure as a process that is useful for explaining the displacement of its population, but also for understanding how new senses of community and family belonging are constituted (Torres 2009).

At the same time, this history of the cultural production of the place of departure is complemented with a genealogy of care-giving, attempting to follow the clues of family meaning in the area, their daily social reproduction practices as well as their forms of collective presentation and their transformations with the migratory experience. With this perspective, we attempted to inquire into the very constitution of the migratory experience, that is, we did not take as given a specific 'experience'. According to Scott, individuals do not have experiences but, rather, subjects are constituted through experiences" (Scott 2008, p. 273) and their agency is not determined by the free exercise of will but created in specific situations.

This historical perspective, shared by both studies/researchers, is complemented by a comparative approach as a strategy for managing complexity. Once the strategy of analyzing origin and destination had been abandoned, comparison arose as the way to balance the degree of importance owe assigned to the dynamics of population mobility in our interpretation of the changes and continuities in gender arrangement related to care-giving and in processes of ethnic identification. In this sense, the ways of being and belonging, of migrant and non-migrant families and of indigenous and mestizo communities, are the units we have chosen to compare.

Why can comparison be useful in approaching complexity? Maintaining the mobility of persons as an independent variable, comparison allows, in the first place, the inclusion of actors that constitute the social transnational space, that is, in terms of Glick Schiller's formulation, this is constructed with migrants but also with their families and non-migrating individuals, groups in which the categories of gender, class, and ethnicity play a decisive role. Thus, on approaching the dynamic of the area of study, with the inclusion of non-migrant families, analyzing class, gender, and ethnic roles in this process, it is possible to become aware of the social density of the region.

On the other hand, this inclusion allows for the opening of a the range of migration's time-place relations since, as indicated, Cañar's population combines different migratory times and different destinations by these migrations; times-places that imply, at the same time, different explanations and practices, and differences in social organization.

Finally, this comparative strategy involving times, places, and actors allows us to take into account how the construction of the political has been influenced by class and ethnic relations, but also by the mobility of the region's inhabitants.

In summary, adopting a comparative view of Cañar has allowed us to take into account and analytically situate the "place" of origin of emigration and attempt to reconstruct its complexity in order, at the same time, to conceive the mobilities of persons as a process.

In the case of transnational arrangements surrounding care-giving, the historic and comparative dimension will be approached through the reconstruction of social reproduction strategies in families with three generations, in order to be able to observe the place of mobility in each of the periods under consideration: 1960–1970, with its predominance of internal male migration; the 1985–1999 period, when international migration to the United States takes off full force and coexists with internal migration; and from 2000 on, when destinations diversify and women as well as men leave. The goal is to reconstruct the different conceptions and practices surrounding motherhood and fatherhood present in care arrangements displayed by families. We have elected to concentrate only on care-giving and not on other aspects of social reproduction, such as education, health, and so on, because we can thus focus the study on a domain in which gender relations are widely deployed.

As for the reconstruction of processes of ethnic identification, to respond to the questions raised and in play with the new theoretical elements, it has been necessary to pose two units of analysis: that of community-identity and that of community-territory upon which to undertake an ethnographic history that reconstructs the discursive trajectories, understanding these as both oral and written discourses, as well as the practices of actors.

The reconstruction of the community-territory axis allows for inquiring about the way *place* is historically constituted, that is, how perceptions of locality and territoriality are generated, how a space becomes a place. Thus, the goal is to describe the political economy of that place.

For this purpose, in the first place, a temporal boundary is defined, the years from 1950 to 1960, because the interest is in recovering the relations of the community with the hacienda, of the community with migration, and of the community with resources at the time the first Agrarian Reform law was passed, and that implies changes in the socioeconomic dynamic of the area. In this period, it is relevant to understand family reconfigurations surrounding internal migration processes by males and the redefinition of family structures which leaving the hacienda signified. The reconstruction of the community-identity axis is for the purpose of examining discourses that politicize ethnicity, the definition of community, and the ways that this has been recreated and is recreated historically as a 'place' conferring identity. We also seek to examine the differentiated roles of men and women in these processes of ethnic identification. To take into account the dialectic between territoriality-dis-territoriality in the constitution of identity, we propose to choose a community with high rates of emigration and one with lower rates to undertake the task of systematic observation that will allow us to register practices that contribute to the reconstruction of the community as an identitary anchor.

## 7.6 Conclusions: From Typology to Process

The trajectory of the study we have described makes it possible to identify how both analytic categories and methodological strategy have had to be reformulated throughout the research process. This reformulation has been possible due to the dialogue and debate that have been maintained between analytical categories and the empirical information that the approach to the study area offered; that is, we have constantly gone back and forth between theoretical formulation, methodology, and data, and while they could have generated constant restatements of the matter under study, in this case, the flexibility has made possible a more complex look that enriches reflection on the processes under analysis, maintaining the problematic initially proposed as well as the units of analysis.

The initial proposal contemplated a study universe synchronically conceptualized, that is, it appeared as an area of migration in which each destination corresponded to a time, to certain social actors, and to certain practices; that is, a set of dynamics that corresponded to a stage. The initial goal was to find in Cañar evidence of differences among the different migratory states and to take into account the changes that the last of these signified for family and community arrangements.

However, the setting we found presented us with a variegated set of phases and processes that did not correspond to the initial proposal; that implied, thus, reformulations, both in conceptual tools as well as in methodology that made it possible to escape from the typologizing we intended to construct and allowed us to approach and look at the dynamics of the area as a complex set of times, destinations, actors, and practices.

Thus, the constant permeability posed by information from the field has made possible a denser approach, reading, and interpretation of the complex processes taking place in Cañar.

This complexity led, at the same time, to our abandoning the initial proposal of analyzing origin and destination and adopting a comparative strategy that permitted the inclusion of direct actors in the everyday construction of place, of identifications, and of senses of belonging; that is, migrant and non-migrant families, and indigenous and non-indigenous persons, which made possible emphasizing the meaning of mobility in the processes described.

On the other hand, this constant coming and going between text and data could have meant the dispersion of themes initially proposed and led to a change in the problematic, or an aspect of the problematic selected, or, finally, it could have led to a product that did not take into account the surroundings and the plurality of the processes that are developing there. However, the dialogue established had, as its objective, finding solutions to the challenges posed by the setting in which the different disciplinary formations of the researchers have also been a relevant tool. In this respect, instead of seeking interdisciplinarity, disciplinary reaffirmation is what has allowed us to set off in search of a perspective that involves the two ways of investigating, analyzing, and interpreting. The historization of processes was the element that gave way to a complex disciplinary view.

In addition, historicizing "origin," that is, making explicit the social and cultural construction of the contexts of leaving-taking makes possible the rethinking of transnational space as a place that is in a constant process of construction. We thus opted for the spatialization and historization of the transnational from two dynamics: the transformation and recreation of the senses of family and communal belonging.

Finally, it is important to point out an element that requires further analysis as a constituent part of these theoretical-methodological reflections: that which could be called the 'politics' of the investigative task and of the generation of knowledge. In effect, as described, during the study various changes and adjustments have been made on the way that have been the product, especially, of the confrontation with information from the field, but also with factors that could be situated in the objective conditions involved in carrying out the study, in reference to financing, times, participation, and conflicts. The adoption of some strategies has been related to political events, since this project, at the outset, was part of a cooperation project between states, which suffered the ups and downs of politics, making it impossible to maintain the cooperation proposed at the beginning with associates overseas, and the carrying out of a transnational study that would serve as a source of information for policies to be implemented in the two states. Some of these objectives fell by the wayside.

We point out this element in order to call attention to the need to include, in theoretical and methodological reflections, ways of 'doing research', in response to questions about the historically situated character in which ways of knowing are constructed.

## References

Bakker, Isabella; Gill, Stephen, 2003: *Power, Production and Social Reproduction. Human Insecurity in the Global Political Economy* (Basingstoke–New York: Palgrave–Macmillan).

Brubaker, R., 2000: Beyond 'Identity', in: *Theory and Society*, 29,1: 1–47.

Bryceson Deborah and Vuorela Ulla, 2001: *The Transnational Family: New European Frontiers and Global Networks*. Oxford University Press.

Camacho, Gloria, 2005: *Cambio mi vida* (Quito: UNIFEM).

D'Aubeterre, María Eugenia, 2001: ¿Todos estamos bien? Género y parentesco en familias de transmigrantes poblanos, LASA, Washington, September 6–8.

Fitzgerald, D., 2006: Towards a Theoretical Ethnography of Migration, in: *Qualitative Sociology*, 29,1.

Glick Schiller, N., 2004: Transnationality, in: Nugent, David; Vincent, Joan (Eds.): *A Companion to the Anthropology of Politics* (Malden—Oxford—Carlton: Blackwell).

Glick Schiller, N.; Çağlar, Ayse, 2009: Towards a Comparative Theory of Locality in Migration Studies: Migrant Incorporation and City Scale, in: *Journal of Ethnic and Migration Studies*, 35,2: 177–202.

Glick Schiller, N.; Salazar, N., 2013: "Regimes of Mobility Across the Globe", in: *Journal of Ethnic and Migration Studies*, 39,2: 183–200.

Guerrero, A., 2010: El proceso de identificación: sentido común ciudadano, ventriloquía y transescritura. Del tributo de indios a la administración de poblaciones en el Ecuador, siglo XIX, in: *Administración de poblaciones, ventriloquía y tranescritura.* (Lima-Quito: Instituto de Estudios Peruanos—FLACSO Ecuador): 161–238.

Gupta, A.; Ferguson, J., 1997: Beyond 'Culture': Space, Identity and the Politics of Difference, in: Gupta, Akhil; Ferguson, James: *Culture, Power, Place. Explorations in Critical Anthropology*, (Durham—London: Duke University Press).

Herrera, Gioconda; Carrillo, María C.; Torres, Alicia, 2005: *La migración ecuatoriana: transnacionalismo, redes e identidades* (Quito: FLACSO—Plan Migración, Comunicación y Desarrollo).

Herrera, Gioconda, 2006: Precarización del trabajo, crisis de reproducción social y migración femenina: ecuatorianas en España y Estados Unidos, in: Herrera, Gioconda (Ed.): *La persistencia de la desigualdad. Género, trabajo y pobreza en América Latina* (Quito: FLACSO- Secretaria Técnica del Frente Social).

Herrera, Gioconda, 2007: Mujeres ecuatorianas en el trabajo doméstico en España. Prácticas y representaciones de exclusión e inclusión, in: Bretón, Víctor et al. (Eds.): *España y Ecuador frente a un espejo* (Madrid: Editorial Catarata).

Hondagneu-Sotelo, Pierrette; Ávila, Ernestine, 2003: Ím Here but Ím There. The Meanings of Latina Transnational Motherhood, in: Hondagneu-Sotelo, Pierrette (Ed.): *Gender and U.S. Inmigration. Contemporary Trends* (Berkeley—Los Angeles—London: University of California Press).

Hondagneu-Sotelo, Pierrette, 2001: *Doméstica: Immigrant Workers Cleaning and Caring in the Shadows of Affluence* (Los Angeles: University of California Press).

Kyle, David, 2000: *The Transnational Peasant: Migration Networks and Ethnicity in Andean Ecuador* (Baltimore: John Hopkins University Press).

Lagormasino, Francesca, 2006: *Esodi ed approdi di genere. Famiglie transnazionali e nuove migrazioni dall Ecuador* (Milan: Franco Angeli, Fondazione ISMU).

Low, Setha; Lawrence-Zúñiga, D., 2003: Locating Culture, in: *The Anthropology of Space and Place* (Blackwell).

Miles, Ann, 2004: *From Cuenca to Queens. An Anthropological Story of Transnational Migration* (Austin: University of Texas).

Moore, Henrietta, 1988: *Feminism and Anthropology* (Cambridge: Polity).

Observatorio de los Derechos de la Niñez y Adolescencia—ODNA, 2008: *Niñez y migración en el cantón Cañar* (Quito: UNICEF and others).

Pedone, Claudia, 2006: *Estrategias migratorias y poder. Tú siempre jalas a los tuyos* (Quito: Abya Yala, AECI, Plan Migración, Comunicación y Desarrollo).

Pribilsky, Jason, 2007: *La Chulla Vida. Gender, Migration and the Family in Andean Ecuador and New York City* (Syracuse: Syracuse University Press).

Ramírez, Franklin; Ramírez, J., 2006: *La estampida migratoria* (Quito: Abya Yala, CIUDAD).

Salazar Parreñas, Rhacel, 2001: *Servants of Globalization: Women, Migration and Domestic Work* (Stanford: Stanford University Press).

Scott, Joan, 2008, 1991: Experience, in: Jaggar, Allison M.: *Just Methods. An Interdisciplinary Feminist Reader* (Boulder—London: Paradigm): 272–281.

Torres, Alicia, 2009: Quilloac: memoria, etnicidad y migración entre los kañaris, Ecuador (MA thesis in Anthropology, Quito: FLACSO—Ecuador).

Ward, Sally, 2003: On Shifting Ground: Changing Formulations of Place in Anthropology, in: *The Australian Journal of Anthropology,* 14,1: 80–96.

# On UNAM and CRIM

## Universidad Nacional Autonoma de Mexico

The National Autonomous University of Mexico (UNAM) was founded on 21 September 1551 under the name 'Royal and Pontifical University of Mexico'. It is the biggest and most important university in Mexico and in Ibero-America.

As part of the *Centennial Celebrations of Mexican Independence*, the National University was officially created on 22 September 1919. With the intention of widening educational opportunities in the country, the effort to launch the National University, though often hampered by adversity, was initially spearheaded by Congressman Justo Sierra in 1881. His vision finally materialized in 1910 with the inauguration of the *National University of Mexico* at a ceremony held in the National Preparatory School Amphitheatre, where as Secretary of Public Instruction, Sierra told the audience that the thrust of the National University's educational project was to concentrate, systematize and disseminate knowledge in order to prepare the Mexican people for the future. One hundred years after the creation of the University, Justo Sierra's inaugural address still rings true: (…) *we are telling the university community today that truth is unfolding: go seek it* (…) *you have been charged with the realization of a political and social ideal which can be summed up thus: democracy and liberty.*

The fundamental aim of UNAM is to serve both the country and humanity, to train professionals, to organize and carry out research, mainly on national problems and conditions, and to offer cultural benefits in the broadest sense possible.

*Website*: www.unam.mx.

L. Rivera-Sánchez and F. Lozano-Ascencio (eds.), *The Practice of Research on Migration and Mobilities*, SpringerBriefs in Environment, Security, Development and Peace 14, DOI:10.1007/978-3-319-02693-0, The Author(s) 2014

## Centro Regional de Investigaciones Multidisciplinarias

The Regional Center for Multidisciplinary Research (CRIM) is an academic institution ascribed to the Coordination of Humanities at the National Autonomous University of Mexico (UNAM). It is located in the City of Cuernavaca on the Morelos Campus of UNAM. Its objectives are:

1. Focus on multidisciplinary research in social sciences, humanities and other disciplines, mostly aimed at tackling specific problems at the local, regional, national and international levels, and their implications within globalization processes.
2. Contribute to the creation of knowledge in relevant and innovative arenas addressing social problems that require the convergence of different disciplines for their study.
3. Contribute to the development of a multidisciplinary approach to humanities, and focus on the development of innovative theoretical and methodological perspectives.
4. Participate in educational programs so as to contribute to the academic training of professionals in social sciences, humanities and other disciplines.
5. Disseminate by all possible means the results of CRIM's research projects.

*Website*: http://www.crim.unam.mx.

# About the Authors

Marina Ariza is a Professor at the *Instituto de Investigaciones Sociales, Universidad Autónoma de México*. Her main areas of research include female migration, family, gender, urban labor markets, demographic processes and methodological reflection. Her main publications focus on Dominican (*Ya no soy la que dejé atrás.....Mujeres migrantes en República Dominicana*, UNAM–IIS/ Plaza y Valdés, 2000) and Mexican international migration (*El País Transnacional: Migración mexicana y cambio social a través de la frontera*, UNAM–IIS, 2007, reprinted in 2010, coedited with Alejandro Portes); family sociodemographic transformations (*Imágenes de la familia en el cambio de siglo*, UNAM–IIS, 2004, coedited with Orlandina de Oliveira); and, more recently, methodological issues in migration research (*Métodos cualitativos y su aplicación empírica. Por los caminos de la investigación sobre migración internacional*, UNAM–COLEF, 2012, coedited with Laura Velasco).

*Address*: Prof. Dr. Marina Ariza, Instituto de Investigaciones Sociales, Universidad Nacional Autónoma de México [full postal address]

*Email*: ariza@unam.mx.

*Website*: http://www.iis.unam.mx/index.php/investigacion/investigadores/30-investigacion/investigadores/54 and http://www.humanindex.unam.mx/humanindex/consultas/detalle_investigadores.php?rfc=AIMA590228

Marie-Laure Coubês is Professor–Researcher in the Population Studies Department at *El Colegio de la Frontera Norte*, Tijuana, México. She obtained a doctoral degree in demography at the Paris Ouest-Nanterre University. Her research focuses on employment and mobility in Mexico, with a regional emphasis on the Mexico-US border. Since October 2010, she has coordinated the Migration Survey project in Mexico's northern and southern borders (EMIF Norte and EMIF Sur). One of her latest publications is "Crise internationale et emploi industriel féminin au Mexique" in: *Travail, genre et sociétés*, No. 25: 41–59, April 2011.

L. Rivera-Sánchez and F. Lozano-Ascencio (eds.), *The Practice of Research on Migration and Mobilities*, SpringerBriefs in Environment, Security, Development and Peace 14, DOI:10.1007/978-3-319-02693-0, The Author(s) 2014

*Address*: Prof. Dr. Marie-Laure Coubès, Departamento de Estudios de Población, El Colegio de la Frontera Norte, Blvd. Abelardo L. Rodríguez No. 2925, Zona Río, C. P. 22010, Tijuana Baja California; *Mailing address*: P.O. Box "L", Chula Vista, CA. 91912-1257, USA.

*E-mail*: mcoubes@colef.mx.

Luin Goldring is Associate Professor of Sociology at York University (Toronto). Her current research addresses immigrants and precarious work, non-citizenship and precarious legal status. She has published in the areas of immigrant incorporation, Latin American community organizing in Toronto, transnational studies, Mexican migration, and migration and development. She is affiliated with York's *Centre for Research on Latin America and the Caribbean* (CERLAC) and a founding member of *International Network on Migration and Development.*

*Address*: Prof. Dr. Luin Goldring, Associate Professor, Sociology, CERLAC, 8th Floor, Kaneff Tower, York University, 4700 Keele St., Toronto, ON M3J 1P3, Canada.

*Email*: goldring@yorku.ca

*Website*: http://www.yorku.ca/goldring/ and http://www.arts.yorku.ca/research/ine/index.php.

Gioconda Herrera is currently Professor of Sociology and Gender Studies at the Latin American Faculty of Social Sciences (FLACSO) in Quito, Ecuador. She received her Ph.D. at Columbia University. Her research interests and publications have focused on the relationship between gender and international migration from Ecuador to Spain and the US. Her most recent book is: *Lejos de tus pupilas. Familias transnacionales, cuidados y desigualdad social en Ecuador* (Quito: FLACSO, 2013) that examines migrant women and families in the Ecuador-Spain circuit. She has also recently published about the effects of the global economic crisis on migrant family strategies (*Feminist Economics, 2012*). Her current research deals with Ecuadorian indigenous families in New York City.

*Address*: Prof. Dr. Gioconda Herrera, FLACSO sede Ecuador, La Pradera E7-174 y Diego de Almagro, Quito, Ecuador.

*Email*: gherrera@flacso.edu.ec

Patricia Landolt is Associate Professor and Chair of Sociology at the University of Toronto Scarborough and Research Associate at the University of Toronto's Cities Centre. Her research examines the production and reproduction of systems of social exclusion and inequality associated with global migrations. Specific themes and topics include: refugee-migrant political incorporation, precarious work and income insecurity, non-citizenship and precarious legal status. She teaches courses in international migration, immigrant incorporation and transnationalism, ethnicity and racialization, social inequality and qualitative methods.

*Address*: Prof. Dr. Patricia Landolt, Professor and Chair, Sociology, UTSC, Research Associate, Cities Centre, 455 Spadina Ave., Suite 400, Toronto, Ontario M5S 2G8, Canada.

*Email*: landolt@utsc.utoronto.ca

*Website*: http://www.utsc.utoronto.ca/~socsci/landolt/ and http://www.arts.yorku.ca/research/ine/index.php.

Lozano-Ascencio, Fernando is full time Professor of Sociology and Demography at the Regional Center of Multidisciplinary Research Center, National Autonomous University of Mexico (CRIM-UNAM). See for details under on the coeditors.

*Address*: Prof. Dr. Fernando Lozano-Ascencio, The Regional Center of Multidisciplinary Research-CRIM, National Autonomous University of Mexico-UNAM, Av. Universidad s/n, circuito no. 2, Campus Morelos, Colonia Chamilpa. Cuernavaca, Morelos, 62431, Mexico.

*Email*: lozano@correo.crim.unam.mx

Pilar Riaño-Alcalá (Ph.D. in Anthropology) is an Associate Professor at the School of Social Work and Faculty Fellow in Residence at the Liu Institute for Global Issues, University of British Columbia, Canada. She is also a researcher with the Colombian Commission of Historical Memory working for the last four years in documenting emblematic cases of war related violence in Colombia (gender violence, forced displacement, massacres, and civil resistance). Her scholarly work is primarily concerned with three broad themes: the lived experience of violence and forced displacement, the politics of memory, and the ethnography of social repair. Pilar has also led the development of a methodological strategy and resource material for the documentation of historical memory in zones of armed conflict and from a victim-centred perspective. She is the author of: *Dwellers of Memory. Youth and Violence in Medellin, Colombia* (Transaction Publishers, 2006). She edited with Martha Villa: *Poniendo Tierra de por Medio. Migración forzada de colombianos en Colombia, Ecuador y Canadá* (Corporación Región and University of British Columbia, 2008) and with Erin Baines, the Special Issue *Transitional Justice and the Everyday* of the: *International Journal of Transitional Justice* (November 2012).

*Address*: Prof. Dr. Pilar Riaño-Alcalá, Liu Institute for Global Issues, 6476 NW Marine Dr. Vancouver, BC, Canada, V6T 1Z2.

*Email*: pilar.riano@ubc.ca.

Liliana Rivera-Sánchez is a Sociologist. She received her Ph.D. in 2004 from the New School for Social Research, New York. Currently she is a researcher at the *Regional Center of Multidisciplinary Research*, at the *National Autonomous University of Mexico* (CRIM-UNAM). For more biographical information see below On the Editors.

*Address*: Dr. Liliana Rivera-Sánchez. The Regional Center of Multidisciplinary Research-CRIM, National Autonomous University of Mexico-UNAM, Av. Universidad s/n, circuito no. 2, Campus Morelos, Colonia Chamilpa, Cuernavaca, Morelos, 62431, Mexico.

*Email*: rivesanl@correo.crim.unam.mx.

Alicia Torres P., Anthropologist, is a Doctoral Student in History; Professor and Researcher, Anthropology Program at the Latin American Faculty of Social Sciences (FLACSO-Sede Ecuador). She has conducted ethnographic research with indigenous peoples in Ecuador on ethnicity, racism, social and political organization. Currently her research examines the relationship between migration and ethnicity, migration and development, migration and identity. Relevant publications include: "Ecuador Modern Era Migrations", in: Immanuel Ness (Ed.): *The Encyclopedia of Global Human Migration* (New York: Wiley, 2013); *Niñez indígena en migración. Derechos en riesgo y tramas culturales* (Quito: FLACSO, UNICEF [TACRO], AECID, 2010); with Almudena Cortés: *El codesarrollo en los Andes* (Quito: FLACSO—Universidad Autónoma de Madrid, 2009).

*Address*: Prof. Alicia Torres P., FLACSO sede Ecuador, La Pradera E7-174 y Diego de Almagro, Quito, Ecuador.

*Email*: atorres@flacso.edu.ec.

Laura Velasco Ortiz is Professor–Researcher in the Department of Cultural Studies at *El Colegio de la Frontera Norte*, Mexico. Her research focuses on the study of identity and migration, transnational ethnicities and migrant's grassroots organizations, and identity formation in the México-US border region. She is author of: *Mixtec Transnational Identity* (Arizona University Press, 2005), and: *Mexican Voices of the Border Region* (with Oscar Contreras, Temple University Press, 2011).

*Address*: Prof. Laura Velasco Ortiz, Departamento de Estudios Culturales, El Colegio de la Frontera Norte, Blvd. Abelardo L. Rodríguez No. 2925, Zona Río, C. P. 22010, Tijuana Baja California, *Mailing address*: P.O. Box "L", Chula Vista, CA. 91912-1257, USA.

Marta Ines Villa Martínez is a Historian (Universidad Nacional de Colombia) and she obtained a Masters in Culture of the Metropolis (University of Catalonia). Her academic and research experience has been in the fields of migrations, forced displacement, violence, and public policy. She coordinates the Migration and Human Rights Program of Corporación Region (Medellin-Colombia), is the lead researcher of the group on "Conflict, Citizenship and Social Policy" and is the co-coordinator of the group on 'Migration' of the Latin American Council of Social Sciences (CLACSO). She has led and participated in several research studies including: "Memories of the return in the Antioquia's Northwest"; "Memory and Displacement: the case of San Carlos and Comuna 13"; and on "Forced Migration of Colombians in Colombia, Ecuador and Canada".

*Address*: Ms. Marta Ines Villa Martínez, Corporación Región, Calle 55 N. 41-10, Colombia

*Email*: marvima@une.net.co.

Christian Zlolniski, an Anthropologist by training, is Associate Professor of Anthropology and Mexican American Studies at the University of Texas at Arlington. His research focuses on the study of economic globalization, work, and transnational migration in Mexico and the United States. Between 1995 and 2000 he was professor and researcher in the Department of Social Studies at *El Colegio de la Frontera Norte in Tijuana*, Mexico. He is the author of: *Janitors, Street Vendors and Activists: The Lives of Mexican Immigrants in Silicon Valley* (University of California Press, 2006).

*Address*: Mr. Christian Zlolniski, Department of Sociology and Anthropology and Center for Mexican American Studies, University of Texas at Arlington, Arlington, TX 76019, USA.

*Email*: chrisz@uta.edu.

# About the Editors

**Liliana Rivera-Sánchez** is a Sociologist. She received her Ph.D. in 2004 from the New School for Social Research, New York. Currently she is a researcher at the *Regional Center of Multidisciplinary Research*, at the *National Autonomous University of Mexico* (CRIM-UNAM). Her geographic areas of study are Mexico and the United States, with an emphasis in so-called emergent regions of Mexican migration and new destination points in the United States. During the last decade, she has worked on two research tracks: migration and social transformation, and transnational practices and processes in migratory contexts. Her current work addresses these issues and challenges of how contemporary Mexican migrants are dealing with return migration. Her recent books are: *Vínculos y prácticas de interconexión en un circuito migratorio entre México y Nueva York* (Buenos Aires, Argentina: Consejo Latinoamericano de Ciencias Sociales [CLACSO] 2012); *Entre contextos locales y ciudades globales. La configuración de circuitos migratorios Puebla-Nueva York* [Coeditor: Marcela Ibarra Mateos] (Puebla, Puebla: Universidad Iberoamericana Puebla, 2011); Bela Feldman-Bianco, Liliana Rivera-Sánchez, Carolina Stefoni and Marta Inés Villa (Eds.): *La construcción social del sujeto migrante en América Latina: Prácticas, representaciones y categorías* (Quito, Ecuador: Consejo Latinoamericano de Ciencias Sociales [CLACSO], FLACSO and Universidad Alberto Hurtado, 2011).

*Address*: Dr. Liliana Rivera-Sánchez. The Regional Center of Multidisciplinary Research-CRIM, National Autonomous University of Mexico-UNAM, Av. Universidad s/n, circuito no. 2, Campus Morelos, Colonia Chamilpa, Cuernavaca, Morelos, 62431, Mexico.

*Email*: rivesanl@correo.crim.unam.mx.

**Fernando Lozano-Ascencio** is full time Professor of Sociology and Demography at the Regional Center of Multidisciplinary Research Center, National Autonomous University of Mexico (CRIM-UNAM). He received his Ph.D. in Sociology from The University of Texas at Austin. He has done work on the Mexican migration to the United States and migrant remittances for over 20 years. His current research interest is the new origins of Mexican migration to the US linked to the use of individual and collective remittances; interna-tional migration, remittances and development in Latin America; migration polices and international migration; and high skilled emigration from Latin America.

His most recent books are: *Remesas y recaudación tributaria en México* (2011) and *Migrantes calificados de América Latina y el Caribe ¿Capacidades desaprovechadas?* (2010), both published by CRIM-UNAM. Professor Lozano-Ascencio was the President of the Population Association of Latin American, ALAP (2011–2012) and is member of the International Network on Migration and Development.

*Address*: Prof. Dr. Fernando Lozano-Ascencio, The Regional Center of Multidisciplinary Research-CRIM, National Autonomous University of Mexico-UNAM, Av. Universidad s/n, circuito no. 2, Campus Morelos, Colonia Chamilpa. Cuernavaca, Morelos, 62431, Mexico.

*Email*: lozano@correo.crim.unam.mx.

# About the Book

The migration process is interpreted in a different way when researchers live in so-called societies of origin, than when it is interpreted from societies of destination—even when research work is multi-situated. The localization of researchers in this field involves numerous factors that influence the modalities for conducting research. Research agendas are clearly mediated by these localizations. This book on contemporary social sciences creates awareness on these mediations, and breaks with the dichotomic readings that are implicit in this migration process (origin-destination, north-south, cause-effect, to mention a few). This book prioritizes the modalities through which research is conducted in multidisciplinary or interdisciplinary teams in the American Continent. This book focsues on the narrative of methodological experience of the research practice on migration and mobility.

L. Rivera-Sánchez and F. Lozano-Ascencio (eds.), *The Practice of Research on Migration and Mobilities*, SpringerBriefs in Environment, Security, Development and Peace 14, DOI:10.1007/978-3-319-02693-0, The Author(s) 2014 

MIX
Papier aus verantwortungsvollen Quellen
Paper from responsible sources
FSC® C105338

If you have any concerns about our products,
you can contact us on
**ProductSafety@springernature.com**

In case Publisher is established outside the EU,
the EU authorized representative is:
**Springer Nature Customer Service Center GmbH**
**Europaplatz 3, 69115 Heidelberg, Germany**

Printed by Libri Plureos GmbH
in Hamburg, Germany